Ben Shahn's American Scene

University of Illinois Press • Urbana, Chicago, and Springfield

Ben Shahn's American Scene

PHOTOGRAPHS

1938

Shahn's

American

Scene

JOHN RAEBURN

© 2010 by the Board of Trustees
of the University of Illinois
All rights reserved
Manufactured in the United States of America
1 2 3 4 5 C P 5 4 3 2 1
♾ This book is printed on acid-free paper.

Library of Congress Cataloging-in-Publication Data
Raeburn, John.
Ben Shahn's American scene : photographs, 1938 / John Raeburn.
p.   cm.
Includes bibliographical references and index.
ISBN 978-0-252-03530-2 (cloth : alk. paper)
ISBN 978-0-252-07715-9 (pbk. : alk. paper)
1. Documentary photography—Ohio—History. 2. Villages—Ohio—
Social life and customs—History—Pictorial works. 3. Social problems in art.
4. Shahn, Ben, 1898–1969—Criticism and interpretation.
I. Title. II. Title: American scene.
TR820.5.R34   2010
770.9771—dc22   2010007691

For my sons
Nick and Dan,
and Rebekah
and Willa

Contents

Illustrations

Acknowledgments

BEN SHAHN'S photographs are reprinted courtesy of the Library of Congress.

The Office of the Vice-President for Research at the University of Iowa generously subsidized the expense of securing the photographs.

Matt Nelson and Cinda Nofziger ably provided research assistance, and I am grateful to the University of Iowa American Studies Department for making their work for me possible. Doris Friedensohn and Eric Sandeen supplied helpful advice about the manuscript, as did the members of my 2008 graduate seminar on FSA photography. The support of my wife, Kathleen Kamerick, was, as in all things, unstinting and indispensable.

Ben Shahn's American Scene

Introduction

BEN SHAHN IS most renowned as one of the leading American painters, muralists, and graphic artists of the twentieth century's middle decades. But during the 1930s, he alternated these fine arts activities with photography, first in New York and then, beginning in 1935, for the New Deal's Resettlement Administration (RA), renamed the Farm Security Administration (FSA) two years later. His first assignment with the agency was a three-month trip through the South to make photographs as *aide-mémoire* for the fine arts work the RA had hired him to do. As a member of its Special Skills Division, he was responsible for creating lithographs and posters to publicize the RA's programs and eventually painting a mural for its Jersey Homesteads project, where the agency had resettled Jewish needle-workers in a newly built cooperative community. But the strength of the photographs he made in the South so surpassed the instrumental uses Special Skills had envisioned for them that Roy Stryker, the director of the agency's photography unit, the Historical Section, arranged for them to be included in its archive alongside images by its own staff at the time, Walker Evans, Dorothea Lange, Carl Mydans, and Arthur Rothstein. Even in this illustrious company, Shahn's photographs rank among the Historical Section's—and the thirties'—most accomplished. They are as distinguished as his fine arts work, and deserve as wide an audience.[1]

After his tenure with Special Skills ended in the spring of 1938, Shahn brokered with Stryker a short-term appointment with the Historical Section to photograph exclusively in central Ohio during the summer months. Being authorized to work in such a limited geographical area for a prolonged period was an unusual arrangement inasmuch as the Section's modus operandi was for the photographers to stay just a few days—rarely as long as a week or two—in any one location before moving on. In Ohio, Shahn made numerous countryside views, but he gave his most concentrated attention to photographing a dozen small towns all located near Columbus.

Being permitted to work so deliberatively not only made Shahn's Ohio assignment uncommon in the annals of FSA photography, but it also provided him exceptional scope to develop in depth his inquiry into the circumstances of small-town life. While many of his pictures can confidently stand on their own as examples of superior photographic artistry, the incisiveness of his cultural analysis is more evident when individual images are seen alongside the others he made that summer. A superb close-in portrait of two female welfare recipients awaiting a dole of foodstuffs, for example—one of them elderly in an old-fashioned bonnet, the other young with her hair fashionably bobbed (fig. 80)—has been reproduced a number of times, to become perhaps the best-known of Shahn's Ohio pictures, but only when viewed in conjunction with his other photographs of that relief distribution and of the poor's desperate living conditions does his acid critique of institutional contempt and public scorn for the needy become apparent.

The ensemble of his Ohio photographs also reveals more clearly than any single image the key role Shahn's formal strategies played in conveying his interpretation of small-town culture. His diagnosis of these communities cannot be summarized adequately by a categorical itemization of the topics he addressed, but requires an assessment of the compositional decisions he made prior to depressing his shutter release because these choices perforce shaped how viewers would perceive what a photograph depicted. A recurring motif in a number of his views of the towns' business districts, for instance, is the torpor of their central squares and nearly deserted sidewalks. The impression of civic stagnation these photographs convey was determined by the decisions he made in formally organizing them, and the cumulative effect of so many employing a perspective that emphasized disused public spaces intimated Shahn's perception that the American small town had entered into a period of decline, a heterodox observation in 1938. These studies both depict those sites and interpret them, and as with all of Shahn's photographs, his compositional decisions here are the surest index of that interpretation. He was documenting the small towns' everyday activities, but actively appraising their implications as well, performing the gifted artist's social role of deploying his acute perceptive capabilities to clarify the significance of emerging cultural developments and what they portended.

But if Shahn intuited that decline was to be the American small town's fate, he was more intent on assessing the symbolic standing such towns enjoyed in contemporary popular culture and public memory as the exemplar of democratic community. Stryker's conviction that this reputation was unimpeachable had led him, a few months before Shahn's Ohio stint, to make small-town studies a priority for the Historical Section's photographers and to draw up a detailed shooting script to assist them in that undertaking. As authoritarian regimes abroad went from triumph to triumph in the late thirties, Stryker sensed that there would be an increasing demand for pictures emphasizing the strength and durability of American democratic traditions, and he believed that studies of small-town culture would best meet it. As a dedicated anti-fascist, Shahn shared Stryker's dismay about political developments overseas and the director's conviction that the threat authoritarianism posed to democratic ideals mandated an amendment to the Section's priorities. Shahn thus announced that in Ohio he intended to focus on "the average American," because he believed that the FSA photographers had too singularly concentrated on the Depression's casualties and needed to broaden their scope to include more sympathetic portrayals of everyday community life.

That resolution led him to make numerous photographs supporting Stryker's view of the small town as a bastion of democratic community. But in addition to his anti-fascism, Shahn brought to his Ohio work a longer-standing commitment to social justice that made him unable to dissemble the violations of democratic ideals he also discovered there, notably racial bigotry and a disregard for the community's most economically disadvantaged citizens that edged into insidious contempt. His politics thus influenced his survey in contrasting, sometimes paradoxical ways. He also hedged about the degree to which the accelerating forces of modernity had altered the towns' traditional cultural patterns, as mass entertainment and communications networks, consumer culture, and the greater mobility afforded to townspeople by nearly universal car ownership played an increasingly larger role in their everyday life. Some of his photographs call attention to these transformative developments, but others neglect and even obscure them. And while a fair number of his photographs do hint at a decline in the American small town's fortunes, a minority emphasize instead its abiding sturdiness and solidity.

In short, Shahn's photographs do not present a singular, monolithic view of these communities. The small-town script with which Stryker had equipped him did, however, conveying the perspective that they were fundamentally healthy, unfalteringly democratic, and largely faithful to their traditional ways. Shahn's ambivalent survey of Ohio's small towns thus illuminates a key question in the historiography of the Historical Section: the degree to which the photographers' autonomy was compromised by Stryker's direction of their work, notably by means of the shooting scripts he issued to guide them in making their photographs. With Shahn's project, that issue is further complicated by his sympathy with the ideological impetus that lay behind Stryker's making small-town studies a priority for the Section's photographers.

While Shahn's survey did not, as a whole, conform to the celebratory tone of Stryker's script and put forward an equivocal interpretation of small-town life, its duality was neither careless nor inadvertent. Working over an extended period in a discrete area granted him the latitude to develop groupings of related photographs that exposed the conflicts between cultural values that he discovered in Ohio's towns and the freedom to explore them with a thoroughness not possible for the other, more itinerant Section photographers. The esthetic distinction of Shahn's photographs alone justifies their reproduction in this volume, but their acuteness in highlighting key tensions of the late 1930s equally makes them an invaluable contribution to a more nuanced understanding of that pivotal moment in American history.

IN MARCH 1938, Ben Shahn had just finished his first mural, commissioned by the Farm Security Administration to adorn the community center of Jersey Homesteads, New Jersey, and his appointment with the federal agency's Special Skills Division, his employer since 1935, was about to be terminated. Inasmuch as his earlier Special Skills photographs had been archived by the FSA's photographic unit, the Historical Section, he wrote as an honorary member to its director, Roy Stryker, asking for an appointment while he sorted out what to do next. Stryker proposed a three-month stint during which Shahn would photograph in the Corn Belt as far west as Iowa for $50 per week, less than he had made with Special Skills but the standard for Historical Section photographers. In May, while the appointment was making its way through channels, the Treasury Department awarded Shahn a new mural commission, for the Bronx General Post Office, with lines from Walt Whitman to supply its theme. By that time he was in Ohio, staying with his in-laws in Worthington, a suburb of Columbus; his wife, Bernarda Bryson Shahn, was expecting their second child in June and planned to deliver the baby there. Stryker wrote to congratulate Shahn for the commission, which, he said, probably meant that "now you won't have time to do photographic work. But in case you decide not to do the mural it will be our luck; but after all, this other thing is much more important to you."[1] Shahn split the difference: he proposed to postpone work on the mural until autumn if he could photograph exclusively in central Ohio during the summer. Stryker agreed, and Shahn joined the Historical Section staff for the first and only time.

Their correspondence ended without a determination of what he would photograph, which was settled by telephone. Shahn later said that his assignment had been "to cover what [Stryker] called Harvest in Ohio," and Bernarda remembered that "Ben called Roy from Ohio and said he had been doing enough photography of the Depression. 'I want to photograph the average American,' he said."[2] He did cover the wheat harvest, and most of the people he photographed were not self-evidently victims of the Depression, but his summer's work was considerably more varied than these recollections suggest. Nearly 900 of his Ohio pictures were printed for the FSA archive, and they break out into five distinct if geographically related subject categories: the harvest and farm life (about 225 printed); a farmstead auction (85); roadside views (85); fairs, carnivals, and an amusement park (140); and, most thematically complex, a survey of small-town life (320).[3]

Photographing "small town stuff" was among the topics Stryker had proposed when Shahn's assignment was to be in the Corn Belt, so it is unsurprising that he made more pictures in central Ohio towns than at other sites. Eight county seats and a number of smaller towns were conveniently located within a fifty-mile radius of his Worthington base and no more than an hour's drive by car. Never having learned to drive, he depended on Bernarda to chauffeur him. Her parents apparently provided child care, but with a newborn, some flexibility in the Shahns' schedule was necessary: the harvest, auction, and fairs were time specific, but the towns could be visited whenever opportunity permitted. Ohio's towns, moreover, offered exceptional possibilities for photographing "the average American," which also anticipated Shahn's plan for the Whitman mural to feature a range of ordinary citizens. Finally, for his exploration of these communities, he had the benefit of knowledgeable local informants: Bernarda was a native Ohioan who had attended college in the state, and his father-in-law published a small-town newspaper.

But that emphasis dovetailed as well with an initiative—to undertake a "Documentary Photographic Study of the Small Town in America"—that had recently become a key priority for the Historical Section, one that Shahn's sojourn in Ohio presented an outstanding opportunity to expedite. As the Section's director, Stryker had two primary goals: to encourage the staff to augment the photographic file's breadth and depth, so that it would achieve permanent significance as a historical archive of the 1930s; and, of more immediate utility, to make certain it included pictures that could serve contemporary publicity purposes. He believed that photographs of small towns would further both ends, by recording for posterity the distinctive way of life of quintessentially American communities, and by supplying timely pictures that would emphasize the underlying stability of democratic culture.

When the Section was established in 1935, its propaganda efforts centered on publicizing the programs of the federal agency housing it, but almost immediately it enlarged its purview to include documentary photographs of the broader social conditions that were making New Deal reforms necessary. By 1938, as political developments in Europe and Asia became increasingly ominous, it began to widen its horizons yet again, to propagandizing for the soundness of American democracy and the political, social, and material benefits the nation's citizens enjoyed. Raised near a small Colorado town himself, and having retained a nostalgic affection for it, Stryker believed that a photographic survey of the characteristic features of small-town life would reflect these American benisons and reveal the still-tensile sinews of national vigor.

To implement this initiative, he composed an elaborate shooting script, identifying twenty-two sites and institutions characteristic of small towns and itemizing the distinctive features of their cultural life that each category revealed. Sometime later he supplemented the list with additional topics, and then redacted the script, possibly around the time Shahn was in Ohio.[4] The redaction declared that "every Farm Security Administration photographer carries a permanent small-town shooting-script" as "a perennial rather than a special assignment," and both versions regretted that the photographers' tight scheduling permitted only piecemeal coverage of any specific locale—a limitation that Shahn's Ohio sojourn that summer would allow him to overcome.[5]

In an interview years later, Shahn claimed that he would have resented it had Stryker prescribed background preparation for his assignments—as he did with the other photographers—and that working for Special Skills had shielded him from it. When he photographed in Ohio, Stryker's only directive, Shahn said, "was just as vague as that: to do the harvests." But that Stryker, with his commitment to small-town coverage, would not have urged photographing Ohio's towns seems an impossibility, as does the idea that he would have failed to supply Shahn with the otherwise ubiquitous shooting script. And the interview indirectly confirms that Stryker and Shahn agreed that he would survey the towns, because immediately after mentioning the vagueness of his assignment, Shahn launched into an apparent digression about Robert Lynd, the co-author of *Middletown*, to the effect that Lynd had asked Stryker whether Shahn knew how greatly women's clubs influenced a town's social structure, and when Stryker reported this observation, Shahn sardonically asked to be sent a "psychologic lens and philosophic film" in order to photograph them.[6]

Stryker's script assumes that small towns are intrinsically democratic and fundamentally sound. Not only would the activities of their sturdy citizens provide strong photographic opportunities, but so would their compact built environment, and the script urges "close ups of the more important buildings" and panoramic surveys of main streets. It glancingly acknowledges class distinctions—"show the better home areas and the area where the poorer people live"—but it assumes that daily life will reveal a pervasive atmosphere of egalitarianism, and it is symptomatic that a suggestion to photograph "shack town" appears as an inconspicuous afterthought in its concluding "Miscellaneous" section, between "Getting the mail" and "Hitching racks for teams and horses." In the script, "the American institution SMALL TOWN" has no clouds on its horizon, and it distills the democratic temper and enduring resilience of the national character, undiminished by the Depression.[7]

The cultural geographer D. W. Meinig identifies three townscapes that seriatim have served as a "model setting for the American community." Until the mid-nineteenth century, that model was the New England town, centered on a church and common ringed by residences and shops. For nearly a century after the Civil War, its successor was "Main Street," a concentrated commercial area with adjacent streets occupied by churches, lodges, and public institutions, residential areas beginning just beyond this hub and thinning out until they met the prosperous surrounding farmland. Ohio's small towns, Meinig says, epitomized that symbolic townscape. In the mid-twentieth century, the California-style suburb became the new dominant form, residentially diffuse and commercially decentralized, linked to urban centers by high-speed highways.[8]

In hindsight we can see that by the thirties, Main Street was already in decline. Although agriculture in central Ohio did not suffer the drought and dust storms that ravaged farmers farther west, the depressed commodities market reduced farm income and resulted in numerous foreclosures, with damaging consequences for town businesses, as farmers had less to spend and there were fewer of them as bankruptcy drove some off the land. Moreover, the ubiquity of automobile ownership—people would give up nearly anything before their car—and improved highways provided locals with practicable access to larger retail and entertainment centers offering greater variety and lower prices, with harmful effects on the vitality of smaller places' downtowns. The perception that the cities offered better opportunities siphoned off some of the most ambitious young people, too; and increased exposure to and embrace of urban culture on radio and in the movies and magazines subtly adulterated townspeople's confidence that they belonged to a singularly self-contained, self-sufficient, and—they likely felt—superior community.

Meinig observes that "for many people over many decades of our national life [Main Street] was the landscape of 'small town virtues,' the 'backbone of America,' 'the real America,'" and it is unsurprising that the uncertainties of the Depression intensified this attachment and obscured the already gathering forces that in the century's latter half would make more visible the small town's decline. Contemporary filmmakers traded heavily on the Main Street model of community—Frank Capra successfully staked his films' popularity on it, and the Andy Hardy and Jones Family series idealized it in more than thirty installments—as did short-story writers for popular magazines such as the *Saturday Evening Post* and advertising agencies that repetitively purveyed idealized versions of it to reassure consumers, as Roland Marchand has observed, that "their society still retained the qualities suggested by 'village America.'"[9] Stryker's conviction that the small town retained its vitality undiminished may have been historically shortsighted, but in the thirties he had a good deal of company.

Shahn's survey of Ohio towns corresponds to Stryker's script in many particulars, as could scarcely fail to be the case with so methodical an outline. But a number of photographs supply circumstantial evidence that this overlap was not merely fortuitous and the script influenced his shooting agenda, as, for instance, do his half-dozen depictions of small factory buildings in outlying areas, distant from the central business districts where he mostly worked. They are among his most prosaic, unexceptional pictures, and it seems certain he made them in response to the script's proposal that "a study of local industries would be of great value."

But if he consulted Stryker's script, he did not slavishly follow it, avoiding some features of town life that it denominated as characteristic and including others that went unmentioned. It proposed, for example, photographing merchants in their stores and residents gathering at lunch counters, but Shahn believed that making documentary pictures with artificial light was "immoral" because it altered a depiction's reality; he resisted using a flash and made almost no interior shots.[10] Nor did he take "a small but selected set of outside photographs of homes," as the script recommended; aside from a pitiful Hooverville, he excluded residential areas almost entirely. The script also urged attention to retailers' window displays as indices of "the purchasing habits of the inhabitants," and to movie theater exteriors because of their prominence on downtown streets. But Shahn's coverage minimizes how pervasive consumer culture had become, and downplays as well the equally ubiquitous mass culture, thus making these Ohio towns appear more immune to modernity than was actually the case. Some photographs dramatize the script's assumption that small communities epitomize the democratic spirit, but a significant fraction qualify it, as do pictures of African Americans and of people on relief—neither of these categories of citizens is even mentioned in the script. Ambivalence characterizes his studies of the built environment. Some emphasize the congeniality of downtown areas—their spaciousness, the solidity of their business blocks, occasionally their engaging quirkiness—but as many suggest a banal utilitarianism or somnolent listlessness. Perhaps so many photographs of such an environment could never compose a uniform attitude, but Shahn's pictures reveal a striking degree of equivocation about the script's assumption that a photographic survey of small towns would reveal their undiminished vitality and ratify their standing as an "American institution." This duality mirrors the competing personas, as propagandist and as artist, that Shahn assumed while working in Ohio.

These personas were competing but not mutually exclusive, and Shahn remarked that "to me the word propaganda is a holy word when it's something I believe in." He felt "very strongly about the efforts that this Resettlement Administration was trying to accomplish," and in the South he had made some exceptional photographs of poverty that could be used as propaganda for it.[11] By the time he transferred to the Historical Section in 1938, though, he had come to believe that its photographs had too narrowly centered on the Depression's calamities, and thus he welcomed its new emphasis on a more balanced representation of American life. At a meeting that Stryker arranged with magazine picture editors to evaluate the unit's priorities, Shahn told the journalists that the FSA photographers had concentrated too exclusively on "just one side of America, the real poverty stricken," and they needed to enlarge their compass to include the "nice little middle class street" and "the family who just bought a new set of furniture from Sears, Roebuck." Photographing such normative subjects with verve was "hard to do," he conceded, but it was imperative that the FSA begin to do so.[12]

As a man of the left and a dedicated anti-fascist, moreover, he had been dismayed by international developments earlier in 1938 that boded such ill for democratic ideals. The horrific rape of Nanking by Japanese invaders had occurred during the winter, in March the *Anschluss* annexed Austria to the Nazi Third Reich, and in April the Spanish Republic was bisected when fascist-led Nationalist armies supported by Germany and Italy reached the Mediterranean and cut off Catalonia from the republic's southeastern strongholds. In the face of these grim political developments, for Shahn to follow Stryker's lead with photographs that advertised the strengths of democracy was not a stretch, especially when doing so would present such excellent opportunities to make the type of photographs he believed the FSA had been remiss in neglecting.

But if he embraced the FSA's propaganda mission, he did not relinquish the artist's prerogative to bring a critical eye to bear on the dominant culture, especially when he perceived blind spots in conventional assumptions. This was less an esthetic discipline than an analytical one, although formal strategies were instrumental in making his critical observations palpable, and it required unblinking honesty and a receptivity to ambiguity, characteristics of the artist if not the propagandist. Stryker, along with other cultural producers in the 1930s, assumed the timeless stability of the small town as the foundation for its democratic traditions, but Shahn's eye detected that decline had set in and that its long reign as a "model setting for the American community" was approaching its end, and that perception qualified if it did not cancel his more positive views of Main Street.

Shahn's earlier FSA assignments had been mostly in the South, and there, he said, "wherever you point there is a picture," but central Ohio seemed so "neat and clean and orderly" that at first he "didn't think it had any photographic opportunities for me." His misgivings disappeared when he realized that it was less antiseptic than he had initially imagined, and that he needed to be more self-consciously selective about where and how to aim his camera. Photographing in Ohio, he said, "you [had] to make some choices."[13] In the South he had mostly exposed poverty and social or racial discrimination, aspiring to make congruent a degrading reality and the photograph's representation of it. The more normative Ohio towns required greater alertness to the potential gap between their stolid ordinariness and what might be glimpsed behind their placid surfaces that might qualify or even be in the process of disrupting it.

Aside from a handful of comments in interviews, the photographs' titles, and a few lengthier captions, Shahn left no verbal record of his Ohio work, no journal, letters, or shooting notes.

The small-town script almost certainly provided a loose template, but perhaps even more important, its uncritical tone supplied an attitude about the small town's well-being against which to test his own perceptions, and in this sense it also influenced the portrait he composed. But the script specified only potential subjects and not how they might be addressed, while managing a photograph's formal elements is the key instrument that photographers employ to *interpret* whatever they have trained their cameras on. Before opening the lens, a photographer must make a number of decisions that will significantly affect how the finished print will be understood, and identifying a subject is just the first of these, as knowing the right moment to trip the shutter is the last. Among these variables are determining the distance and angle from which to shoot; calculating how the intensity and pattern of light and shadow may affect meaning and how to best exploit them; deciding what the picture's frame ought to include— and exclude—as well as where within it the principal subjects will appear; and selecting a horizontal or vertical format. That itemization does not exhaust the decisions that making a photograph requires, but it does suggest how greatly a gifted photographer's subjectivity inflects the apparently objective end result that he or she produces and formally embeds in its composition an interpretation of its subject.[14] For an understanding of Shahn's ambivalent assessment of Ohio's small towns—their present circumstances as well as their future—the structure of his photographs is often as revealing as the subjects he chose to depict.

Of all the visual arts, photography perhaps most greatly depends on the artist's intuition because of the instantaneity with which an image is made. As Shahn's contemporary Edward Weston put it, the photographer must be alert "to capture the moment—not just any moment, but the important one, the one moment out of all time when your subject is revealed to the fullest— that moment of perfection which comes once and is not repeated."[15] Shahn, whose method was to shoot spontaneously and rapidly with a handheld camera, had even less opportunity for premeditation than did Weston, who worked deliberately with a view camera mounted on a tripod. Stryker's script supplied an outline, but Shahn depended on his artist's intuition to shape his compositions, much as a talented jazz soloist improvises on a musical score. Photographers often speak of lucky accidents, and they usually occur because a gifted photographer anticipates where to look for them and instantaneously grasps their expressive potential. "Luck is the residue of design" is an aphorism the baseball magnate Branch Rickey coined to explain why winning teams seem to benefit from lucky breaks, and it applies to photography, too.

Shahn at age eight had emigrated from Lithuania and grown up in New York's bumptious atmosphere of urban bustle and heterogeneity, so dissimilar to the sedate, orderly country towns he would photograph. An outsider's perspective sharpened his alertness to what was distinctive about them, but it also threatened to make his survey no more than a catalog of their deviations from the model of city life he had known. But he believed that his exposure to nonurban locales afforded by his three years with the FSA had weaned him away from succumbing to that temptation, acquainting him with an America he had formerly known only abstractly "via New York and mostly through Union Square," by which he meant through patronizing metropolitan cultural and political criticism unleavened by any actual experience of the nation's hinterlands. While his earlier travels for the agency had helped unburden him of that eastern provinciality, nowhere did he work longer or shoot more film than in central Ohio. His FSA stint, he later said, made him feel "totally in harmony with the times. I don't think I've ever felt that way before or since."[16] And not long after finishing his Ohio assignment, he moved to the small town of Roosevelt, New Jersey—as the FSA's Jersey Homesteads project was renamed—and lived there the rest of his life. But that testimony and his personal preference notwithstanding, his Ohio towns are neither idealized nor debunked; his studies of them exhibit both skepticism and sympathy, but most acutely they intimate, in contrast to Stryker's script and the larger cultural perception it echoed, that the reign of the small town as "a model setting for the American community" was nearing its end. Sometimes singly and certainly as a whole, his Ohio photographs richly exhibit, as Lawrence W. Levine has said of the FSA file more generally, the "tensions and ambiguities [that are] a clue to their essential soundness as guides for the historian."[17]

TWO-THIRDS OF Shahn's small-town studies are of eight county seats in the fertile agricultural region surrounding Columbus. London and Marysville had 4,000 to 5,000 inhabitants, Circleville, Urbana, and Washington Court House 8,000 to 9,000, and Lancaster, Newark, and Marion between 22,000 and 31,000. He also shot twenty-five or so pictures in the considerably larger cities of Columbus and Springfield, and about sixty in smaller towns with populations of around 1,000: Canal Winchester, Plain City, Somerset, and Worthington. In the hamlets of Linworth and Unionville Center he made twenty more, all of churches.[1]

While these communities differed appreciably in size, his photographs do not indicate it. Pictures of larger places resemble those of smaller ones, and he treated the towns as interchangeable. This perception is heightened by his avoidance of most sites that locals would have pointed out as distinctive or unique, and while he photographed handsome central squares in two towns, both with Civil War monuments, such notable sights are rare. And on the few occasions when signage indicates a town's name, what it appears on is generic—a railroad depot, post office, or Rotary Club sign.

His indifference to what distinguished the towns from one another suggests his intention to have the photographs compose a unified survey along the lines of Stryker's script. If this ambition was broadly ethnographic, though, it was not holistic. He did not aspire to address all six of the "main-trunk activities" that the Lynds in *Middletown* itemize as central in all communities: earning a living; making a home; educating the young; participating in leisure; practicing religion; and engaging in community affairs, their catchall category for political arrangements, information diffusion, health care, and assisting the unable.[2] While his photographs depict several of these central activities, documenting them with any thoroughness would have necessitated more than brief visits and required a greater intimacy with residents than his circumstances allowed, a sociological mentality that he had no interest in developing, and a systematic approach that comported poorly with his own preference for improvisatory shooting.[3] He concentrated instead on what he could observe in central business districts where the ordinary round of community life most visibly took place, to discover how residents interacted with their built environment and each other, supplementing these observations with a few forays into peripheral areas where economic and social distinctions were more apparent.

Shahn's camera—a 35 mm Leica compact enough to fit into his back pocket—permitted him to work rapidly with a minimum of fuss and conspicuousness. To further disguise his intentions, he fitted it with a right-angle viewfinder that could be discreetly engaged or switched off; this angle finder, as he called it, allowed him to face ninety degrees away from his unsuspecting human subjects as he made their picture. That deception, he believed, eliminated their self-consciousness and gave his pictures a candidness that "was a very helpful thing in the whole quality of my work."[4] In at least five shots (for example, fig. 1), a reflection reveals him using the angle finder, and while there is no way of knowing how consistently he did so, with nearby human subjects it was likely most of the time.[5]

If Shahn ever felt ethical misgivings about that stratagem, there is no record of it, and it would be surprising if he did. Sophisticated portable cameras permitting candid photography had been available for only about a decade, and as yet few worried over how their flexibility might abet invasions of privacy or misrepresent subjects. A few years after he worked in Ohio, though, James Agee's and Walker Evans's *Let Us Now Praise Famous Men* did assail the ethics of candid photography by reprinting a fatuous newspaper interview with Margaret Bourke-White, the era's best-known photographer, in which she boasted of the utter truthfulness of her depictions of poor Southerners, echoing her claim in *You Have Seen Their Faces,* the best-selling book in which they appeared, that her method of "imprison[ing subjects] on a sheet of film before they knew what had happened" guaranteed the pictures' veracity.[6] Reproducing the interview invited a comparison of her sensational photographs with Evans's restrained ones, including a number of unmistakably posed portraits of impoverished individuals like hers. Reviewing *Famous Men,* Lionel Trilling commended Evans's "perfect respect" for his subjects, which permitted them to "defend [themselves] against the lens" by posing as they wished to be seen.[7] But because Agee's

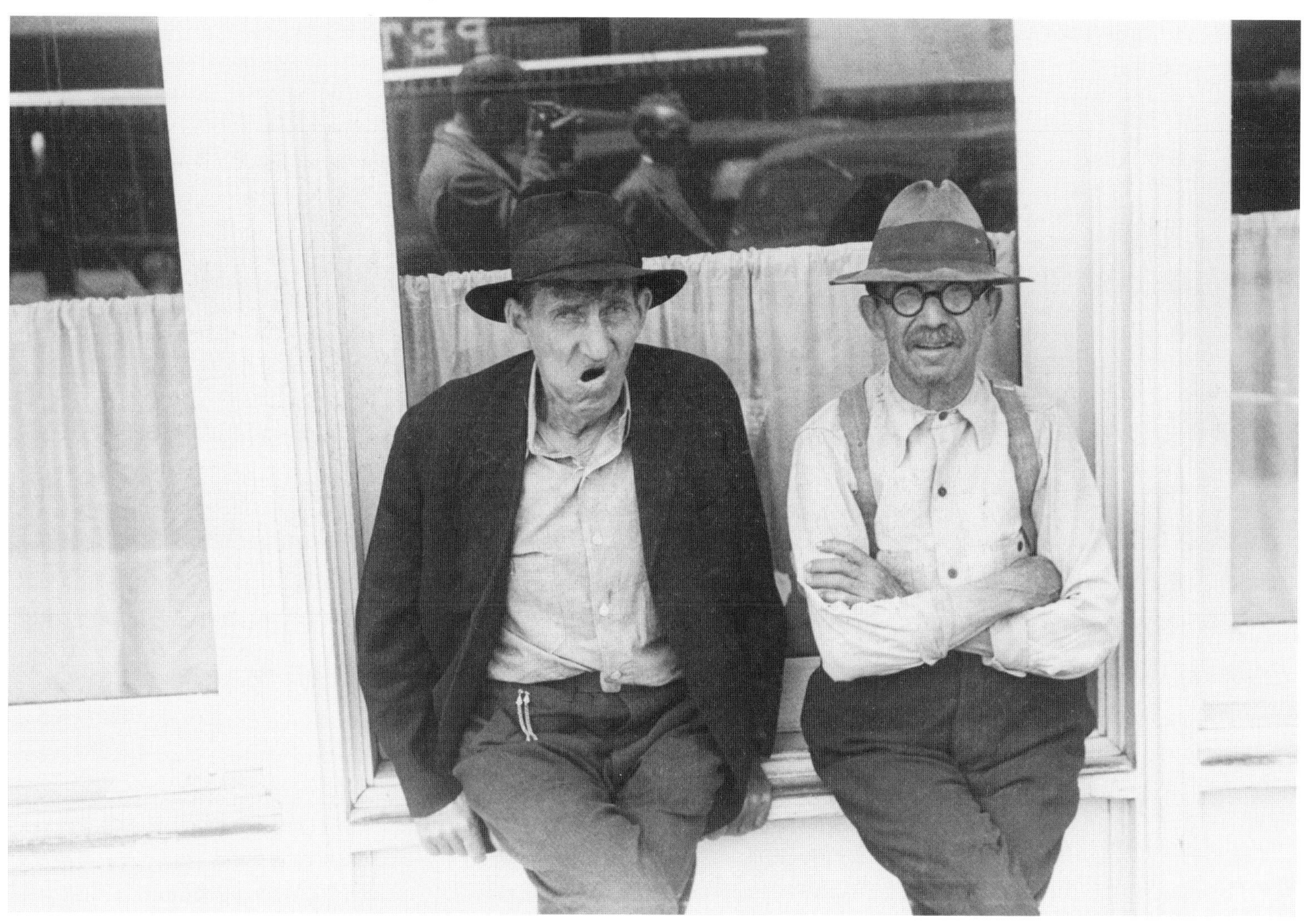

FIG 1 Street scene, Circleville, Ohio

and Evans's book had few readers and quickly dropped from sight, consideration of the ethics of candid photography never gained much traction until Susan Sontag raised it again a generation later in *On Photography*.[8] In any case, even Evans did not scruple at deception: the next year after making the *Famous Men* photographs, he dedicated himself to shooting clandestine (and illegal) portraits of New York subway riders, his 35 mm Contax camera hidden beneath his overcoat with its lens peeping through a gap between buttonholes.

Usually, however, Evans favored an 8 × 10 view camera because it maximized detail and tonality and its ground glass allowed him to seamlessly organize his compositions and previsualize the finished print. Shahn's preference for shooting on the fly militated against such fastidious preparation, and his Leica did not register detail or tonality so faithfully, which was also diminished by the need to enlarge the 35 mm negatives, but it allowed him mobility to range widely and permitted a spontaneity that a larger camera did not. He counted on the camera's inherent capacity to arrest time and isolate subjects from the welter of street activity to underscore the symbolic implications of what the frame encompassed, and on his ability to shoot rapidly enough to make his survey reasonably comprehensive. The Leica's flexibility made it ideally suited to his method of roaming town streets in search of variegated views that would be culturally resonant as well as pictorially compelling. While he respected Evans's meticulousness, for his purposes, Shahn said, "the image was more important than the quality of the image."[9]

Uniting his survey are a number of stylistic consistencies. In many mid-distance shots, the frame is busy with multiple subjects competing for attention—a row of parked cars, a line of buildings, shop windows and signs—while if people on a sidewalk are a picture's central interest, they are often seen closer in and centered in the frame to emphasize facial and body expressions. When human subjects and the built environment compete for attention, or people are absent or negligible, his compositions are frequently asymmetrical. For panoramic views of a business district, he tended to employ two strategies, sighting either along a sidewalk receding into the distance or obliquely across a street to the opposite row of structures angling away from the lens. Less frequently, a head-on perspective picks out one or two buildings for special emphasis. Most noticeably, he almost always employed a horizontal format, even when what he was photographing might have seemed to call for a vertical one.[10] This preference corresponded to his predilection for busy compositions with overlapping subjects, but equally with his survey's ethnographic ambition, because horizontality emphasizes context more.

SHAHN'S AMBITION TO create a unified survey is especially apparent in two sequences, "Saturday afternoon in London, Ohio, 'the main street'" and "Saturday afternoon in London, Ohio, 'the other side of the tracks,'" nineteen and eleven photographs respectively sharing these titles. Like all of his Ohio pictures, they are dated only "Summer" or "August" 1938, but it is reasonably certain that he made them near the outset of his summer's work, and that he meant these linked sequences with uniquely contrasting titles to supply the scaffolding for his project.[1] While he made most of his strongest Ohio photographs later, this circumstance warrants special attention to his London coverage. The forthrightness with which the titles call attention to London's class cleavages implies his misgivings about the script's neglect of them, and most of his photographs of "the other side of the tracks" concentrate on African Americans and foreground caste divisions as well. The "main street" photographs hew more closely to the script's upbeat view of small towns and their egalitarianism, but also intimate that their vitality may be ebbing.

Saturday was the traditional shopping day, and Shahn's coverage of it along the main street resembles a photo-essay, a genre the new picture magazines *Life* and *Look* had pioneered: people arrive downtown and park their cars, do their errands, and then depart with their purchases (figs. 2–4).[2] No one appears impoverished, and all plausibly fit the category of "the average American" that Shahn intended to concentrate on. Farmers are identifiable by overalls, and townsmen by neckties or open shirts; women dress more uniformly in daytime dresses, usually patterned, and low pumps, although the few young women rarely wear hats, whereas older women usually do. Gender and age distinctions are most notable: men are more numerous

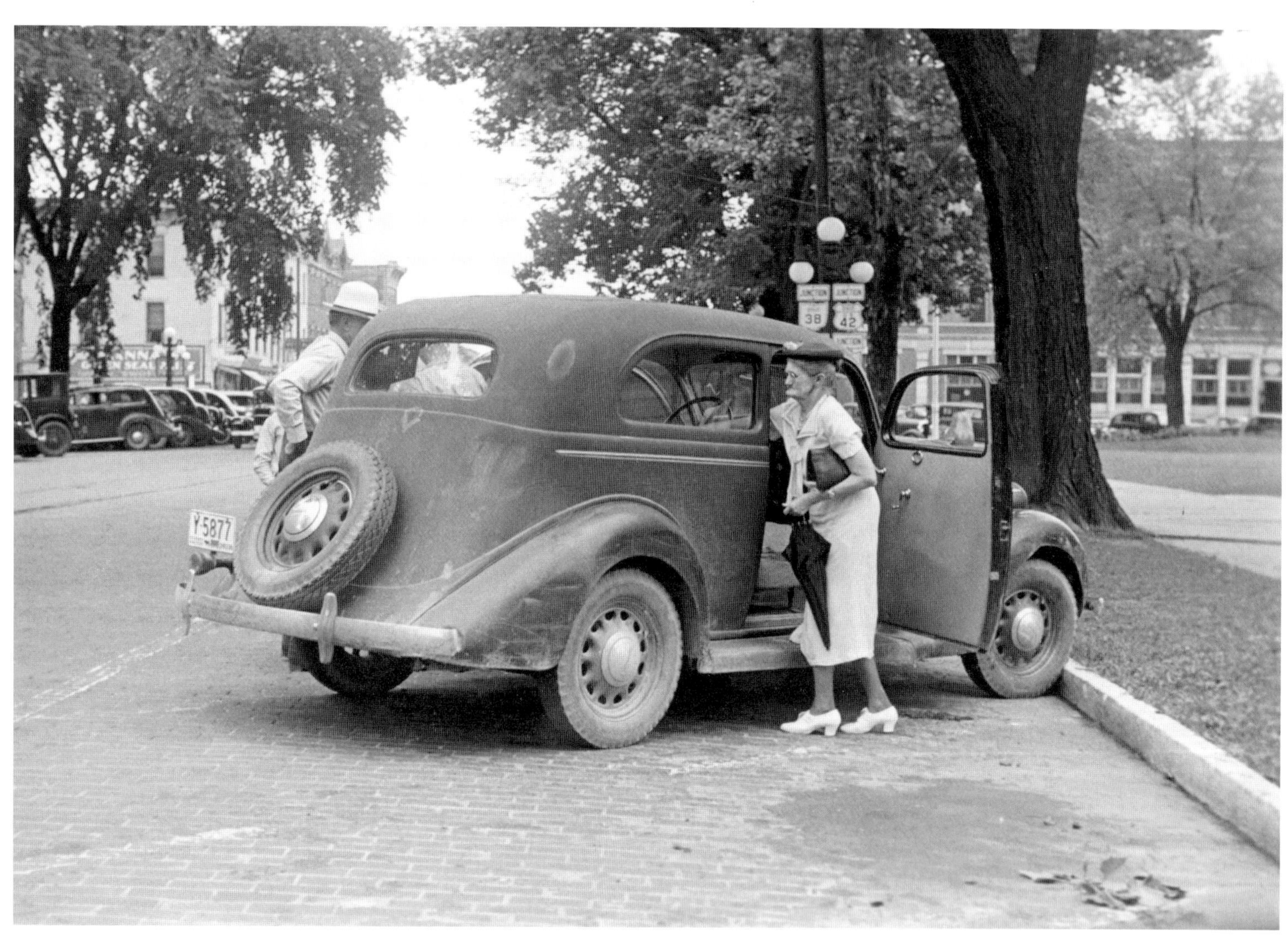

FIG 2 Saturday afternoon in London, Ohio, "the main street"

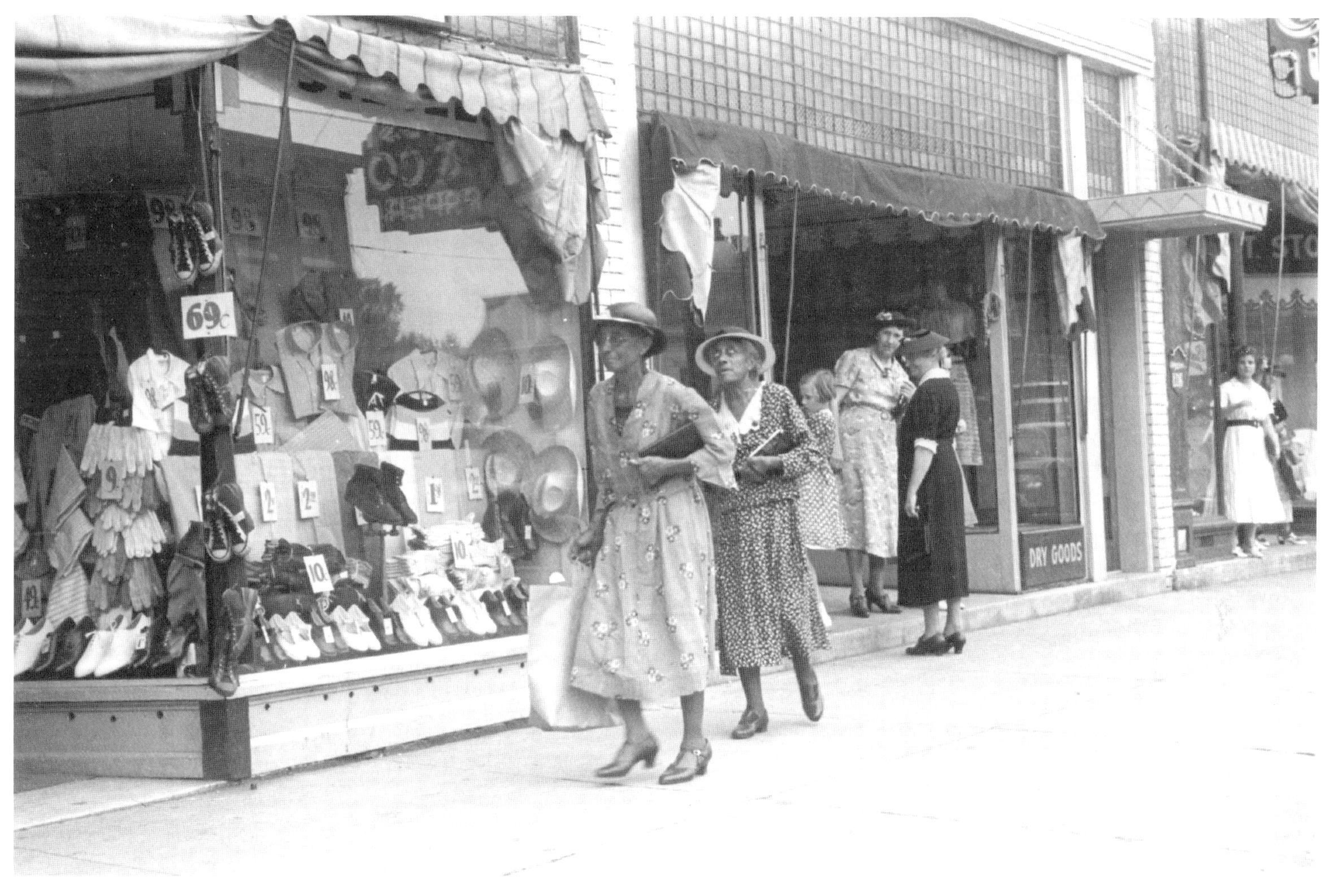

FIG 3 Saturday afternoon in London, Ohio, "the main street"

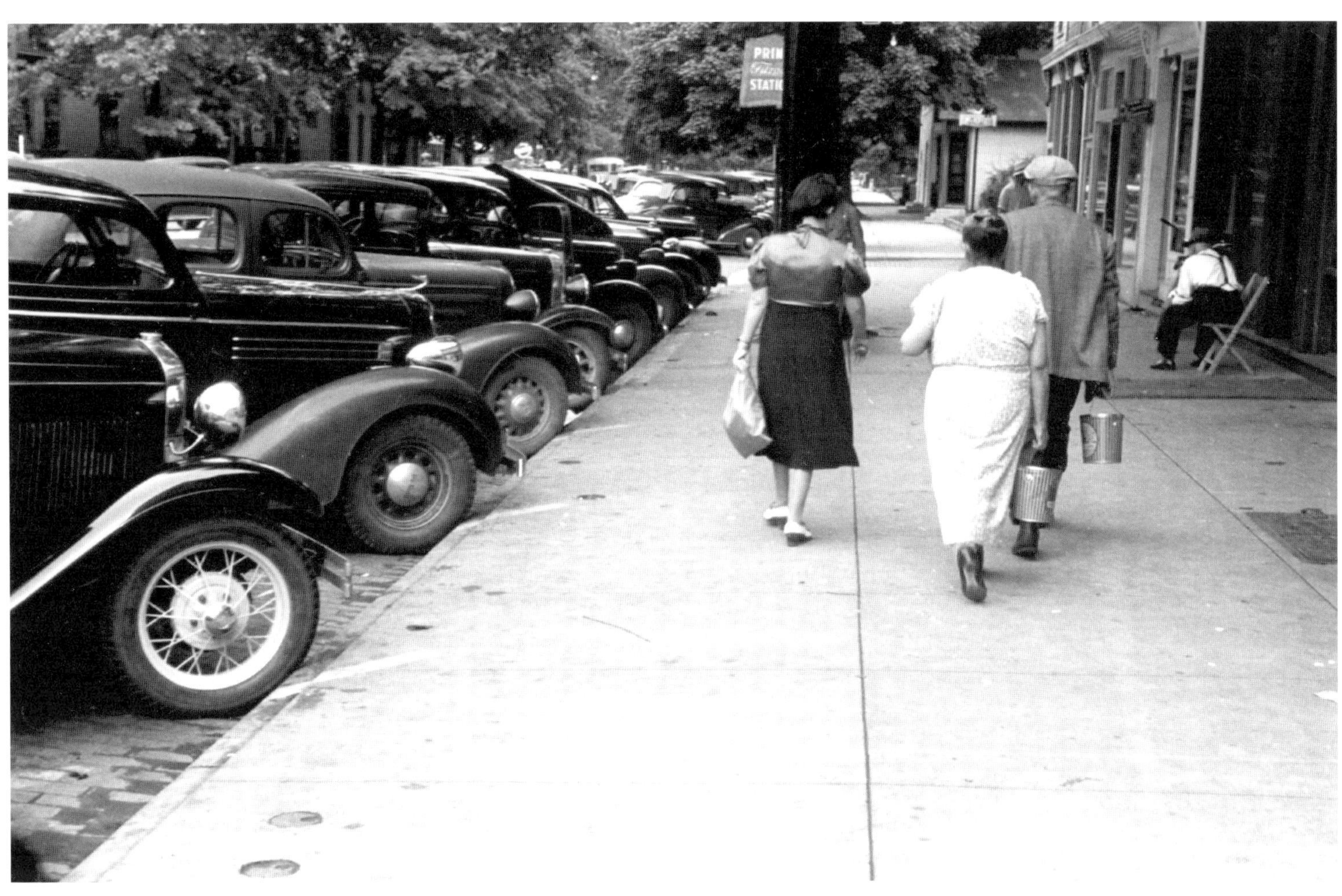

FIG 4 Saturday afternoon in London, Ohio, "the main street"

than women, with social segregation of the sexes almost universally observed, and middle-aged and elderly people far outnumber young adults.

These demographics remained constant throughout Shahn's work that summer. The paucity of younger subjects may indicate only that older residents frequented downtowns in greater numbers, but the effect was to give the impression that the towns were largely populated by aging residents and that their young people had abandoned them for more enticing urban centers. Women may also have been less conspicuous than men on downtown streets, or, perhaps as probable, Shahn shared the era's barely contested assumption that women's activities were less significant than men's, but two features of his project also likely accounted for women's limited representation. Those he did photograph mostly appeared to be shopping, and depicting this activity comported uncomfortably with his impulse to deemphasize the influence of consumer culture; also, the homogeneity of women's street attire did not permit dramatizing the small-town egalitarianism that he found so compelling among dissimilarly dressed males in London and elsewhere.

Seven of the main street photographs feature men congregating in democratic fellowship, foreshadowing the frequency of that motif in his studies of other towns. Most of these gatherings embrace individuals of differing social stations, as their dress indicates. Two of the three men lounging in front of the Underselling Store are garbed in overalls, while the third sports a necktie and dashing straw skimmer (fig. 5). An obliquely angled composition depicts pairs of conversationalists at each flank of the Central National Bank, the foreground twosome a resident in a denim shirt and cloth cap chatting with a spruce townsman sporting a bow tie and fedora (fig. 6). The strongest main street photographs are of two elderly men meeting on a broad sidewalk, one attired in a bow tie and pearly homburg, the other in a double-pocketed work shirt and battered felt hat. In a nearly full-length shot, they cordially shake hands as two unheeding young women in the background walk toward the camera (fig. 7). Shahn then moved in closer to make three waist-length portraits of the men conversing. Two in which they are seen against a store window indicate their facial features most clearly, but he decided not to have them printed for the FSA file, preferring another version in which body language—one participant's hand to his cheek, perhaps in amazement or dismay—emphasizes that the conversationalists' intimacy surpasses a merely polite exchange of salutations (fig. 8). In his studies of such sociability, the main street provides a public arena, at least for males,

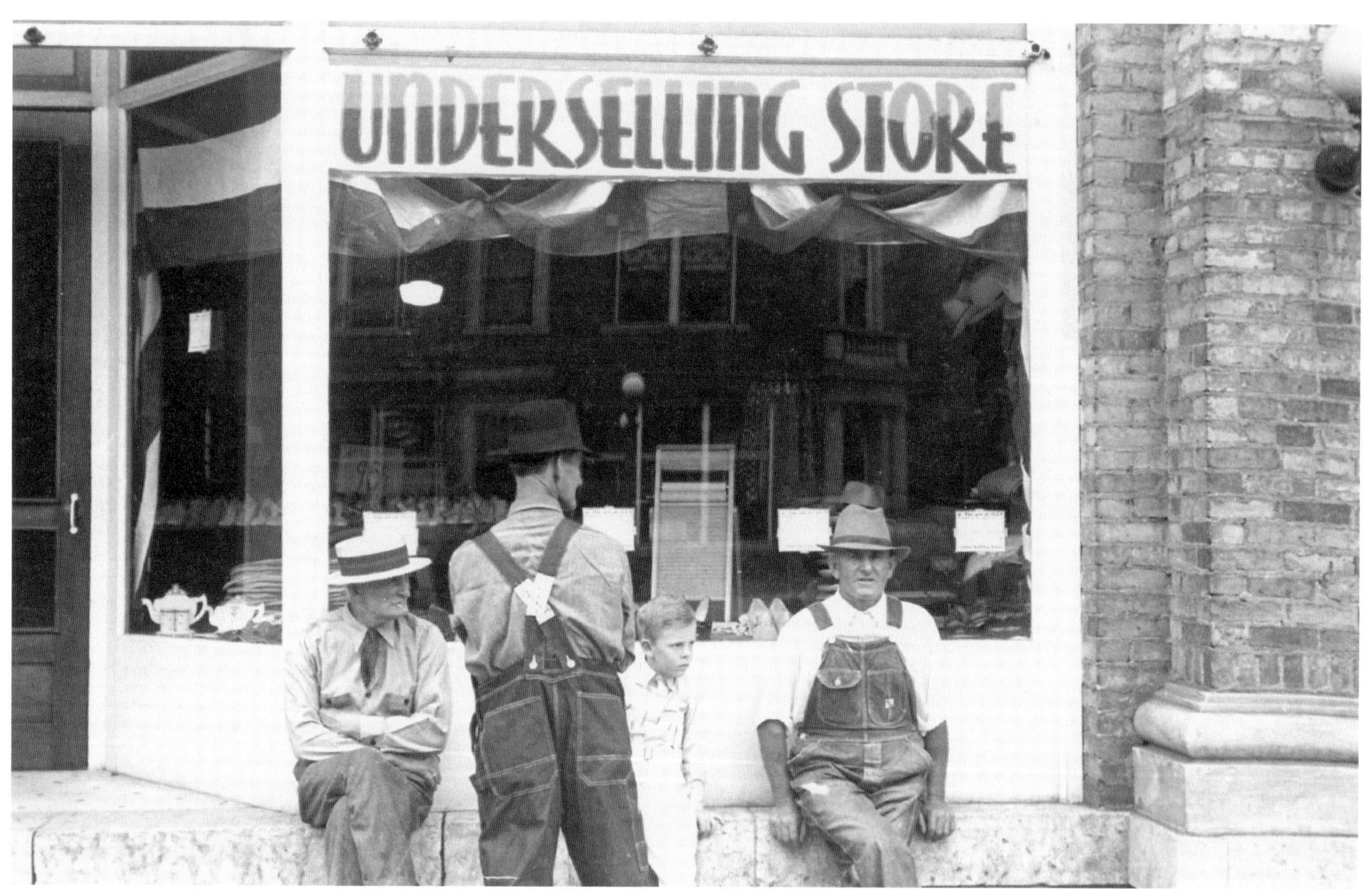

FIG 5 Saturday afternoon in London, Ohio, "the main street"

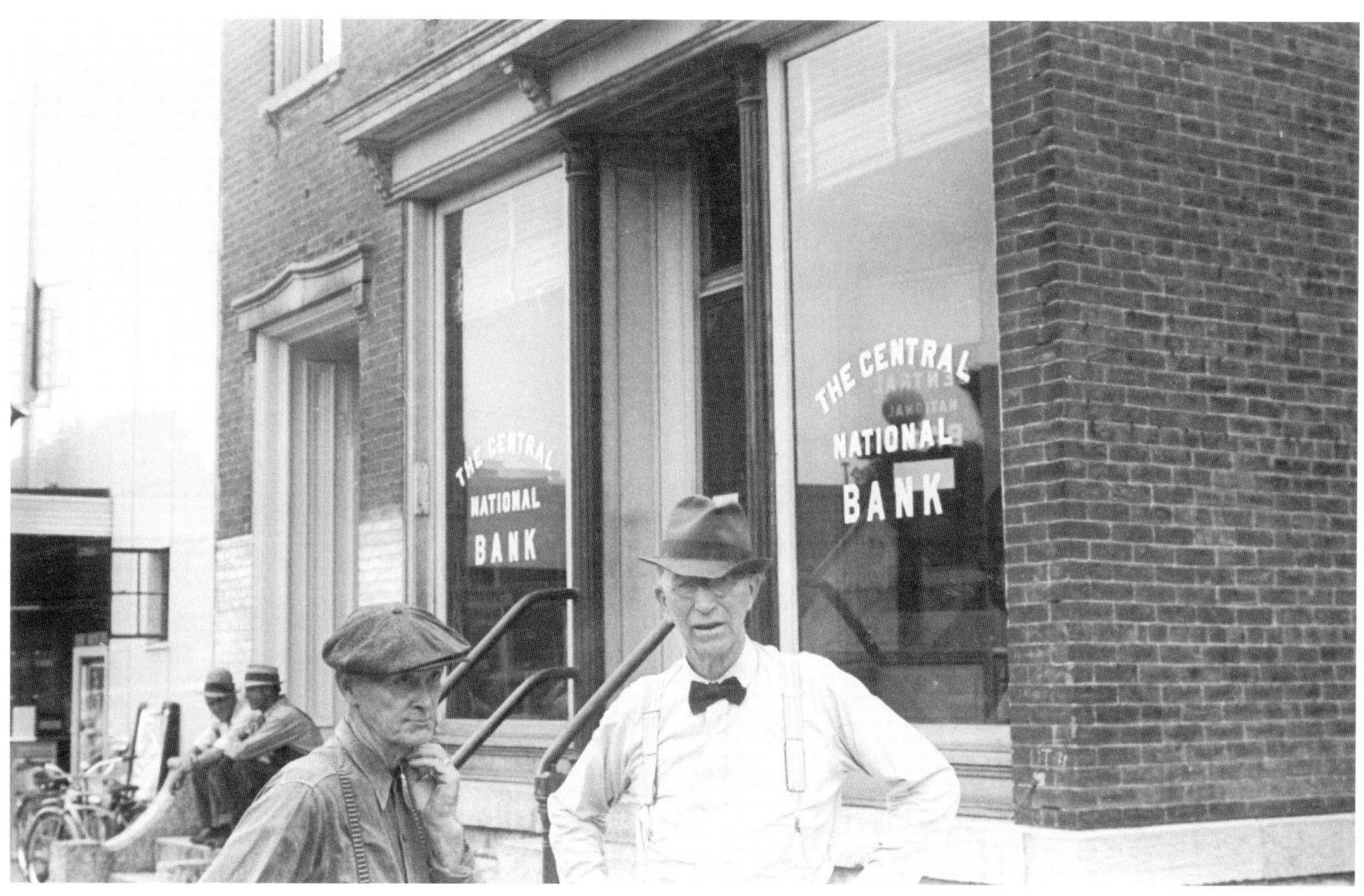

FIG 6 Saturday afternoon in London, Ohio, "the main street"

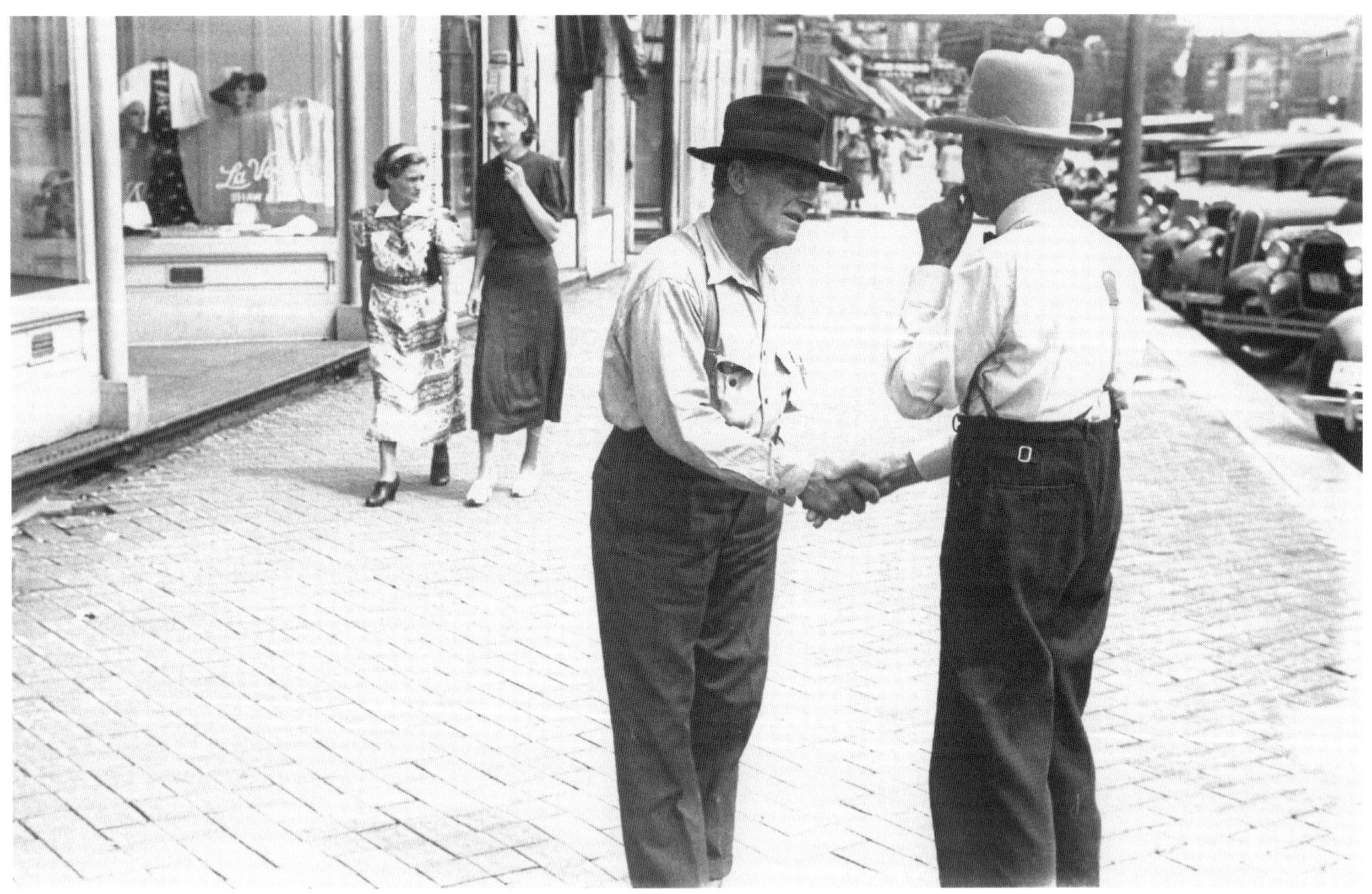

FIG 7 Saturday afternoon in London, Ohio, "the main street"

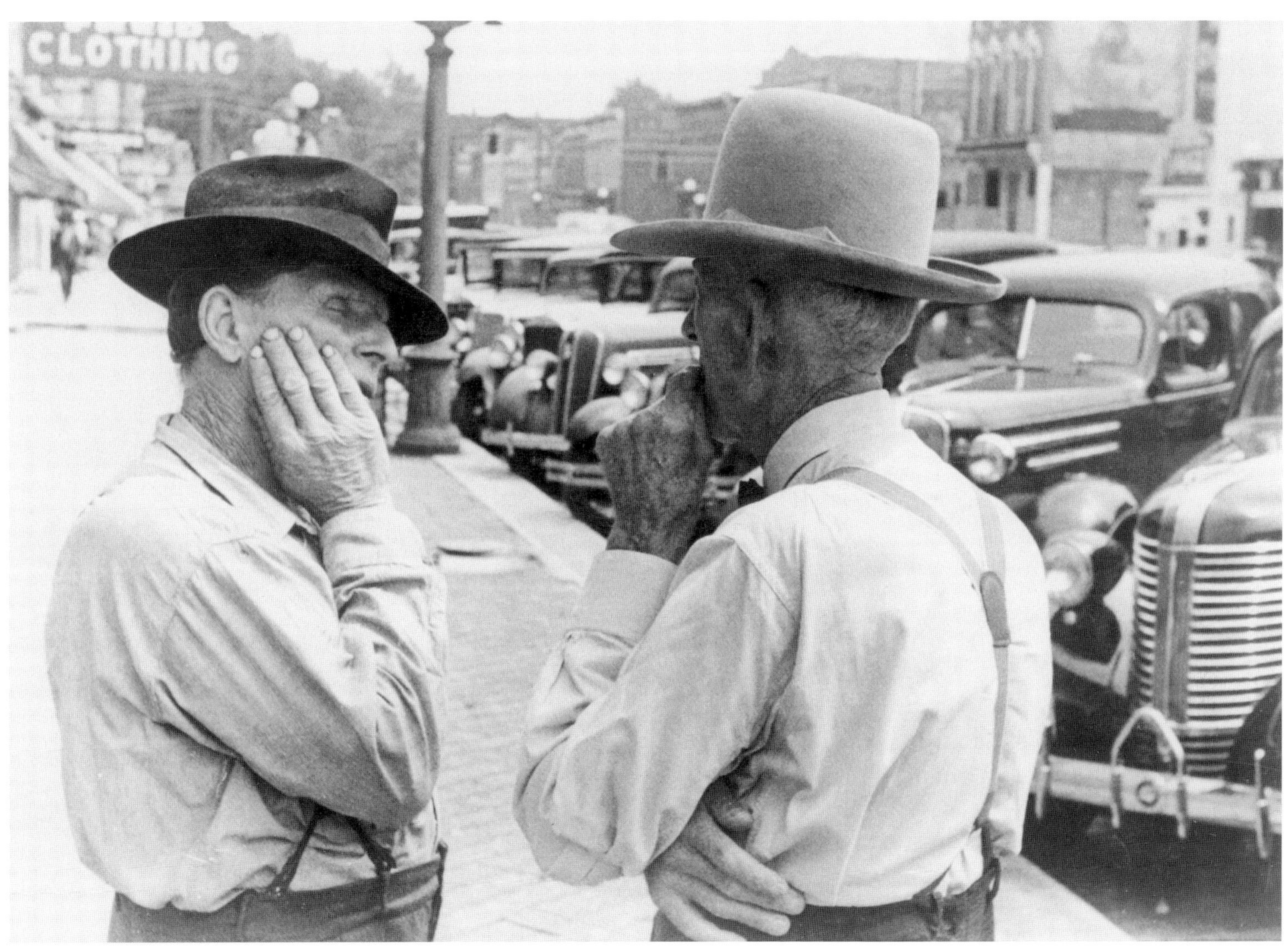

FIG 8 Saturday afternoon in London, Ohio, "the main street"

that transcends social divisions and creates an atmosphere conducive to the democratic spirit that Stryker believed characterized small towns.

General views along or across London's main street establish the physical setting for these activities and portray structural features common to all of the downtowns. Streets and sidewalks are notably wide and lined with late Victorian two- and three-story buildings, mostly brick; commercial enterprises occupy their ground floors, and offices or living quarters their upper levels. Some stores have installed full-length plate glass show windows and recessed entrances to maximize their merchandise displays, although older-fashioned windows that begin a few feet above the sidewalk are also common. There are, however, few instances of the modernized facades then popular with merchants across the nation, with which they contrived to make their brick storefronts appear less dated by superimposing new fronts of terra-cotta or porcelain tile. Files of angle-parked automobiles nose up to the curb, and some stores flaunt perpendicular signs that jut over the sidewalk to be more visible to passing vehicles. Nature is determinedly excluded from the business district—no greenery or flower boxes, even in high summer—and although a few shade trees have escaped removal to accommodate more parking, mostly they begin only at the downtown's periphery. For small-town merchants in the interwar period, John Jakle observes, "trees planted along the street did not symbolize progress."[3] While courthouses usually were situated in a surrounding green space, and some towns had parks just beyond their downtowns, Shahn gave only minimal attention to them, and when he did show them, he usually concentrated on their provision of benches for men (almost always) to idle on, and not on the ways they modified the downtowns' strict utilitarianism.

Shahn's studies of London's built environment reveal an orderly and functional commercial center, but one that is also nondescript and in which human activity is so sparse as to suggest a declining civic vitality, an impression that his compositional choices are decisive in conveying. One expansive view sights across the railway crossing separating the figurative two sides of the tracks and down the main street's broad sidewalk for a distance of several blocks to its vanishing point. Although the sun is high and cars line the curb, the street is somnolent, and the only people out and about are two distant pedestrians and a man lounging against the crossing guard's shack (fig. 9). In a similar but obliquely angled vista, the broad street is likewise deserted and the sidewalk fronting a hotel and car dealer on its opposite side is uninhabited, with a barely visible person in a store's doorway the sole human presence in the picture (fig. 10).

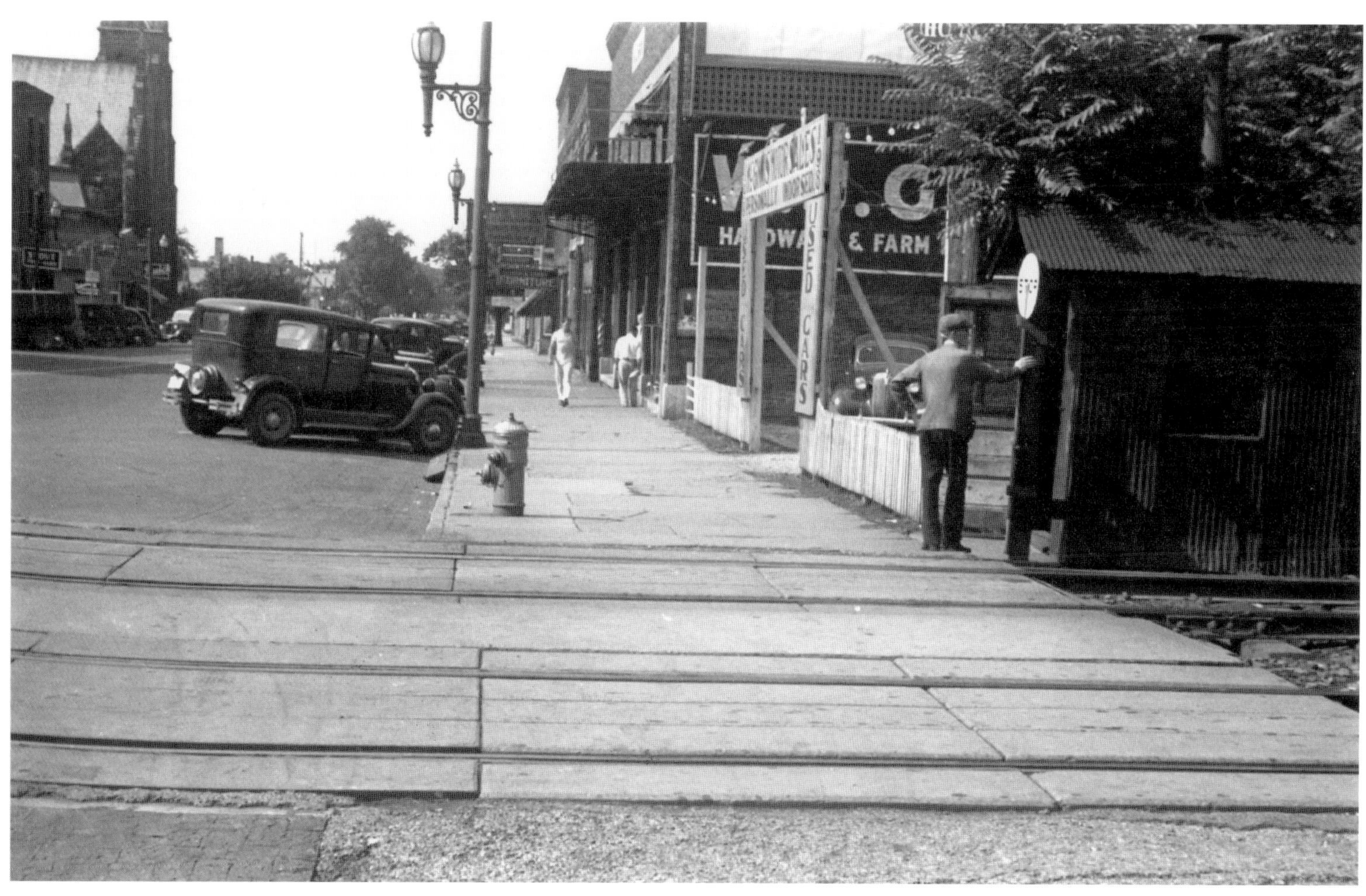

FIG 9 Saturday afternoon in London, Ohio, "the main street"

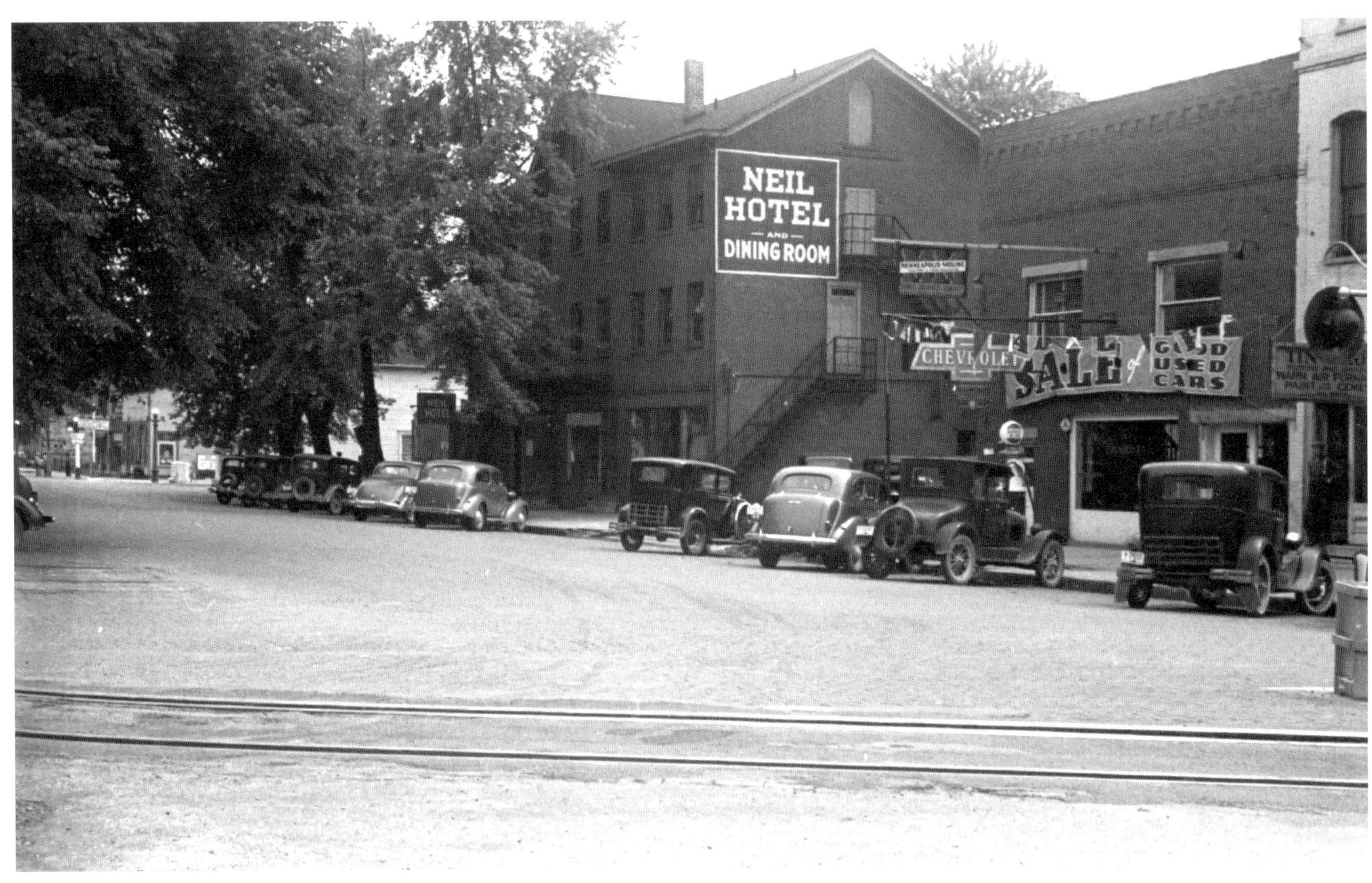

FIG 10 Saturday afternoon in London, Ohio, "the main street"

Two other shots of the main street are more tightly composed, aimed across it at the buildings opposite. In one, Shahn employs an oblique camera angle with the lens tipped slightly down to foreground an expanse of the street's empty pavement, exaggerating its width so that it occupies most of the picture's lower half; this perspective also makes the frame bisect the nineteenth-century brick structures angling away opposite, eliminating or obscuring the ornamentation of their upper windows and cornices and whatever coherence the ensemble may have presented. Instead of the possible visual pleasures afforded by vernacular architecture, this photograph calls attention to the pavement's blankness, a phalanx of angle-parked cars, and a row of first-floor businesses, all spanning the frame. Inasmuch as the scene is deserted and the pavement and cars are so visually dominant, the composition subtly intimates that an increased reliance on automobiles has eroded opportunities for civic sociability (fig. 11). Another shot across the main street is nearly head-on, to emphasize the prosaic architecture of a dime store and a candy emporium, both four-square, single-story buildings flaunting false fronts to bolster their visibility and disguise their lack of solidity compared with other downtown structures. Perhaps Shahn concentrated on them because their old-fashioned plainness was anomalous and could conceivably represent an earlier stage in London's history, but within the sequence, and since they are the only buildings so conspicuously picked out by head-on address, the effect is to hint at the town's fustiness (fig. 12).

Possibly he arrived in London early to make views of the built environment before the day's shopping began, but it seems unlikely inasmuch as many parking spots are taken and the sun is well up, not to mention the titles' specification of "Saturday afternoon." Or we might imagine that he did not want a human presence to distract attention from the townscape and so patiently waited until there was none, but that seems implausible on two counts. His preferred mode of working was rapid, improvisatory shooting; and by his own admission he was uninterested in buildings for their own sake, with his photographs rarely calling attention to their most distinctive architectural features and sometimes, as in figure 9, actually obscuring them. In these studies London's downtown appears not merely undistinguished but also afflicted by a low pulse rate and declining vitality.

In this respect, also significant is what he did not include in his photographs along the main street: neither the neo-Gothic First United Methodist Church nor the High Victorian Madison County Courthouse, London's most prepossessing and architecturally impressive

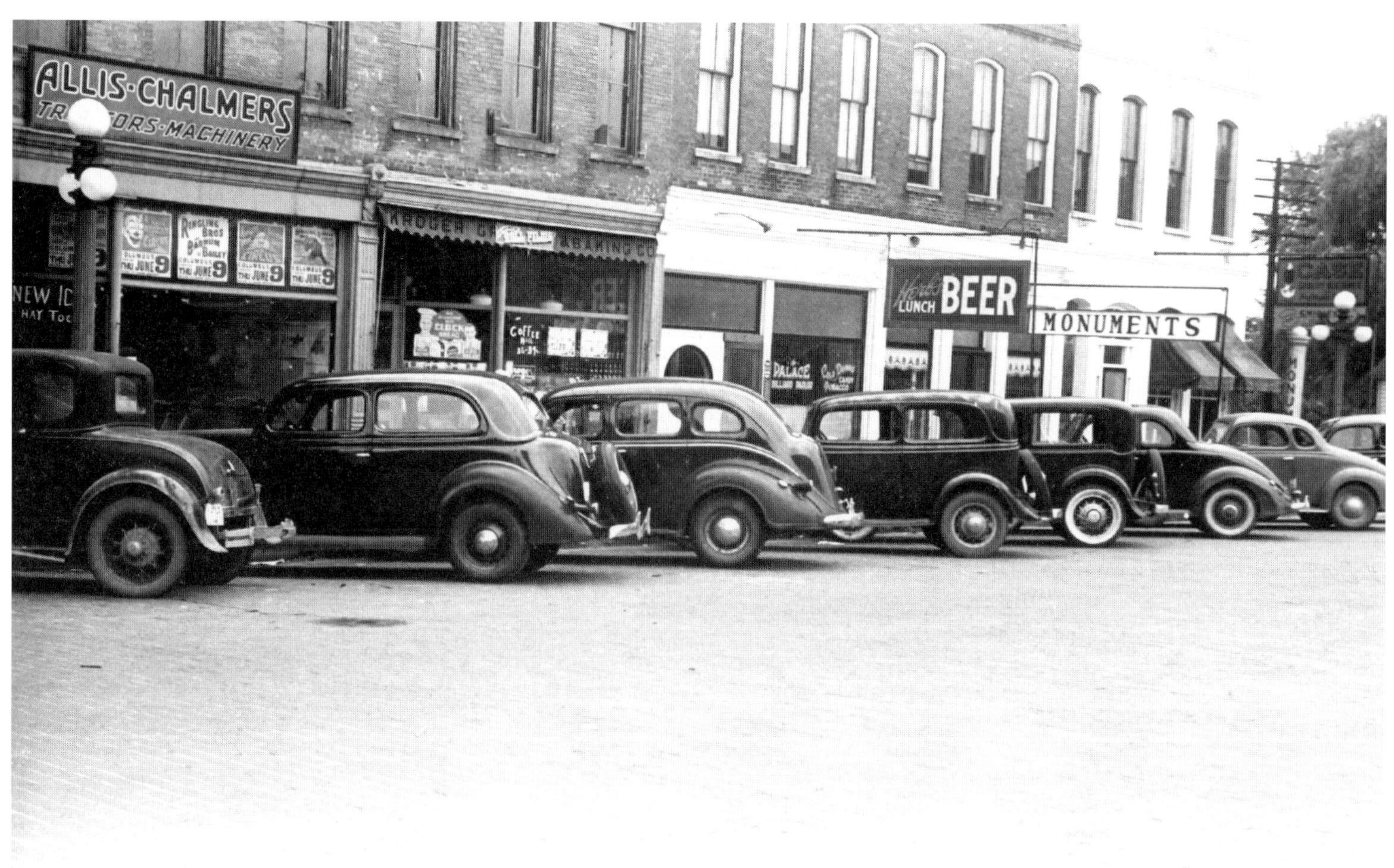

FIG 11 Saturday afternoon in London, Ohio, "the main street"

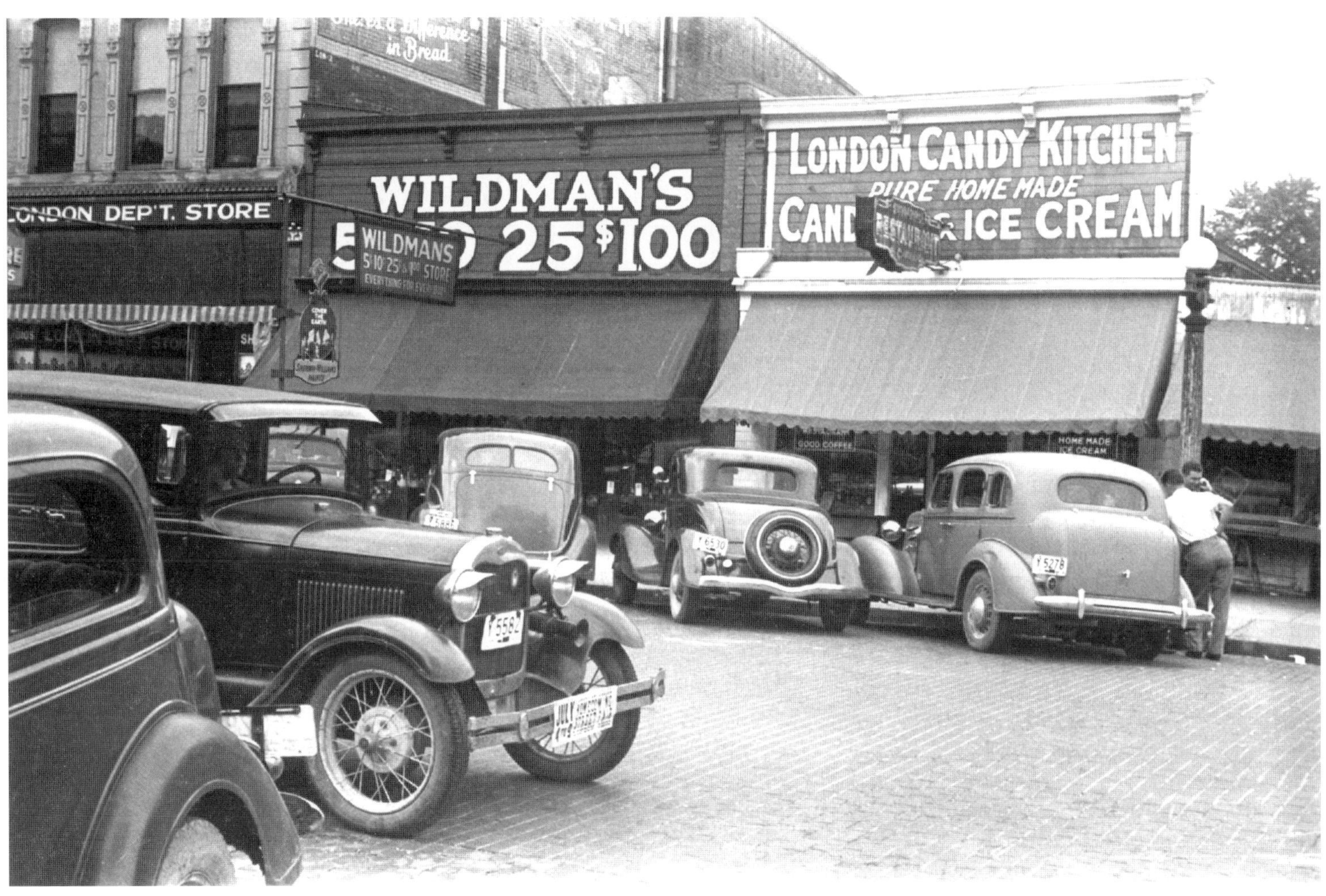

FIG 12 Saturday afternoon in London, Ohio, "the main street"

structures. He also excluded at least two establishments with sleek, modernized facades, the State movie theater and a restaurant with its makeover so recent that it had been trumpeted in the local newspaper the week before he worked in London. Chooman's Restaurant had been equipped with air-conditioning and completely refurbished, the newspaper reported, but the "most conspicuous of the new decoration is the new black and white glass front with the octagonal window."[4] Shahn's dowdy London thus differs markedly from its contemporaneous characterization in the WPA Federal Writers' Project's *Ohio Guide,* which describes its downtown as a "combination of old and new," with "a dazzling movie façade" adjacent to "a dilapidated building hospitably offering a hitching post."[5] Identifying these excluded sites is not to suggest that Shahn was derelict in failing to photograph them, but that choices other than those he did make would have created a less threadbare impression.

His streetscapes thus counterpoint the portraits of citizens actively utilizing these same spaces, and together they divide the main street sequence against itself, some pictures portraying a community that fosters lively, face-to-face, and democratic encounters among its citizens, and others a torpid atmosphere in which civic vitality seems attenuated. This disparity, also apparent in his studies of other towns, mirrors his competing personas as propagandist and artist, the former influenced by Stryker's script, the latter guided by Shahn's confidence in his own eye even when it called into question the script's a priori assumptions.

In addition to his skepticism about London's vitality, he also could not countenance Stryker's disregard of small-town inequalities, and the "other side of the tracks" sequence emphasizes the most blatant and pernicious of them, seven of its eleven pictures centering on African Americans. While these photographs do not arrange themselves into a photo-essay, they nonetheless echo motifs of the main street pictures. Two show a trio of women embarking on a shopping expedition, and all but one of the remainder feature male sidewalk sociability. While similar cultural patterns characterize Saturday on both sides of the tracks, a code of racial separation requires that they usually be enacted separately.

Both shots of the female shoppers are from about fifteen feet and are asymmetrically composed with the women in the pictures' right half, a deviation from his more frequent mode of depicting individuals closer in and centered. That distance and compositional strategy allowed the two photographs to include an ample view of the surroundings the women are walking through, an uninviting area haphazardly dotted with grain elevators, scruffy and littered open spaces, weathered shacks, and outlying businesses. The selectivity imposed by any photograph's frame invites viewers to infer relationships among the elements it encompasses, and perhaps especially when it is so methodically divided as in these two pictures. Their identical composition proposes that the dismalness of this space is not merely incidental but a typical environment for these black women from "the other side of the tracks," and the irony that they are dressed so neatly only accentuates it (fig. 13).

A shot of five men clustered on the sidewalk in front of a cafe was less successful, owing to its haphazard composition that fails to organize satisfactorily its disparate elements. But at the end of the same block, Shahn was so fascinated by a deep two-story frame building with a sloping flat roof that he made four views of it; inasmuch as the men who gather on its front steps vary in personnel and number, it is likely he returned two or three times during the day to shoot it again. Only rarely did he make more than a single view of a building, and that he took four of this one suggests that it had special significance for him. The structure had probably first been a livery stable (its long side walls have just one window between them), then became the General Tire and Battery Shop, and presently it housed the Apostolic Gospel Church, which a sign above its entrance declares to be "The Church Thats [*sic*] Different." All of those who use its front steps to socialize are African Americans, and it seems virtually certain that the church's congregants were, too, especially in an era in which main-line white churches did not welcome black worshippers.

He made a head-on study of it from across the street, a side view along an intersecting street, a mid-distance shot of its lower facade—all with one, two, or three persons included—and a close-in picture from six or so feet of two men sitting on its steps. Besides illustrating that it serves as a site for male sociability, these photographs constitute an architectural survey of the structure and its setting. The side view especially indicates that it is in need of upkeep—broken glass in an upper window has been replaced by a flimsy substitute, the siding is in need of paint, and even the fading sign of its previous business occupant has not been painted over. For this shot Shahn chose an angle that would also take in a billboard advertising chewing gum on the side of the cafe down the street, to suggest that the church's semi-residential neighborhood was too poor and powerless to disallow such gaudy commercial intrusions (fig. 14). A front view indicates that the curb in front of the church has noticeably crumbled in two places as well, indicating civic neglect.

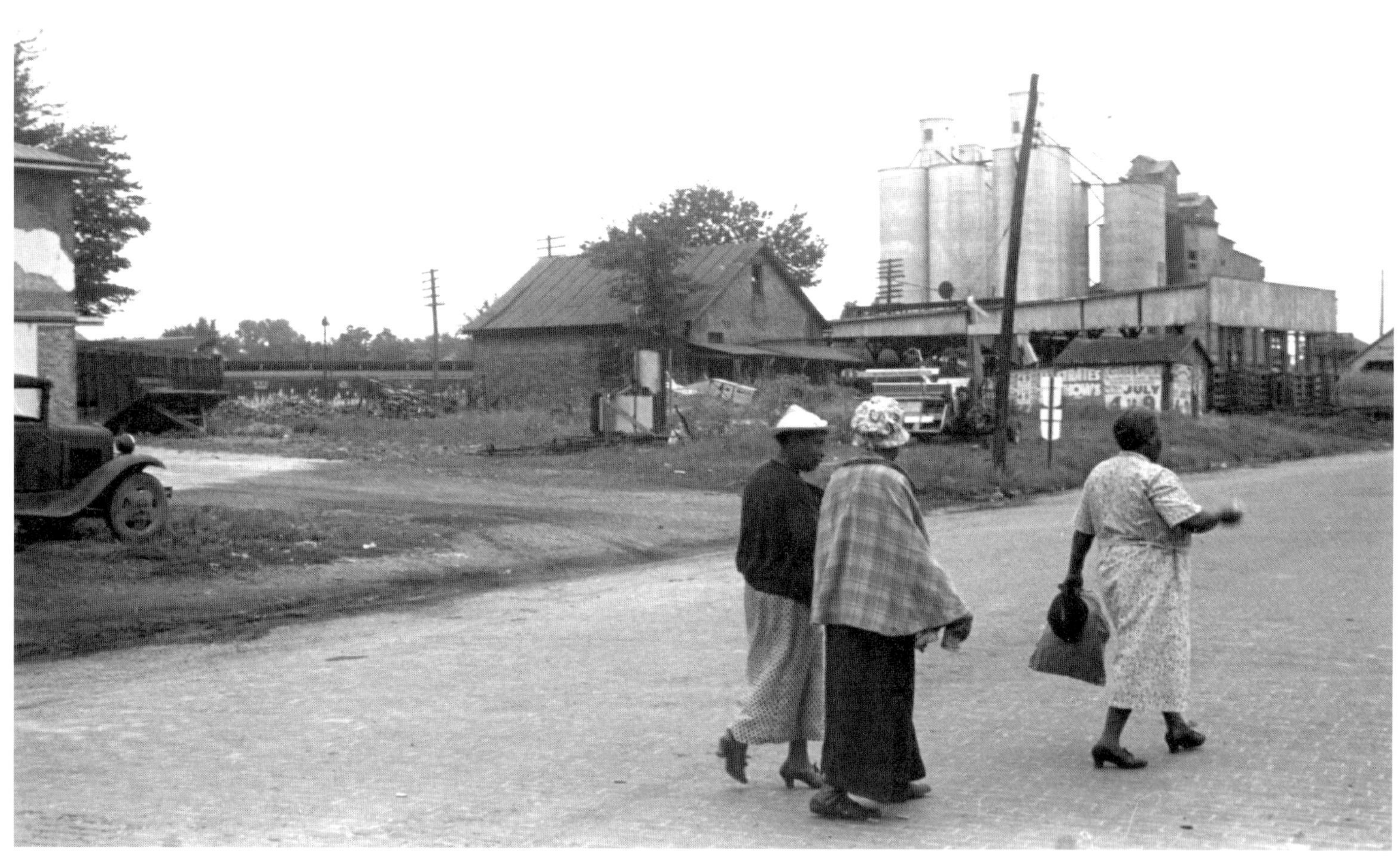

FIG 13 Saturday afternoon in London, Ohio, "the other side of the tracks"

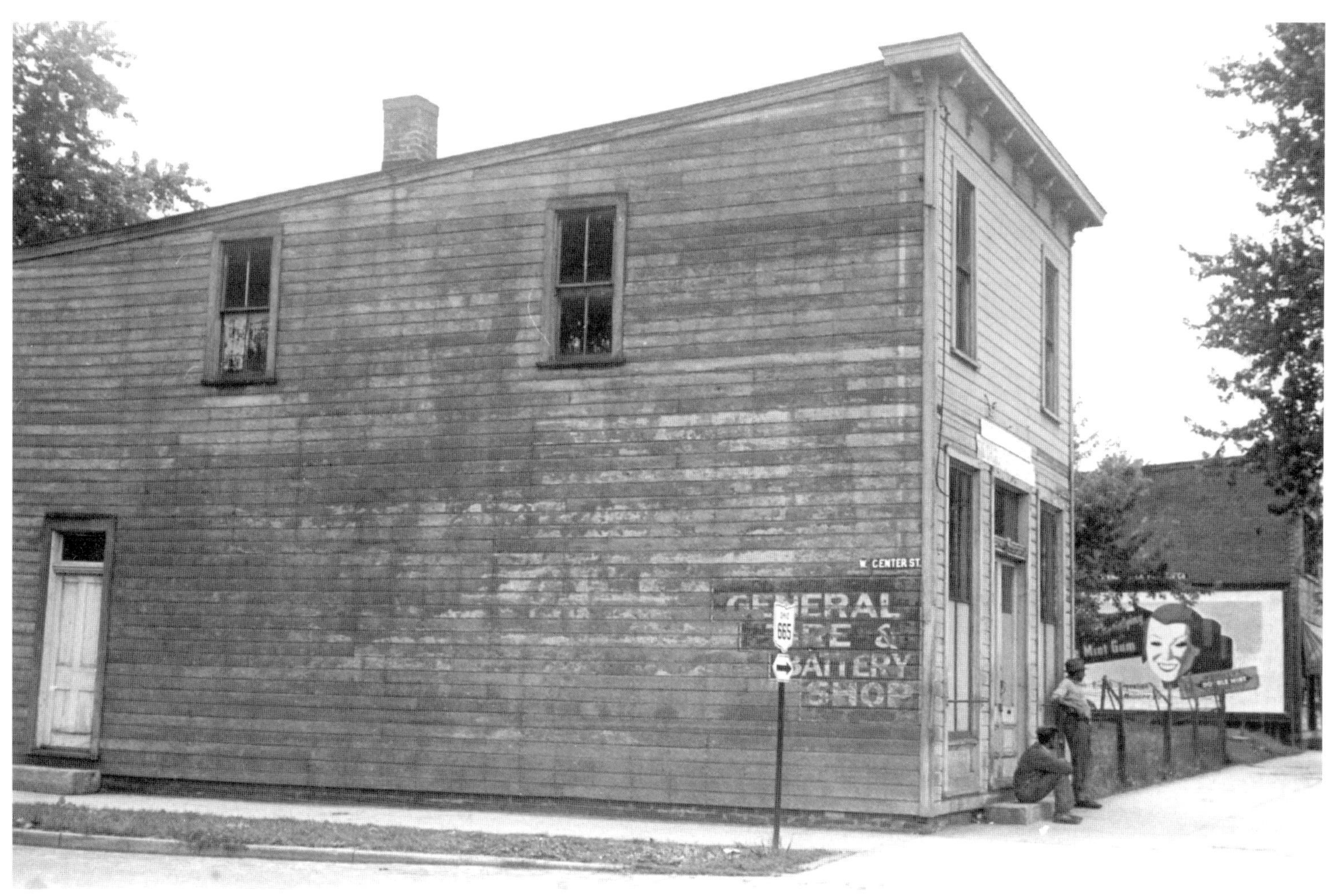

FIG 14 Saturday afternoon in London, Ohio, "the other side of the tracks"

But withal, in its simple dignity the Apostolic Gospel Church is not unlike the similarly four-square churches his friend Walker Evans had photographed in the South, and its artless integrity is particularly evident in Shahn's full-length, head-on view of it. The church is almost horizontally centered in an envelope of space created by the width of an intersecting street on one side and a vacant lot on the other. The slight downward slope of the facing street emphasizes the church's spare uprightness. Marks of disrepair appear on its front, too, but from the camera's distance, the impression of its unembellished serenity is stronger. The men on its steps are not incidental, but except in the nearest shot they are generalized and less significant to the compositions than the church itself (fig. 15).

Since London's African Americans are barely visible on "the main street" and are mostly found on "the other side of the tracks," the sequences' contrasting titles make clear their relegation to this physically substandard area of town. Details of apparel also suggest African Americans' delimited horizons: the black men from "the other side of the tracks" are all garbed in work clothing, whereas on "the main street" several white townsmen sport neckties, with the implication that the economic and social opportunities of black residents are as circumscribed by cultural custom as is their spatial mobility. Shahn's extensive attention to the Apostolic Gospel Church added a further nuance to his depiction of London's racial arrangements. Its plainness connoted the scanty material resources available to congregants, but the church also represented the black community's capacity to resist the dehumanization of segregation, in modest ways by performing public sociability on the church's steps, and in a larger way by sustaining an institution that featured more formal expressions of community solidarity. While London's African Americans were victimized, they were not solely victims.

His observations about American racial practices may now seem self-evident, but they were considerably more novel in 1938, when most white citizens accepted racial discrimination as an unquestioned norm, and the only photographs with black faces they might see would be of entertainers and athletes.[6] That Shahn included African Americans in his studies of Saturday afternoon in London indicates not only his dissent from Stryker's exclusion of race from his vision of small-town egalitarianism, but also how determinedly he embraced the artist's responsibility to expose his culture to what it otherwise did not wish to confront.

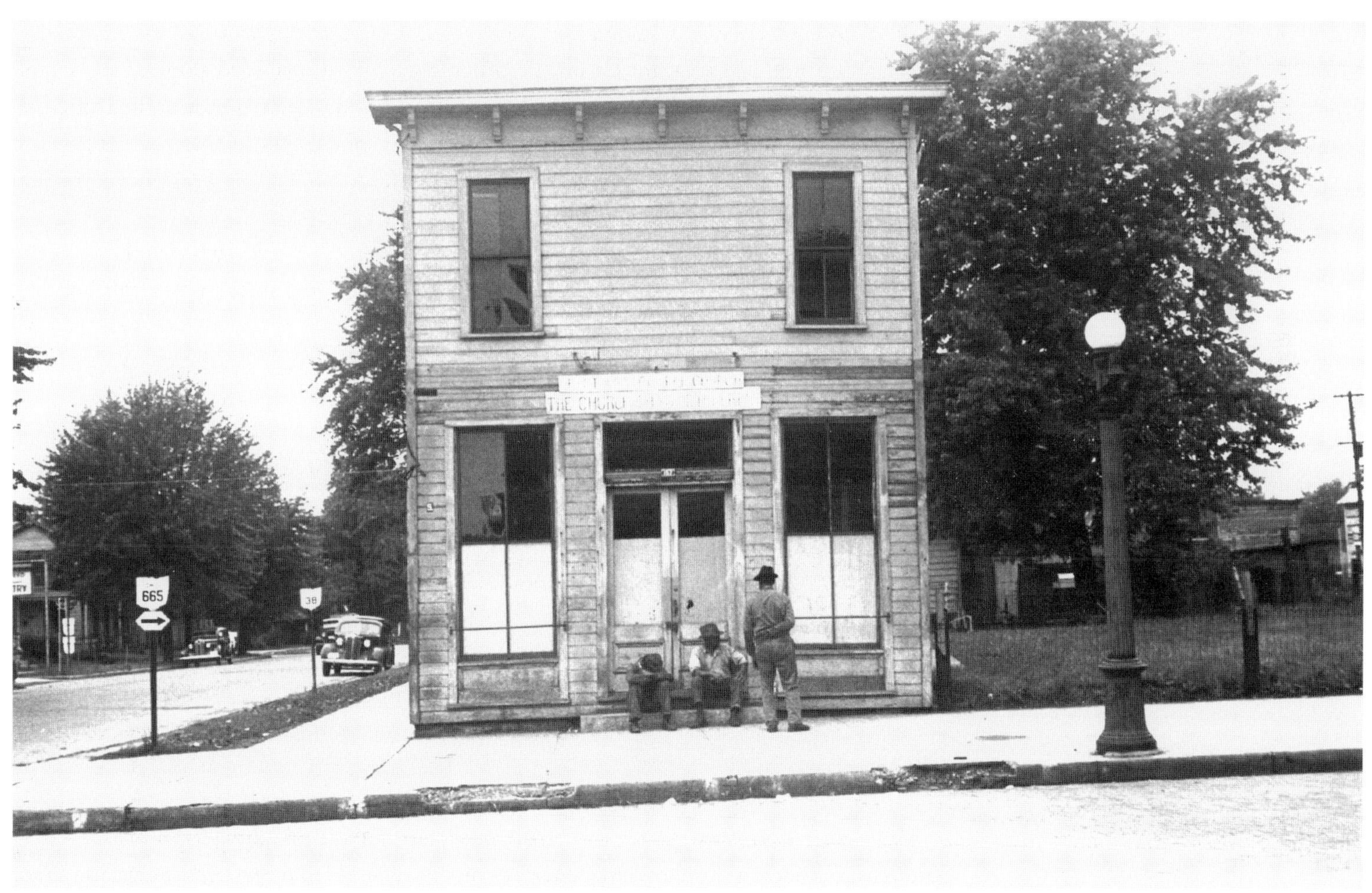

FIG 15 Saturday afternoon in London, Ohio, "the other side of the tracks"

SHAHN'S VIEW OF Lancaster's downtown gives a considerably stronger impression of civic vitality than any of his London photographs. Shoppers throng sidewalks, traffic proceeds along the street, and pedestrians wait to cross a corner. Of all of his downtown studies, this one most fully meets the script's specification of carefully chosen "general views of the main street" that "give an overall impression of the main part of town" and its activities. The vista is both wide and deep, encompassing a broad swath of the physical setting in which community life takes place. Aligning the lens with the receding curb gives equal prominence to the busy sidewalk, the wide street, and the multiform buildings lining its opposite side until the downtown meets the trees at its periphery. And from being shot across an intersection, the view also takes in a cluster of pedestrians on the opposite intersecting sidewalk, implying that just outside the frame's edge lies a comparably busy scene (fig. 16).

Two years later, the editors of the WPA's *Ohio Guide* included this photograph in a portfolio of fifteen of Shahn's pictures making up "a portrait of small town life." Its amalgam of expansiveness and energetic street life was unique in the portfolio, and inevitably so, since he made no other photograph of any downtown that duplicates its bustle. Despite the picture's atypicality, it conformed to a conviction shared by the *Guide*'s editors and Stryker's script that small towns continued to be thriving enterprises. Also symptomatic of that assumption was the portfolio's exclusion of any of Shahn's many shots of barely populated sidewalks such as the ones he had photographed in London and would continue to emphasize in other towns, including Lancaster.[1]

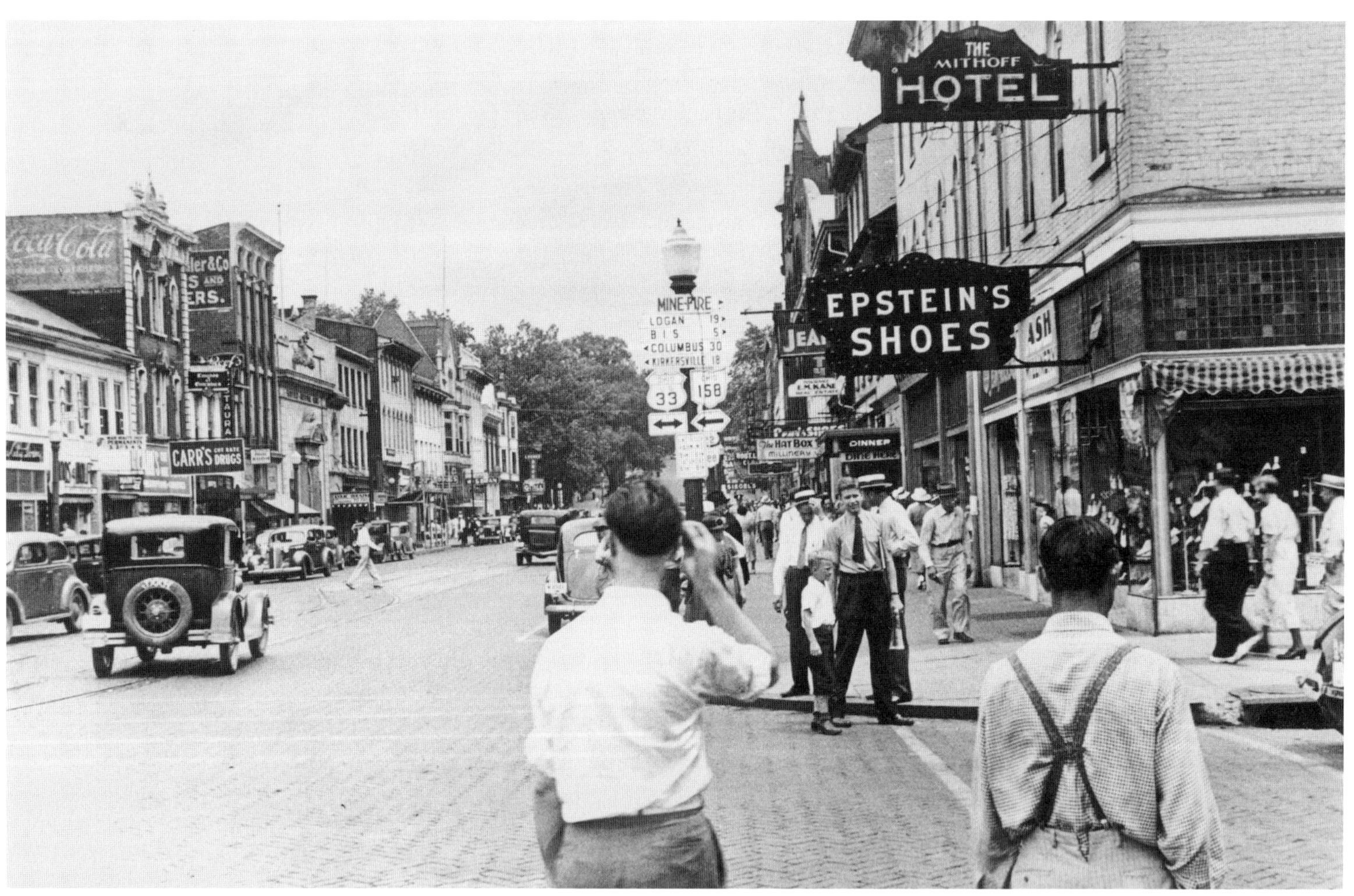

FIG 16 Main street, Lancaster, Ohio

A Newark photograph also includes a busy sidewalk, but it occupies only a receding corner of the composition behind a few pedestrians crossing an intersecting square. The distant sidewalk's activity is visually subordinate to the subdued foreground elements that constitute the primary subjects of the picture—the square's pavement, the two nearest pedestrians, and a bank building. Shahn angled his lens to emphasize the square's spaciousness, so ample that its central area had been transformed into a parking zone. The bank is architecturally the most notable building he photographed: designed by Louis Sullivan in 1915, its facade's dramatic organization of large rectangular shapes, terra-cotta facing, and distinctive floral ornamentation mark it as unique among Main Street structures. Not exactly an architectural photograph—the downward angle of the camera cuts off the bank's second floor—nor a vista, a depiction of a lively shopping area, a study of a civic space, or a portrait of individual citizens, it synthesizes all of these elements into Shahn's most enigmatic representation of the physical context in which community life takes place (fig. 17).[2]

It is now impossible to determine whether Newark's residents in 1938 felt pride in Sullivan's bank as a landmark sight, or whether familiarity had made it more or less anonymous. When it was erected in 1915, the local press hailed it as "Newark's most beautiful building of which every citizen is proud," but two generations later it had become so inconspicuous as to be characterized as a "neglected treasure located in Newark."[3] Shahn was apparently beguiled by it, because he only infrequently photographed a single edifice in a head-on fashion that called special attention to its structural and decorative features, and mostly he excluded architectural landmarks. On the other hand, his compositional foregrounding of such an expanse of the square's pavement not only makes the upper half of Sullivan's building invisible but also gives particular emphasis to the parked cars that partially obscure the view of it, as especially does the sedan nearest the camera. The mid-square parking zone transforms a civic space into an uncongenial setting for both the distinguished building and the pedestrians crossing it, requiring them to be wary because parked cars block their vision. His terse title, "Street crossing," neglects most of what the photograph depicts and supplies little guidance for interpreting it. Is it an avowal of the extraordinary visual pleasure that such an illustrious building afforded Newark's residents, or a critique of the town's expedient utilitarianism that has trumped considerations of esthetic integrity and the civic ideal that such spaces ought to enhance citizens' pleasure and pride in their community? Both ways of understanding the

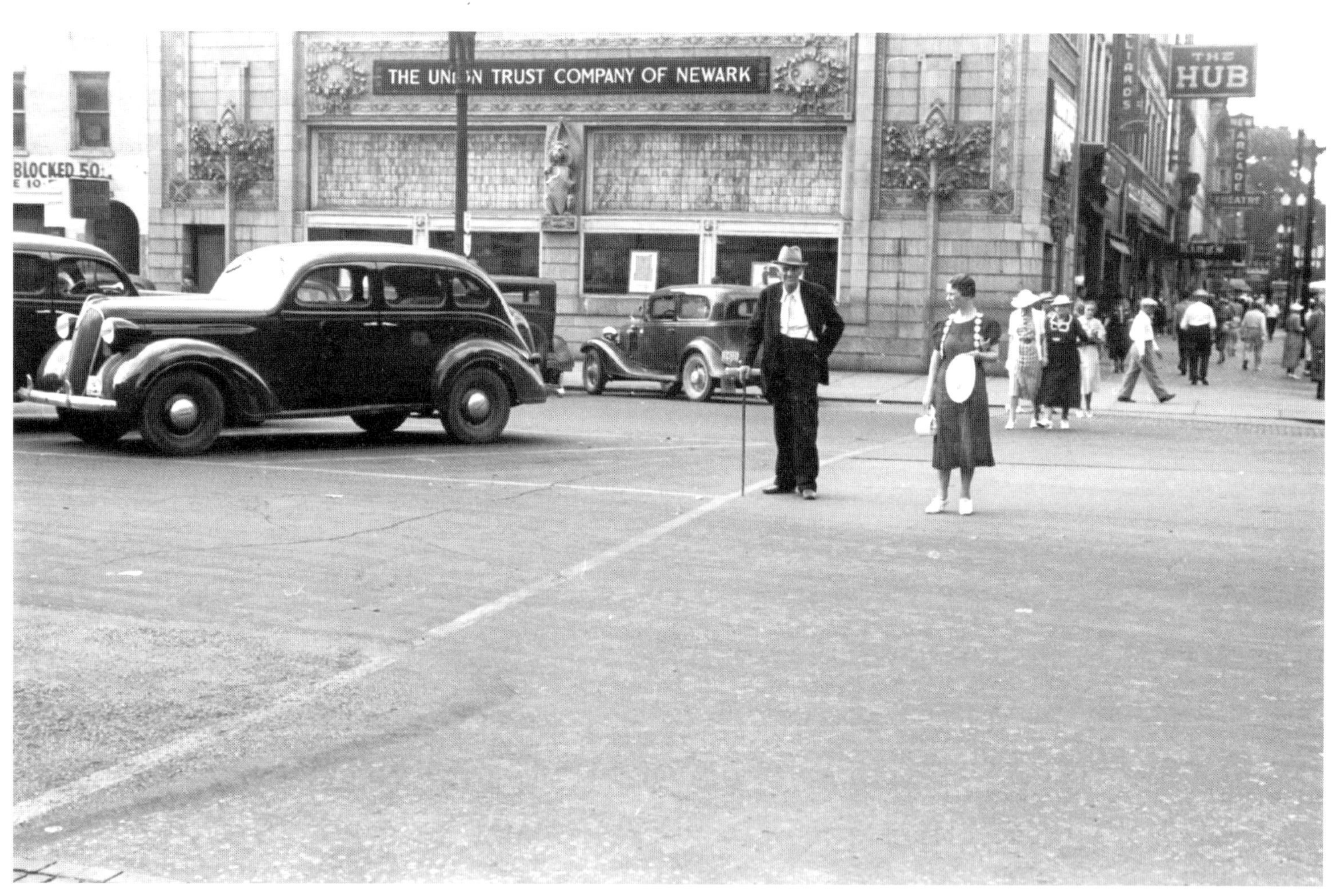

FIG 17 Street crossing, Newark, Ohio

photograph are feasible enough, and the ambivalence Shahn embedded in its formal structure is but a concentrated version of the ambiguities of his small-town survey as a whole.

Urbana's Monument Square and Somerset's Public Square epitomized that civic ideal. Generous, handsome spaces anchoring their communities and representing the continuity of their traditions, these sites exemplified residents' pride of place. Shahn made two studies of Monument Square and three of Public Square—most often in photographing the built environment, he shot a single exposure and moved on—and these pictures also reveal the tensions in his survey. They at once depict how beguiling Ohio's towns could be while hinting at their contemporary stagnation.

Monument Square had been "the central point of Urbana life" since the town's founding in the early nineteenth century, according to a contemporary guidebook to Urbana and its surrounding county. In 1871 citizens erected a statue on an island in the square, sculpted by Urbana's native son John Quincy Adams Ward, of a pensive Union soldier looking homeward, a memorial that in 1938 was still surrounded by "venerable business structures with . . . Victorian facades of painted brick, stone trim, and ornate wooden cornices."[4] Shot from one of the square's corners, Shahn's diagonal view takes in the statue in the middle distance and several of the nineteenth-century buildings beyond it. This prospect, a local favorite, was almost exactly duplicated by an artist's illustration heading the guidebook's "Urbana Points of Interest" section. Unlike the drawing, though, Shahn's photograph includes electrical poles awkwardly jutting up from the statue's island, traffic lights dangling from wires strung across it, and a plethora of highway and directional signs affixed to poles and streetlamps, these twentieth-century additions diminishing the space's coherent, tranquil dignity. As a counterpoint, perhaps, to these indications of the automobile's transformation of the townscape, he included a young family on foot entering the foreground of the picture, one of the rare family groups in any of his downtown photographs. They are the roomy square's only pedestrians (fig. 18).

He then moved to the next corner of the square to aim along the sidewalk toward two of the venerable buildings, now seen head-on unobstructed by the island's distractions. Substantial, well-maintained three-story structures with ground-floor shops, they represent the diverse architectural modes typically found on downtown streets: one in a restrained Federal style, although crowned with a scalloped cornice and small pediment; the other more flamboyantly eclectic, with Gothic and Romanesque windows, lunettes, a balustrade, and a pediment. If the

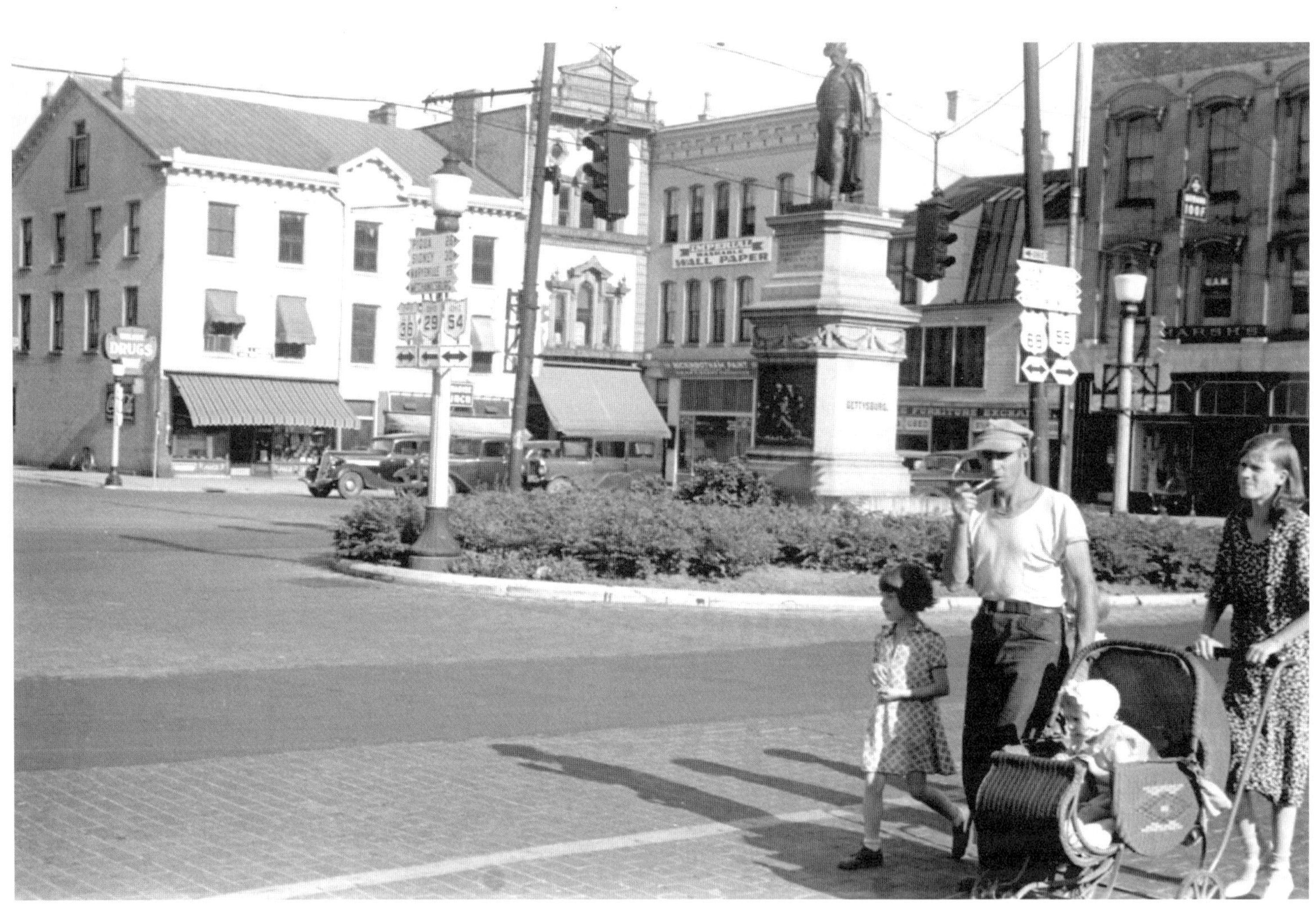

FIG 18 Center of town, Urbana, Ohio

buildings around Monument Square lacked harmony, these two had panache and visual appeal, a perception heightened by his composition, which centered them between a foreground lamppost and the building wall along the perpendicular sidewalk leading to them. On the sidewalk a single pedestrian walks toward the camera, two more pass by stores a block away, and a fourth crosses to an area of the square used for parking, a makeshift transformation not apparent in the first photograph (fig. 19). "On Saturday night," reported the *Ohio Guide,* "farmers and townsfolk alike park their cars around Monument Square and spend the evening gossiping with neighbors and trading with merchants along Main Street," but it was little used on the day Shahn photographed it.[5]

An enisled Civil War statue also dominates Somerset's Public Square, portraying its native son General Philip Sheridan mounted on his rearing horse and histrionically waving his hat toward the downtown shopping district. Shahn shot it from behind, at a distance of twenty-five feet and from the left lane of the broad street leading to it, so as to juxtapose the statue and the stores beyond. Not only did that vantage distinguish his photograph from the standard postcard's conventional head-on address to a noteworthy site, but so did its asymmetrical composition, here employed to reveal the ampleness of the square by including its northern extension demarcated by the side of a dry goods store. Two details in the photograph also contribute to defining the square, the street's off-center lane divider and a traffic directional to "Keep Right" to its invisible southern extension, these traffic markers subtly enlarging the sense of the square's spaciousness. Like Monument Square, Public Square supplies a handsome locus for Somerset's communal life, but as in Urbana, few residents utilize it—a woman crosses it, a child bicycles on its far side, and just one pedestrian is on its sidewalks (fig. 20).

In another study of Public Square, Shahn modified but did not abandon his treatment of Somerset as drowsy. This image concentrates on the square's northern extension; from about ten feet behind, he photographed a half-dozen residents passing time on sidewalk benches, a tree's branches above them increasing the illusion of depth and attractively framing the view across the square. The windows of the opposite store and the line of parked cars echo the idlers' seating arrangement and unify the composition. He stopped down his lens, making the light less intense than in "Statue of Sheridan," contributing to the perception of this corner of Public Square as a quiet, shady spot to wile away an afternoon.[6] The sense of sociability is

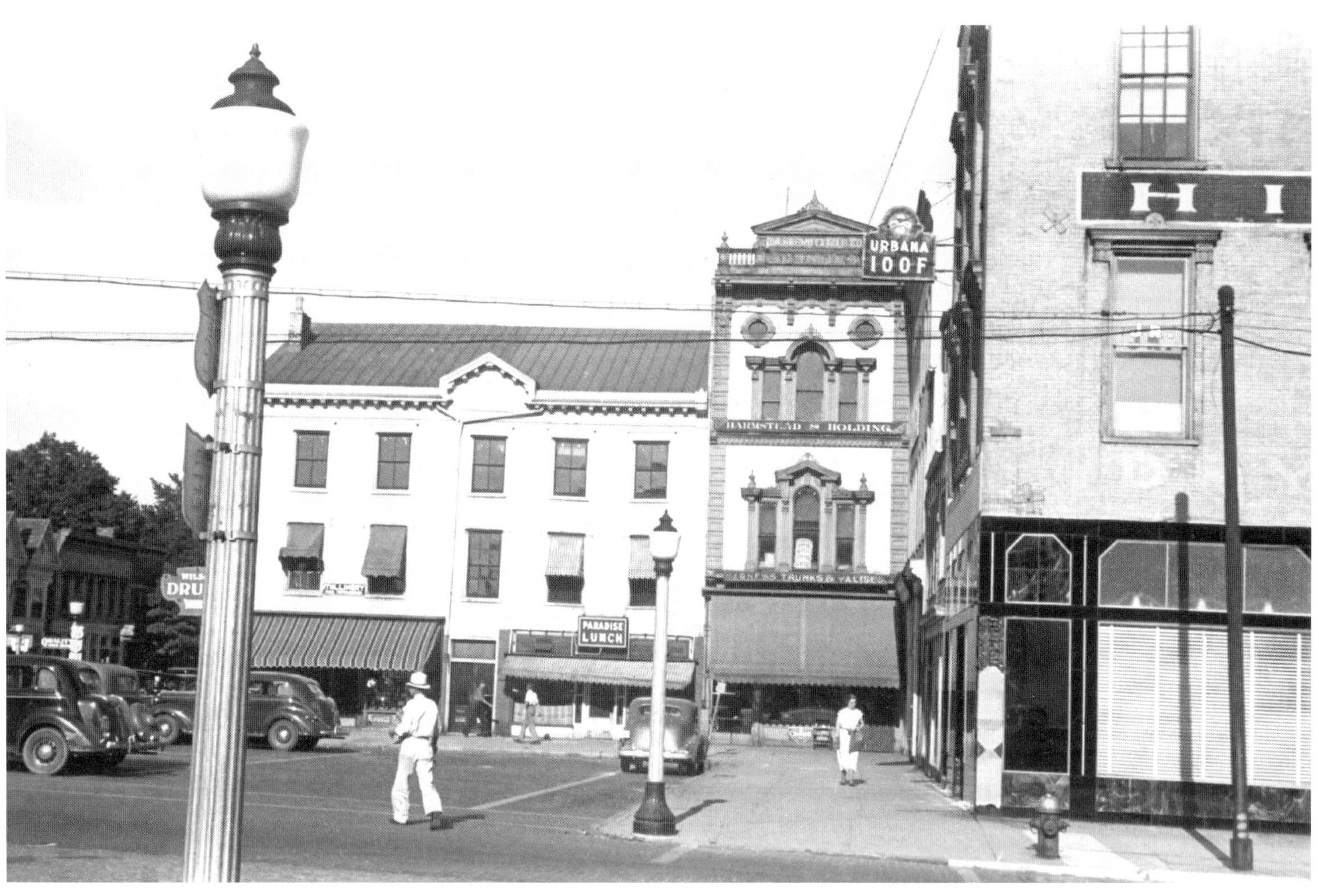

FIG 19 Business district of Urbana, Ohio

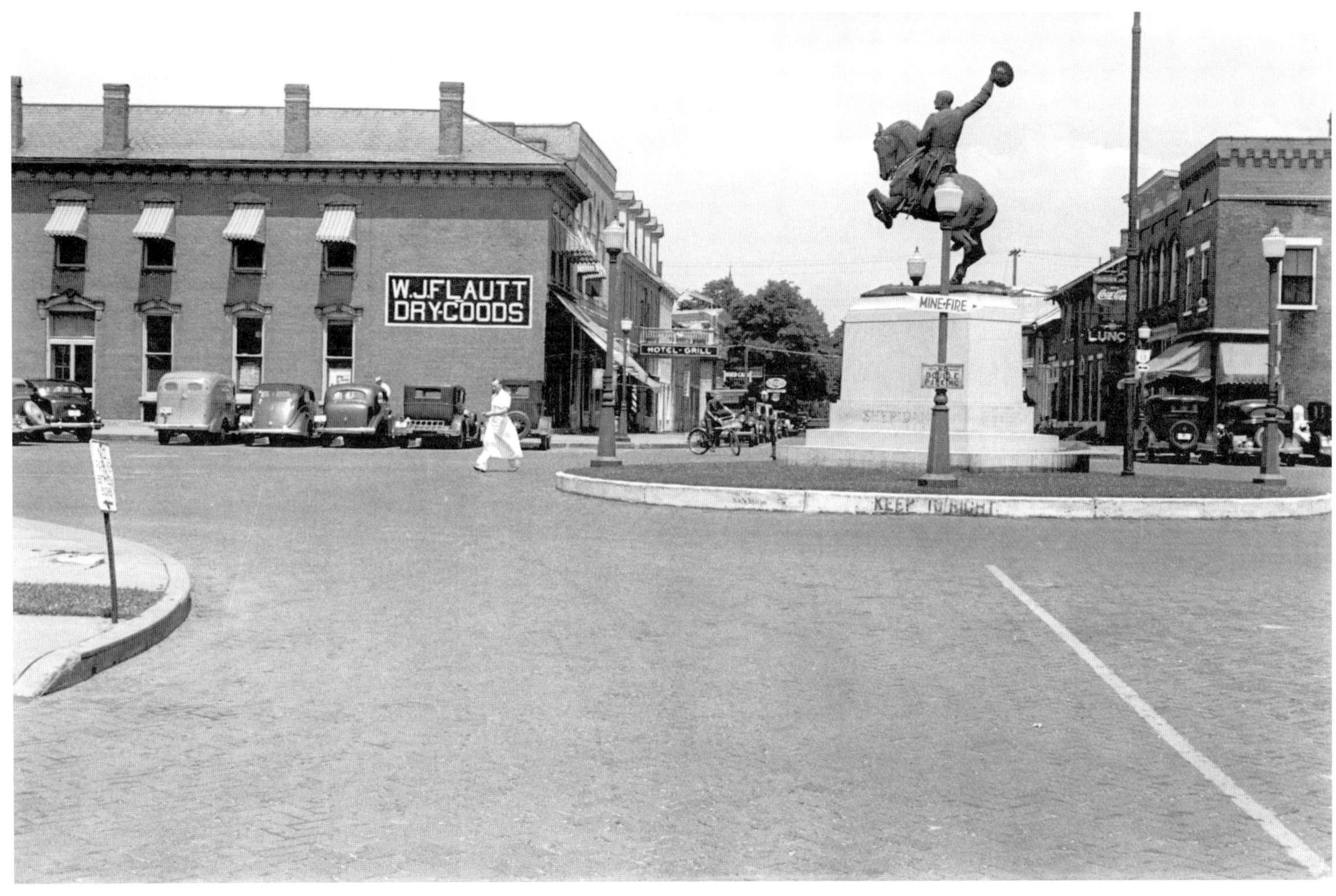

FIG 20 Statue of Sheridan, Somerset, Ohio

strong, but even a background shopper making his way toward a store does not much reduce the impression of lassitude (fig. 21).

Attractive as these photographs make Public Square, another, of its southern extension, is even more winsome. An oblique camera angle foregrounds its brick pavement and the curb gracefully arching toward its boundary, occupied by a hardware store and a few parked cars. Even though it meant bisecting the hardware store, Shahn composed to give prominence to the pavement's brickwork and the dappled patterns cast on it by an unseen tree in order to bring out the appealing tonal contrasts created by the play of shadow and sunlight. The title, "Hardware store," is nominal, because aside from a barrel displaying brooms, only the firm's sign indicates its specialty, and rather than a study of a typical downtown business, the photograph most insistently calls attention to the unassuming beauty that an observant eye can discover in Ohio's towns (fig. 22).

Shahn largely avoided photographing sites that conventionally signified civic culture—city halls, parks, public libraries, and the like—and his studies of these central squares constitute his survey's most sustained examination of representations of it. Besides being intrinsically handsome, the squares allowed him to bring together disparate aspects of community life to create emblematic juxtapositions of past and present. Evoking memory were the squares themselves as souvenirs of the towns' earliest years, when their founders made generous provision of land to create these focal points, while the more recent statues memorialized their communities' contributions to the nation's history. As hubs for commercial enterprise, they continued to be the symbolic nexus of town life, although, as his photographs of their little-used spaces suggest, with diminishing intensity. Still handsome and appealing they were, but the towns they centered seemed to be languishing.

Usually, however, his photographs concentrated on more prosaic sites than the Sullivan bank or the squares. Typical of these was a Washington Court House townscape where he had aimed his camera cater-corner across a deserted intersection at a line of commercial buildings and composed to accentuate the built environment's banality and imply the town's enervation. By foregrounding a sun-struck stretch of blank pavement, locating himself distantly enough to encompass a panoramic view of the utilitarian homeliness of the buildings along the facing block, and shooting when the high sun did not cast any beguiling shadows, he embedded in his study a fundamentally different interpretation of the congeniality of

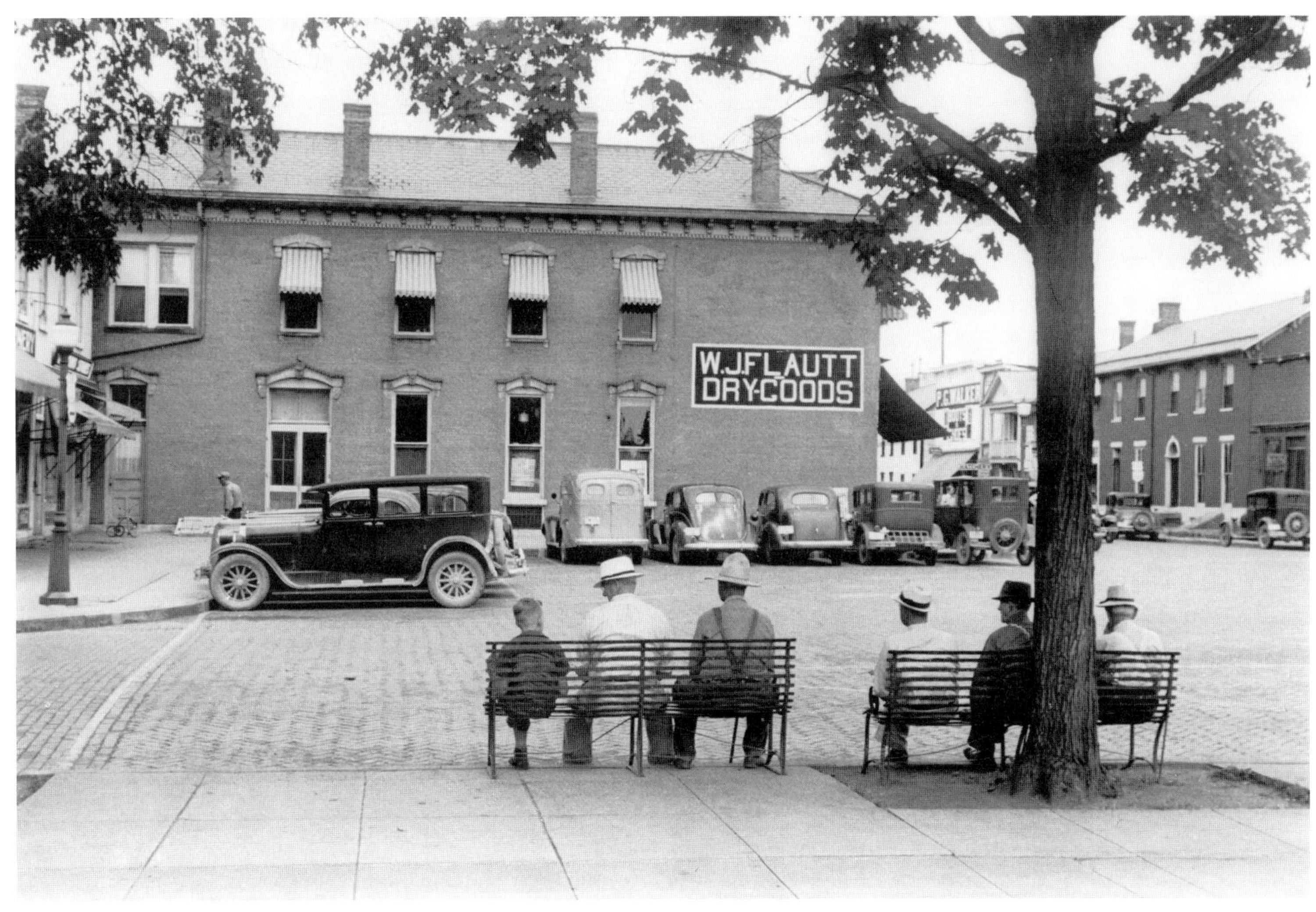

FIG 21 Street scene, Somerset, Ohio

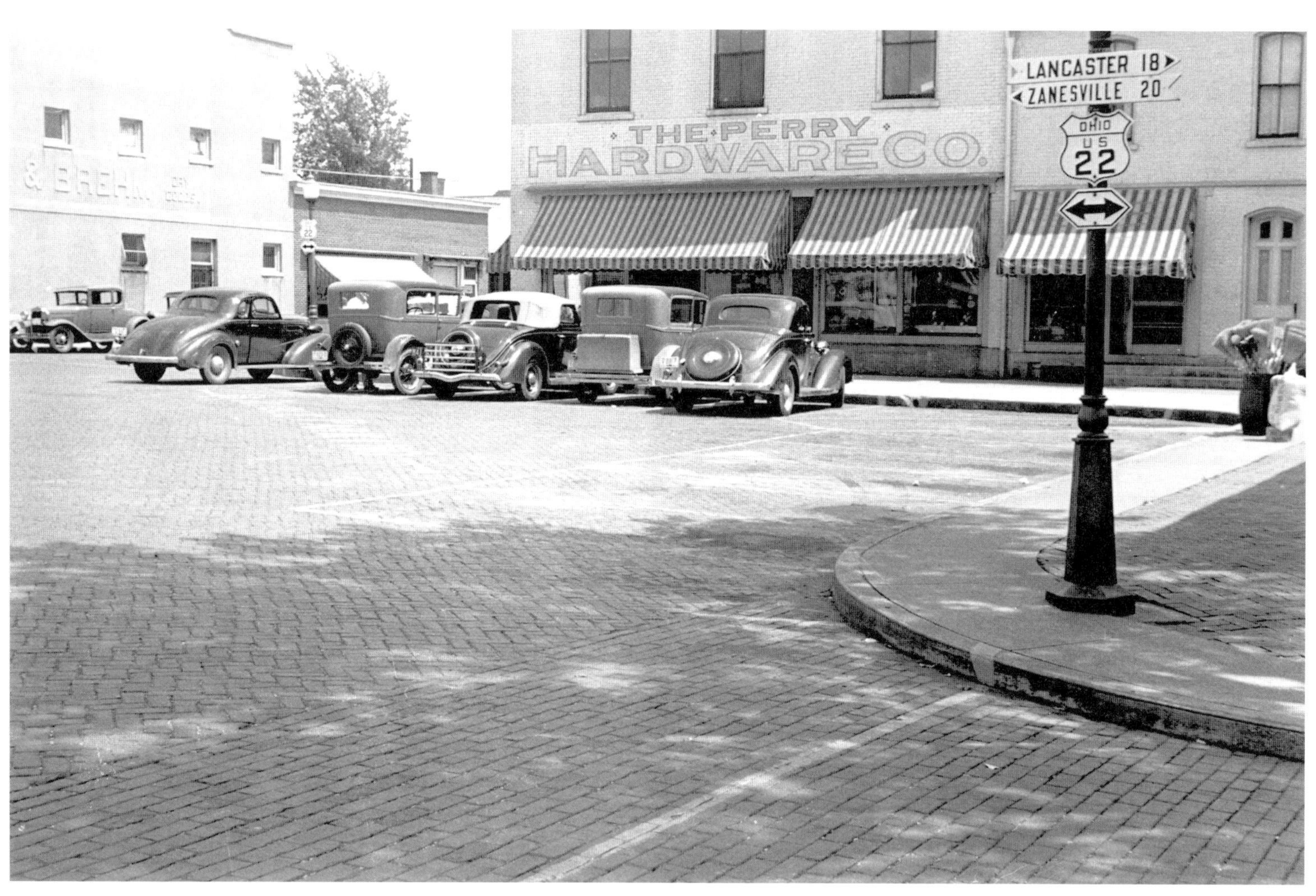

FIG 22 Hardware store, Somerset, Ohio

the small town's built environment than in his photograph of the comparable corner of the Somerset square, where his emphasis on the sinuous line of its arching curb, echoing patterns in brickwork and awnings, and alternations of light and shade had invested it with an atmosphere of inviting gracefulness (fig. 23). His antithetical interpretations of these similar sites indicate how much he resisted adopting the singular point of view of Stryker's script, but also hint at how conflicted his feelings were about its assumption that the small town was a robust "American institution."

Lewis Atherton, in his classic cultural history of the small town *Main Street on the Middle Border*, claims that "no one has ever complimented the architecture of the Midwestern Main Street," which he characterizes as "highly utilitarian and nondescript" and "both grim and drab," but this assessment is perhaps too totalizing, or at least does not entirely square with Shahn's less categorical representation of the built environment.[7] His most concentrated scrutiny of a downtown was in Circleville, where he made nine photographs titled "Main and Court Streets"—the town's central business district—and a few others that prominently feature its buildings, supplementing them with eight pictures all titled "Street scene," shot along these central streets. Some concentrate on individuals or close-in views of storefronts and offices, but several are panoramic streetscapes or head-on architectural studies of key buildings. A number of these photographs corroborate Atherton's judgment about Main Street's banality, but not all do. Neither an endorsement of Stryker's assumption that depictions of the small town's physical setting would represent democracy's material benefits, nor an exposé of its wretchedness, material as well as spiritual, which Sinclair Lewis and others had made a literary staple of the early interbellum era, Shahn's survey is less programmatic. The viability of a small community such as Circleville might be ebbing and its streets nondescript, but still integral to its common life were some conspicuous monuments of its more vigorous past.

A mid-block vista that takes in the central intersection of Main and Court streets and the length of the latter until it meets the trees at the downtown's periphery serves as the establishing shot for Shahn's studies. An older woman approaches the camera; the sidewalk just behind her is empty, although jutting signs make it seem less so, and Court Street, with a pair of jaywalkers and a distant sprinkling of pedestrians, is slightly livelier than most of his business-district shots. The buildings lining the street are serviceable but unexceptional, aside from one on a corner with an elaborate cornice and stone facade facing Main Street.

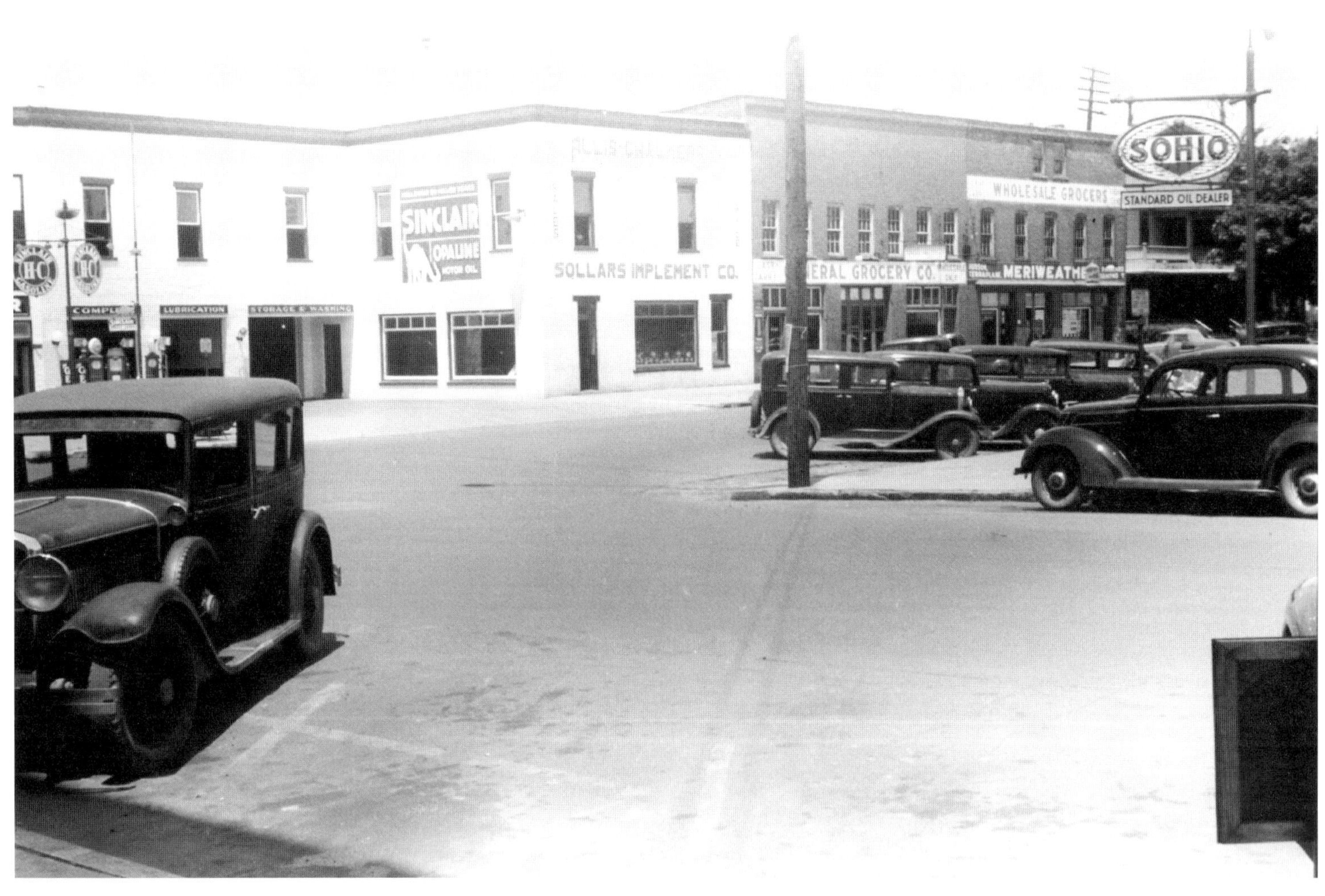

FIG 23 Street scene, Washington Court House, Ohio

Serried files of parked vehicles, as almost always, are among the downtown's most conspicuous earmarks and contribute to making it seem disproportionate, its spaces paradoxically both tightly compacted and more ample than its human activities require (fig. 24).

Automobiles are mostly excluded, though, in a cater-corner view across another intersection, perhaps because it concentrates on a greater number of people than usual, a dozen or so individuals, most idling on its sidewalks. Two groups on the distant corner cluster separately, but what relationship the three persons on the nearer corner might share is tantalizingly unclear. Is the stout woman pausing to greet an older man, as her slightly turned body suggests, or just passing by without either acknowledging the other? And have the two identically dressed men previously been loafing together or, as their turned backs imply, merely been passing time separately on the same corner? Is the photograph a depiction of sociability or a hint that the small town's reputation for it is exaggerated and that ennui is more characteristic of its daily existence? Shahn was drawn by the moment's human interest and its equivocal revelation of small-town behaviors, but his formal strategies also make the physical context in which these activities take place a key element in the photograph's meaning. His framing of the nearby individuals, oblique shooting angle, and asymmetrical composition give special emphasis to the pavement that spans the photograph and extends out of it, so that an inert blank expanse occupies much of it. That organization of the picture's space strengthens a viewer's sense that the banality of the physical setting connotes the town's more general dullness. While so enigmatic a photograph cannot be said to convey a single meaning, Shahn's figuring of space in it suggests that an atmosphere of monotony and perhaps stagnation is an undercurrent in Circleville's everyday life (fig. 25).

A vista of several Main Street buildings and storefronts and of the parked automobiles facing them is a more attractive if not unmixed representation of Circleville's built environment. To make the vista more engagingly intimate, Shahn reduced the impression of the street's width by locating himself in it, aiming diagonally toward a shoe concern occupying the farthest storefront of a white brick building spanning two-thirds of the frame. Austerely handsome in the Federal style, it is embellished only by slim stone lintels and a simple cornice, although the storefronts are less restrained and a few commercial signs are affixed to its facade. The oblique camera angle also takes in, at the photograph's distant edge, two archaic, more insubstantial, and considerably less prepossessing structures, the nearer vainly hoping

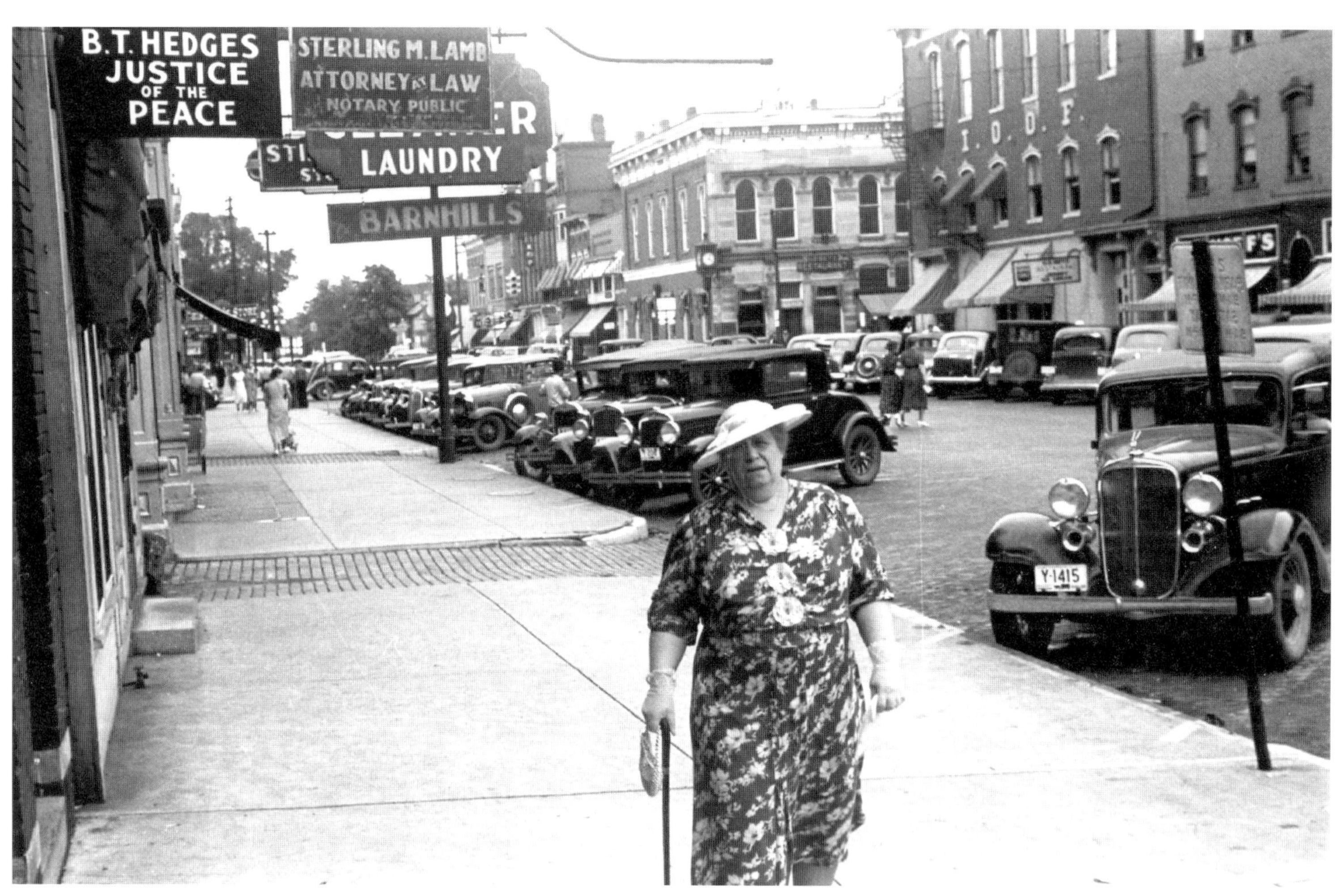

FIG 24 Street scene, Circleville, Ohio

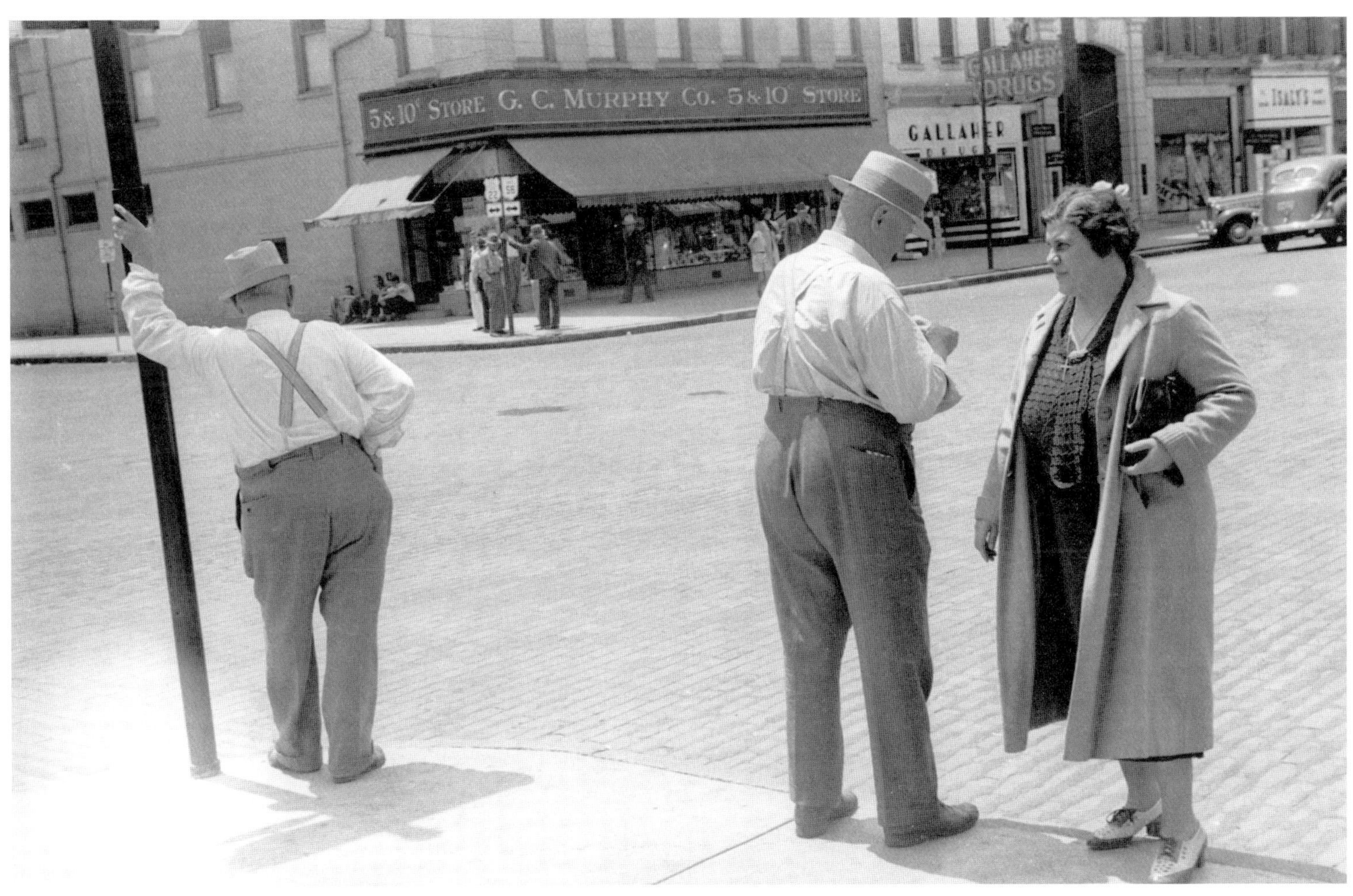

FIG 25 Street scene, Circleville, Ohio

to disguise its ill fit with the row's other buildings by flaunting an ungainly false front. At the photograph's nearest edge is a tile-fronted tavern, one of the few such modernizations in Shahn's photographs.[8] Old and new thus jostle in this part of downtown, as do shabbiness and modest gracefulness, but, most emphatically, the dignified Federal building's conspicuousness gives the streetscape an attractively pleasing air (fig. 26).

Stryker's script emphasized the importance of lodges, hotels, and banks in the life of small towns, and in Circleville Shahn shot head-on studies of each that highlight their institutional significance. The plainest is the Odd Fellows Hall, an impression strengthened by a camera angle that cuts off its roofline and by Shahn's decision to make a side view in which an iron fire escape is a somewhat disfiguring appurtenance. The ground floor of the lodge's more spacious front on Main Street housed a restaurant and shops, which he may have seen as distractions from his documentation of it as a community institution (fig. 27). He photographed the American Hotel with a rare vertical format required by its being shot from a narrow alley across the street, an indication of his determination to include its full elevation. It is a handsome structure, with architectural flourishes that include a delicate second-floor balcony, masonry lintels accenting its tall windows, and a Greek Revival pediment emblazoning its name. A female pedestrian caught in mid-stride crossing the alley's opening is reflected in a puddle from a recent rainstorm, and her vigorous step adds a note of dynamism to what is essentially an architectural view (fig. 28).[9] Flanking the Second National Bank are two more commonplace buildings, and the contrast highlights its scalloped cornice, its elevated masonry entryway, and the tall, arched windows that pierce its upper floor. These architectural flourishes advertise its primacy as a key community institution, as more obviously do the gigantic letters that boldly proclaim its importance (fig. 29).

A present-day historic preservation initiative in Circleville permits an assessment of Shahn's shooting priorities because it identifies on Main and Court streets more than twenty-five structures (or "blocks," several buildings erected simultaneously as a development project) that have survived and are now eligible for landmark status, all of them ornaments of the townscape in the thirties. For a community of its size, Circleville's downtown was generously endowed with handsome edifices exemplifying the architectural styles favored by the late nineteenth and early twentieth century—adaptations of the Federal, Greek Revival, Renaissance, Italianate, and Second Empire styles, eclectically embellished with bracketed cornices,

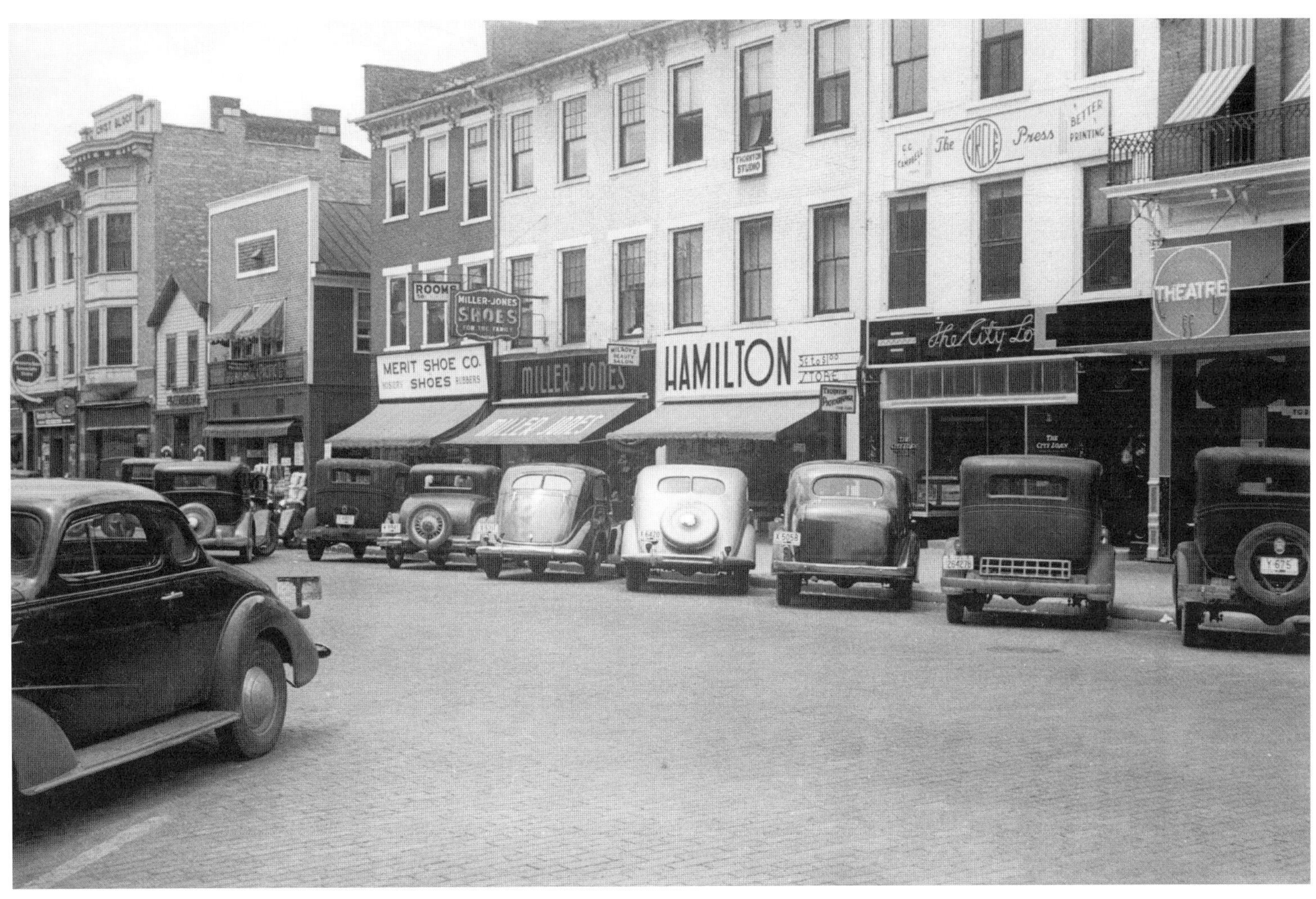

FIG 26 Main and Court Streets, Circleville, Ohio

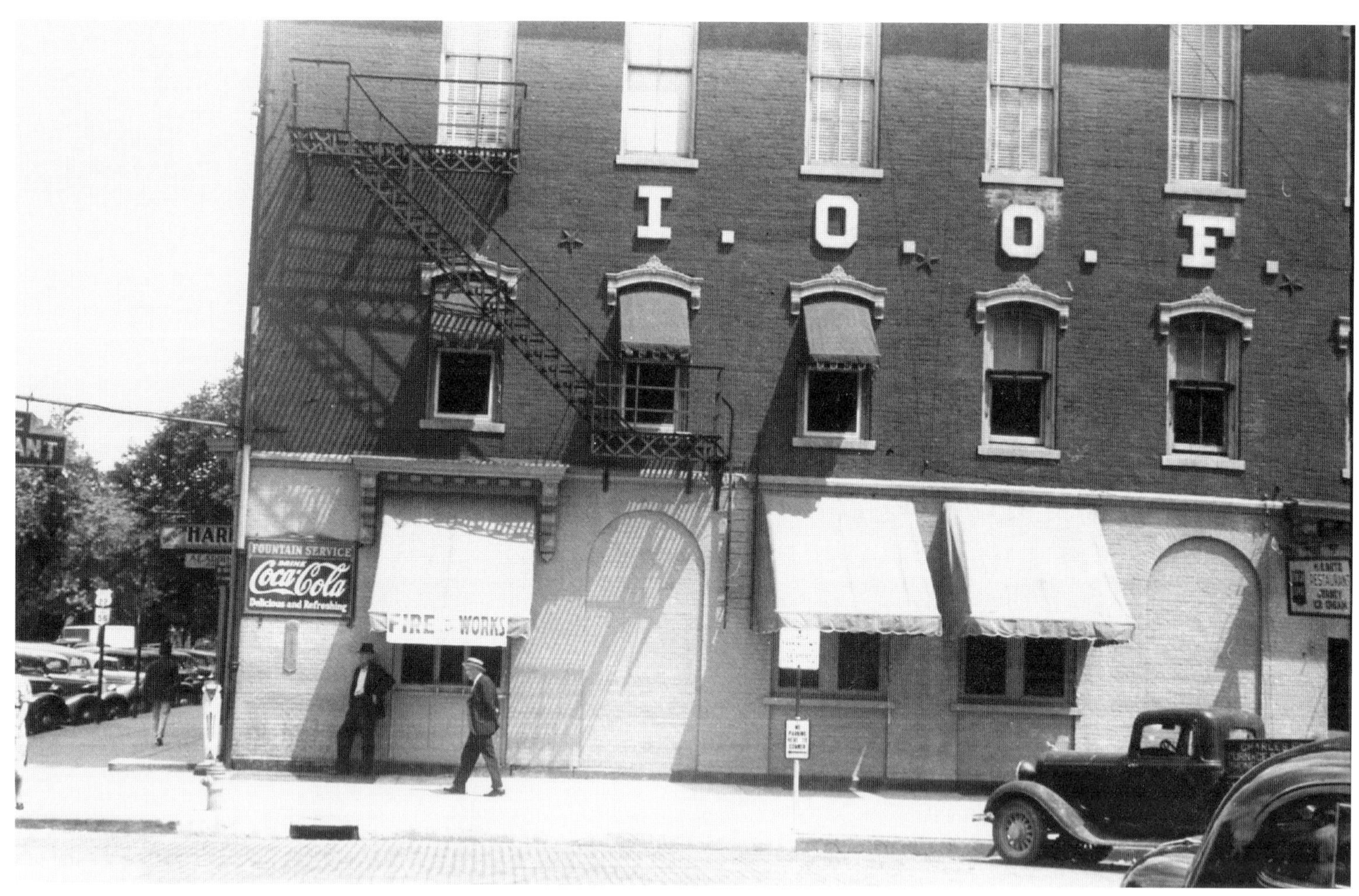

FIG 27 Hall of Independent Odd Fellows, Circleville, Ohio

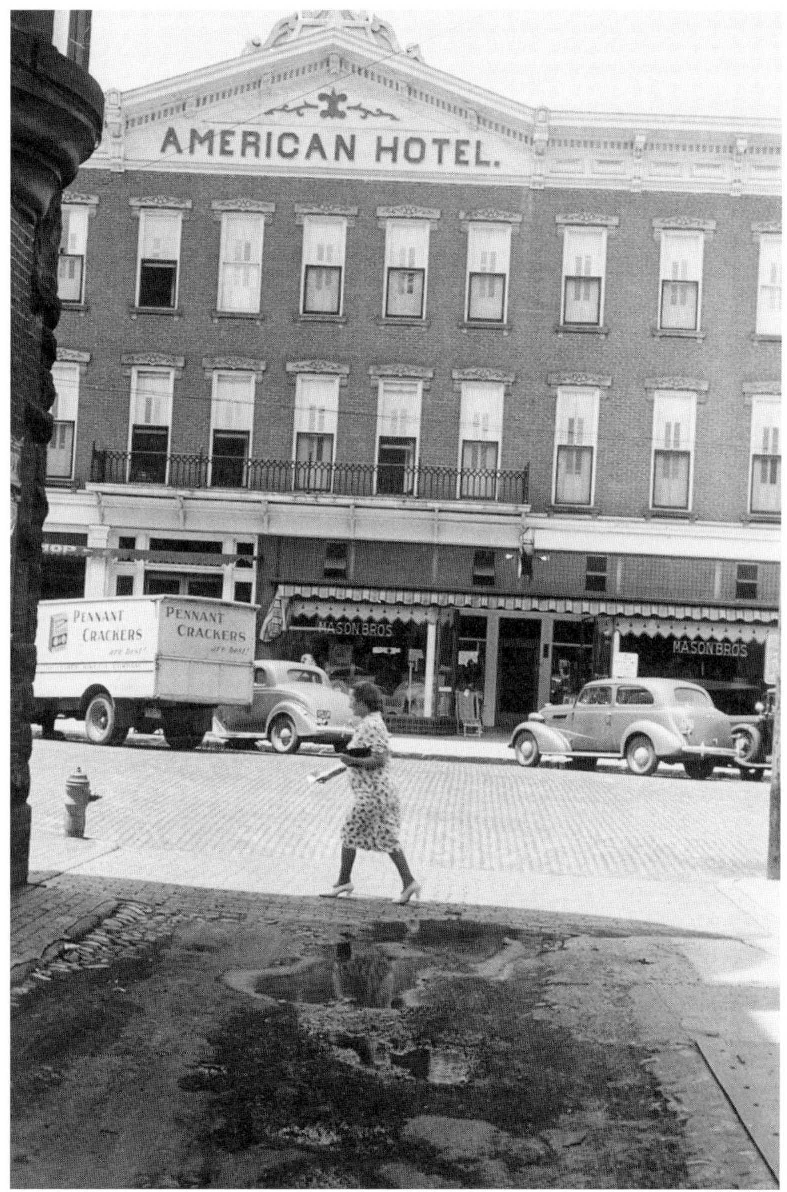

FIG 28 Main and Court Streets, Circleville, Ohio

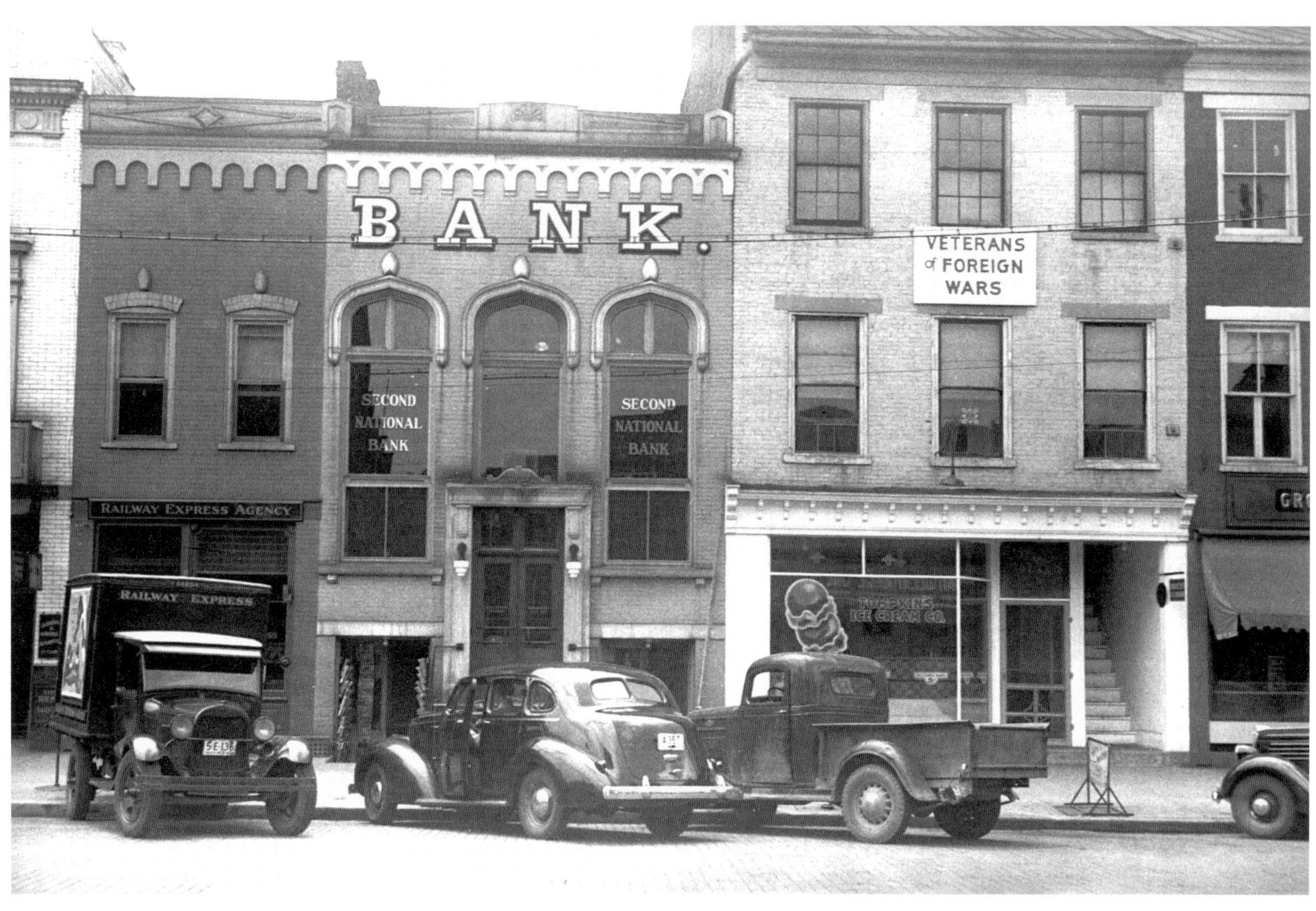

FIG 29 Main and Court Streets, Circleville, Ohio

pediments, lunettes, turrets, upper-floor bay windows, and masonry window arches.[10] Among these notable structures are the Second National Bank, the Odd Fellows Hall, the American Hotel, and probably the Federal-style building in figure 26.[11]

Shahn's photographs of Main and Court streets thus hinted at how attractive Circleville's built environment could be, but not the degree to which it was. By excluding so many of its prepossessing edifices, his canvass made its downtown appear more prosaic than a broader survey would have. Not only were these structures integral to citizens' pride in their community, but handsome, well-kept buildings also signified ongoing civic vitality, the sense of which was diminished by their absence. His goal, of course, was not to produce an architectural survey; on the other hand, the considerable number of conspicuous buildings in Circleville makes the omission of so many noteworthy. Why that should have been so is impossible to know with any certainty, but it may have reflected Shahn's perception that towns such as Circleville had entered a period of decline. If so, that also helps account for why, in the course of the entire summer's work, he made just one photograph of a bustling downtown street, and for the impression of ebbing vitality implicit in his studies of Urbana's and Somerset's handsome central squares.

MANY OF SHAHN'S small-town photographs embroider on the paradoxical circumstance he discovered in London—an egalitarian ethos that encouraged spontaneous mingling by white male citizens in central business districts, but with these democratic gatherings taking place in settings that intimated flagging civic vitality. Both perceptions depended on what he could observe on sidewalks, which featured in his compositions as insistently as the towns' more obviously photogenic storefronts. Because his perception was so acute, however, and his gift for expressive composition keen, these pictures rarely became repetitive or his observations stale.

In most towns, Shahn continued to shoot sidewalk parleys. One such gathering comprised an animated cluster of a half-dozen women in front of a shoe store, but it was the only female group he photographed, so either such assemblies were rare or he believed men's to be more culturally significant (fig. 30). An asymmetrical composition depicts four men huddling on a corner, and beyond them and angling away from the lens, the empty street, a row of parked cars, and a line of storefronts. While a few pedestrians are visible opposite, the asymmetry creates a thematic tension between the intensity of the men's conversation and the drowsy streetscape, as well as a formal one between their tight conversational square and the receding diagonals (fig. 31). He made three studies of a pair of men conversing near a bank: one from behind, a head-on portrait, and the third obliquely framed to include the bank's plate glass window reflecting the buildings opposite and revealing most fully the context for their conversation. The men's clothing—one is in overalls and a battered hat, the other wears a necktie and Panama—unmistakably indicates their differing social stations. Nonetheless, their relaxed

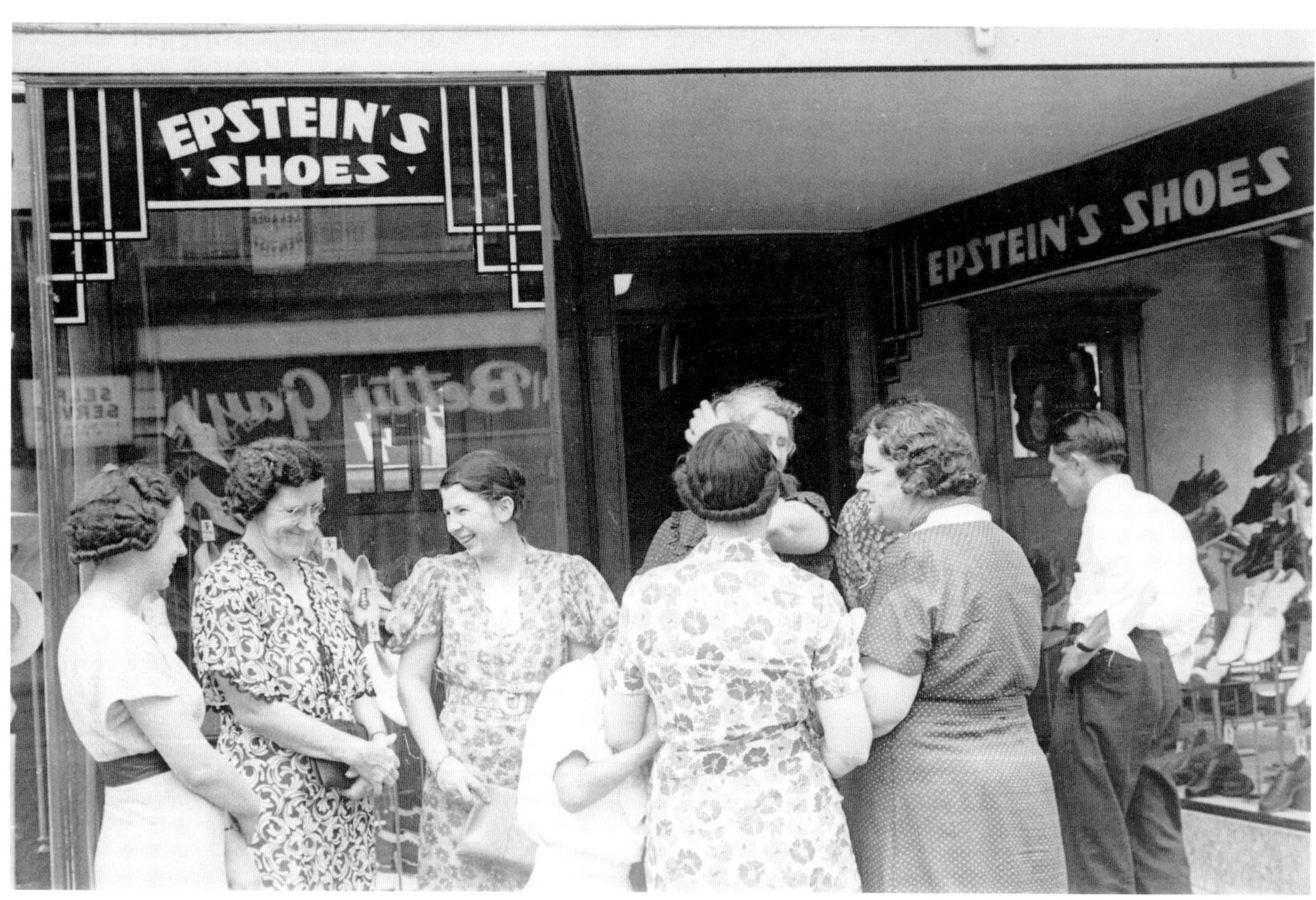

FIG 30 Along main street, Lancaster, Ohio

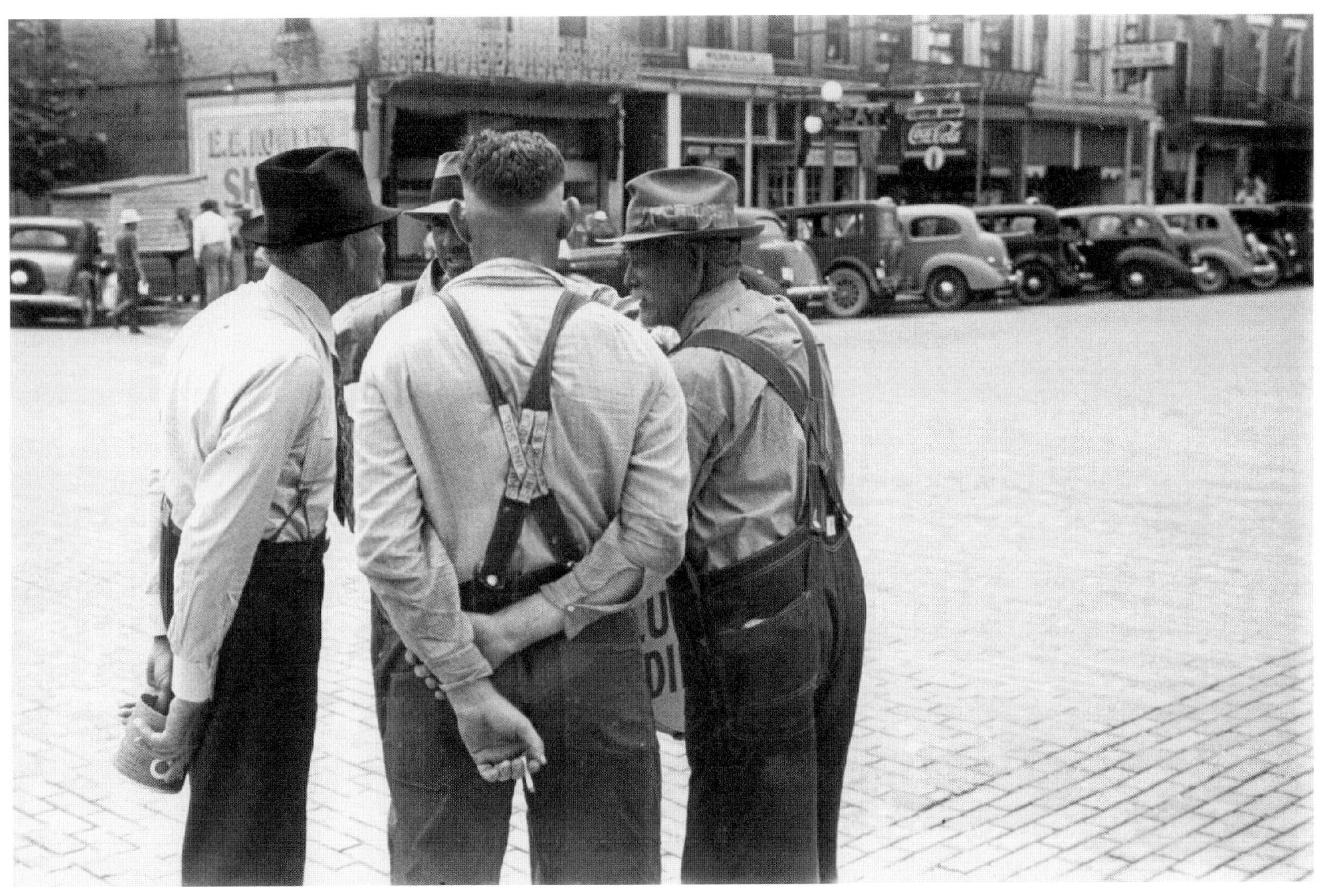

FIG 31 Street scene, Washington Court House, Ohio

body language evinces comfortable familiarity, the egalitarianism of the sidewalk leveling normative distinctions of class and occupation. All three pictures are titled "Farmer and banker," a specification of vocational identities unique in Shahn's sidewalk studies (fig. 32).

A photograph of an animated Marysville group was unique in another way. Among Shahn's numerous depictions of such gatherings, it alone reveals a breach of sexual segregation that otherwise was universally observed (fig. 33). That anomaly notwithstanding, the most visually complex and culturally resonant of his Marysville studies are three photographs made outside a tavern, where he exploited the division its plate glass created between subjects behind and in front of the window to interrogate and then ratify small-town egalitarianism. The first he composed with his lens almost parallel with the window to highlight contrasts of age, class, and perhaps receptiveness to modernity. In front of the window are two older men garbed in ancient, misshapen hats and rumpled workaday clothing, one of them turned with an arm around the other's shoulder to deliver a comment. Behind the glass, a clean-cut young man staring at the camera bears a resemblance to the idealized representation of a jaunty, smart user of El Verso Cigars on a cardboard advertisement just below him in the window. The juxtaposition suggests that he has absorbed notions of personal style from the consumer culture that is powered by such advertisements, as the men outside clearly have not. The photograph also gives off a whiff of the surreal. Behind the glass hovers a disembodied hat, an optical illusion that highlights its modishness and points to the decrepit antiquity of the headgear worn by the pair outside. Within the photograph's rectangle, the tavern window is an internal frame that concentrates the viewer's attention on the contrasts being exposed, differences suggesting Marysville's social disunities (fig. 34).

But that impression is dissolved by a second photograph taken from an oblique camera angle to include a third man outside. The newcomer, dressed in immaculate whites and a dapper Panama, engages in a sidewalk colloquy with the two disheveled men that reaffirms the democracy of small-town ways. The advertisement and the young man are mostly obscured, the photograph's figuring of space is more expansive, and the sense of disparity between those inside and outside the tavern is reduced (fig. 35). Shahn then retreated a few steps up the street for the final shot, which he composed so as to divide it into three distinct planes. Two feature portraits: the young man is now isolated in the tavern's side window, while on its front sidewalk the conversationalists continue to be absorbed in their get-together. But extending into the

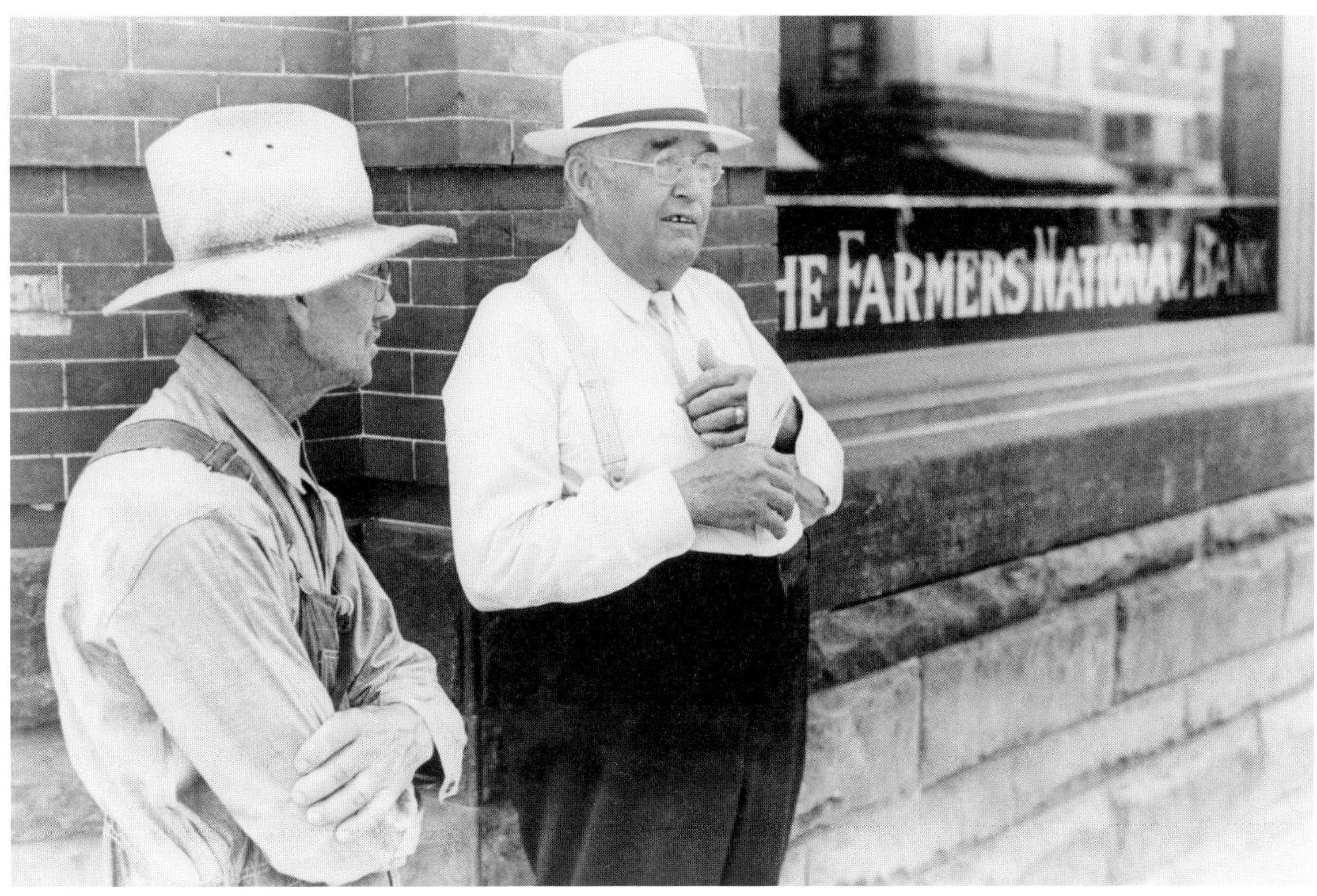

FIG 32 Farmer and banker, Plain City, Ohio

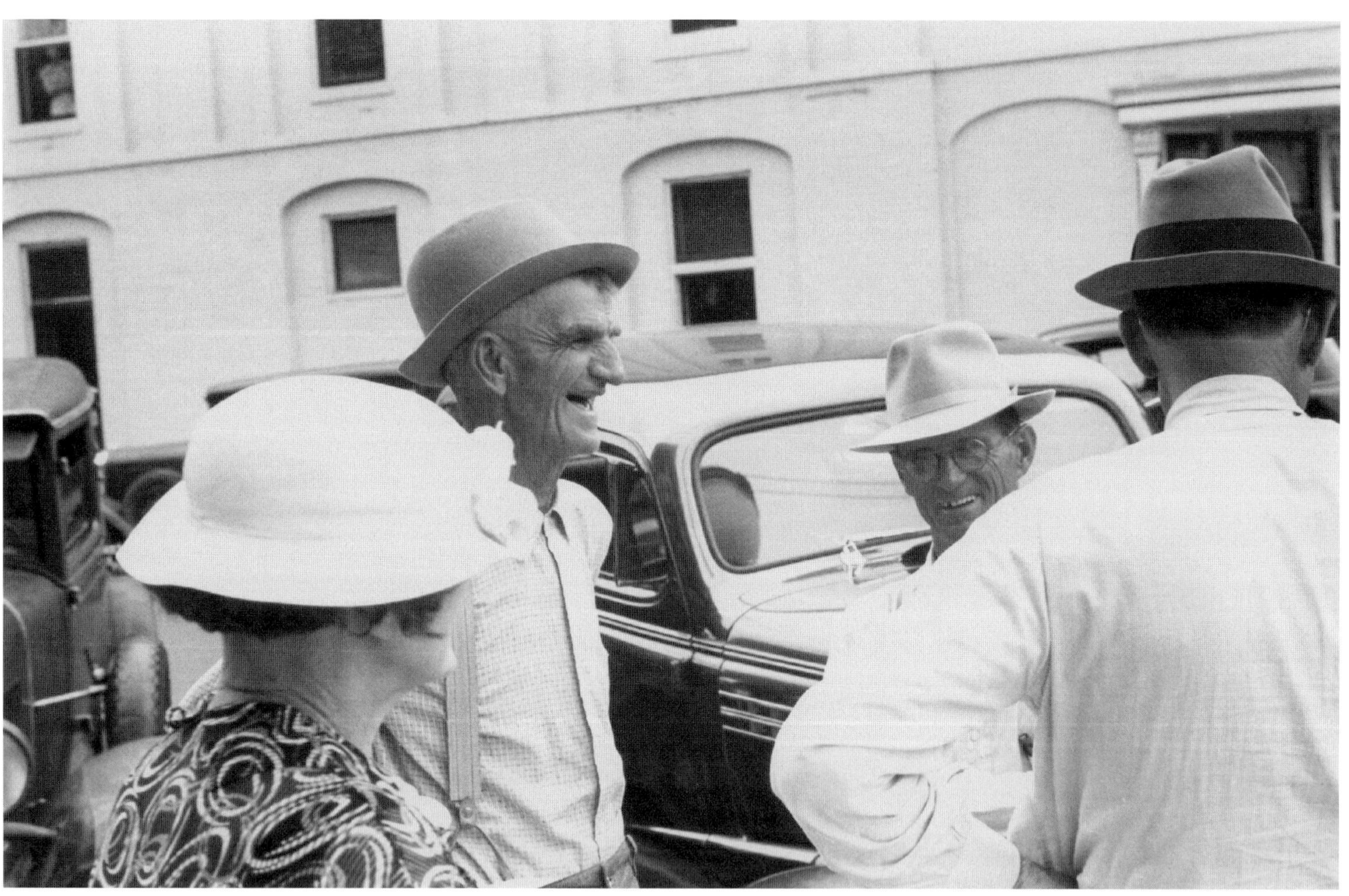

FIG 33 Street scene, Marysville, Ohio

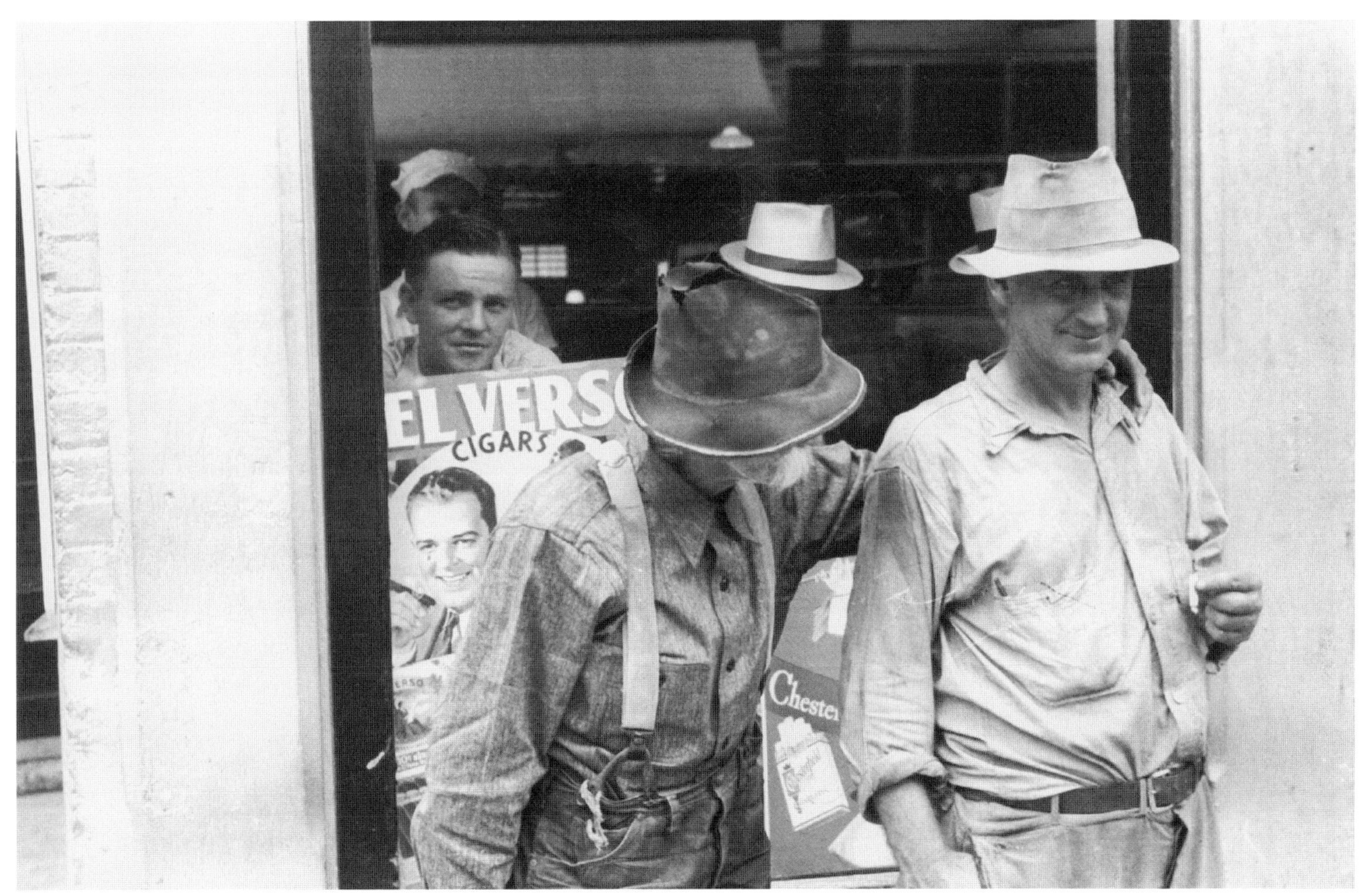

FIG 34 Street scene, Marysville, Ohio

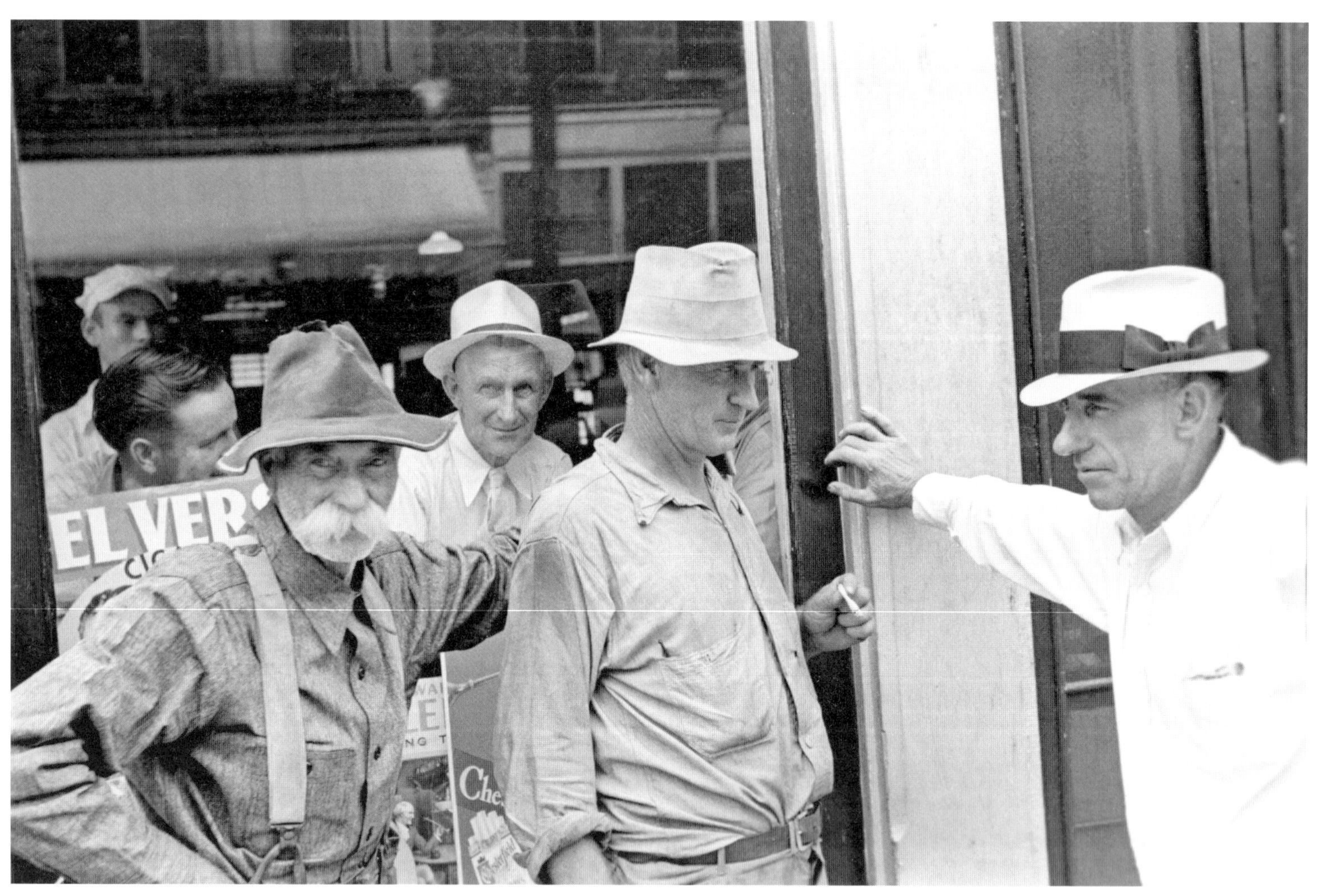

FIG 35 Street scene, Marysville, Ohio

distance in the photograph's third plane, the sidewalk is nearly empty, hinting that opportunities for spontaneous gatherings are less common than these pictures suggest (fig. 36).[1]

Such sparsely used sidewalks stretching into the distance are, if anything, more frequent in Shahn's ensuing coverage than they had been in London. His repetitions of this compositional strategy may have owed something to his angle finder, because while he seemed to be aiming across a street, the lens actually would be pointed along the sidewalk. But in many of these shots his use of the angle finder would have been unlikely, because they depict pedestrians either walking away or too distant to be self-conscious about being photographed (figs. 37–39). Even when subjects were nearby and the angle finder was almost certainly switched on, he only infrequently waited to press the shutter release until they would be seen centered against a storefront—which would have been a simple matter of turning the camera forty-five degrees from its apparent aim across the street. Instead, he usually made the lengthening sidewalk a central feature in the photograph (fig. 40). On those relatively few occasions when he did portray pedestrians against a store's window, its display was usually more essential than the passersby to the picture's meaning.

His repetitive motif of disused sidewalks was not inadvertent but the result of decisions about composition before he opened his lens. A Circleville sidewalk picture in which he made other choices illustrates how they conveyed a contrasting interpretation. Passing by a twelve-foot sidewalk clock advertising an optician's services are two pedestrians (and the leg of a third), a man in overalls and battered hat and a woman wearing a smart outfit and holding an unseen child's hand. The man and woman may or may not be a couple—they are about the same age, and they are abreast of and in step with one another, but their mismatched apparel suggests differing class positions—and this enigma is the picture's most arresting subject. Shahn's organization of the photograph is uncommon in two ways: he aimed at the parked cars, excluding any perception of the sidewalk's extension, and he chose a vertical format to include the clock's full height. Both decisions contribute to the impression of an intimate drama taking place within a bounded, almost theatrical space, as the pedestrians stride into the picture. Had more of his sidewalk pictures been composed as was this one, overtones of the towns' lassitude would have been considerably less frequent. As it happened, though, none other duplicates its formal strategy (fig. 41).

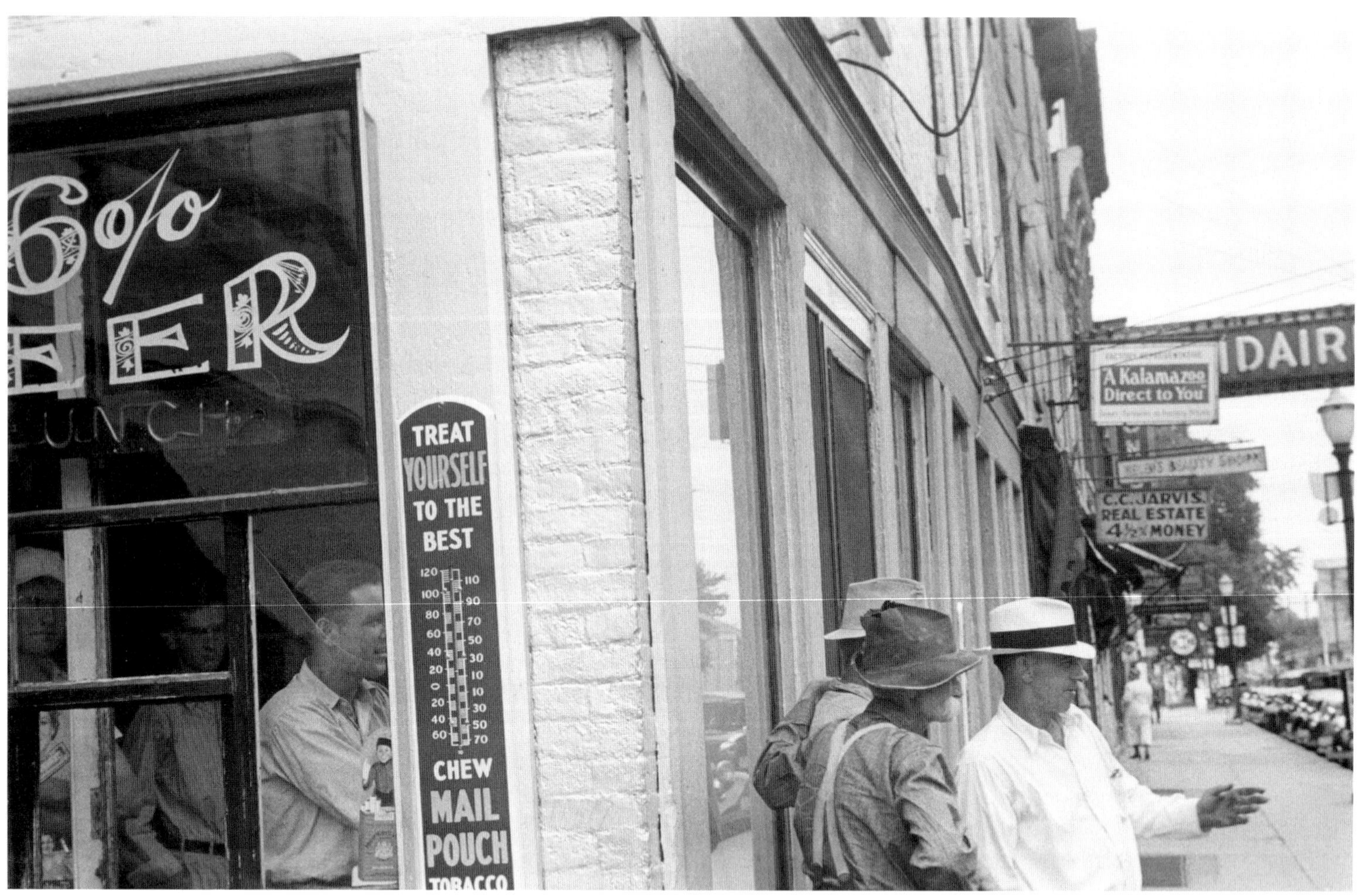

FIG 36 Street corner, Marysville, Ohio

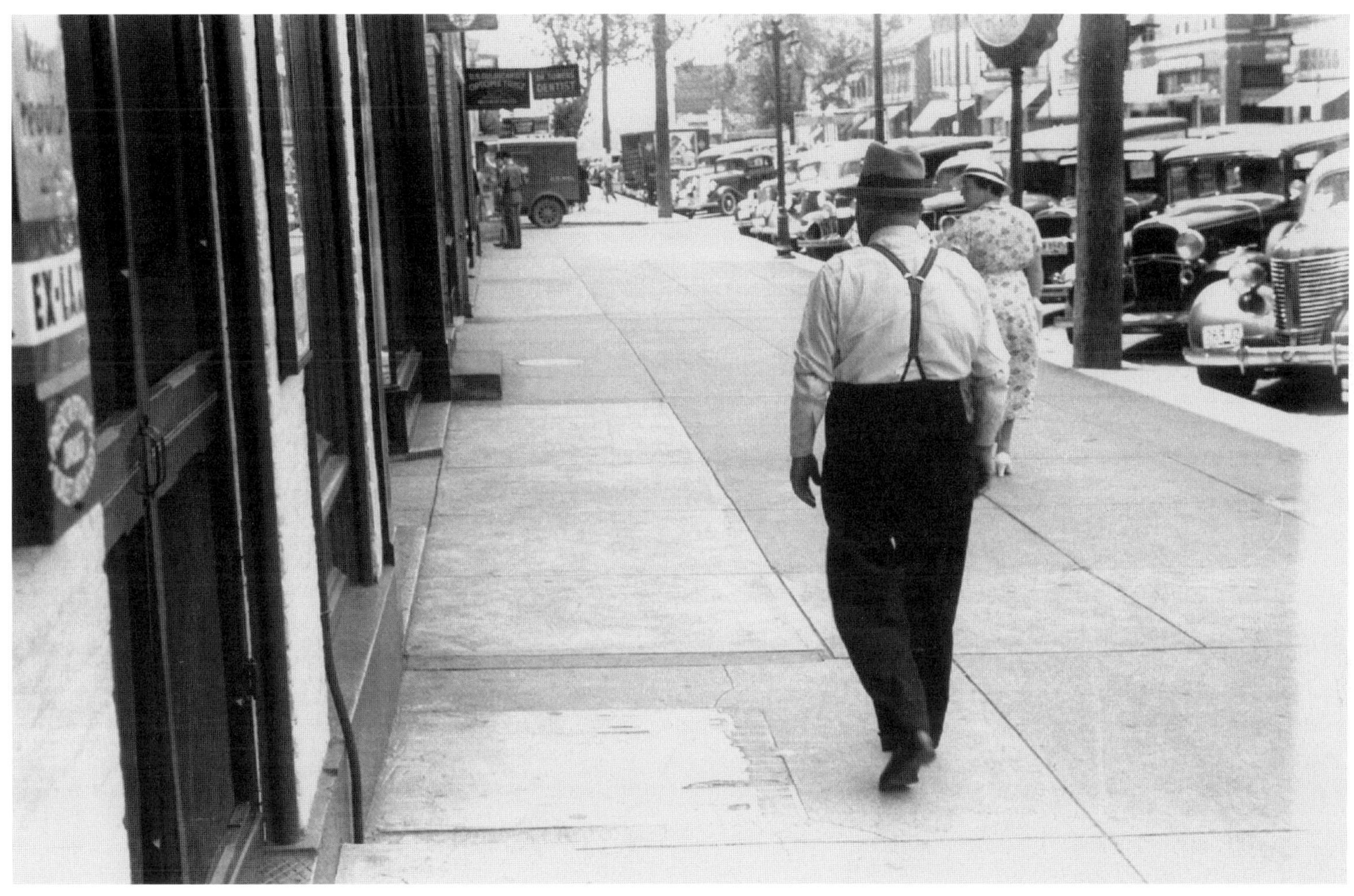

FIG 37 Street scene in central Ohio

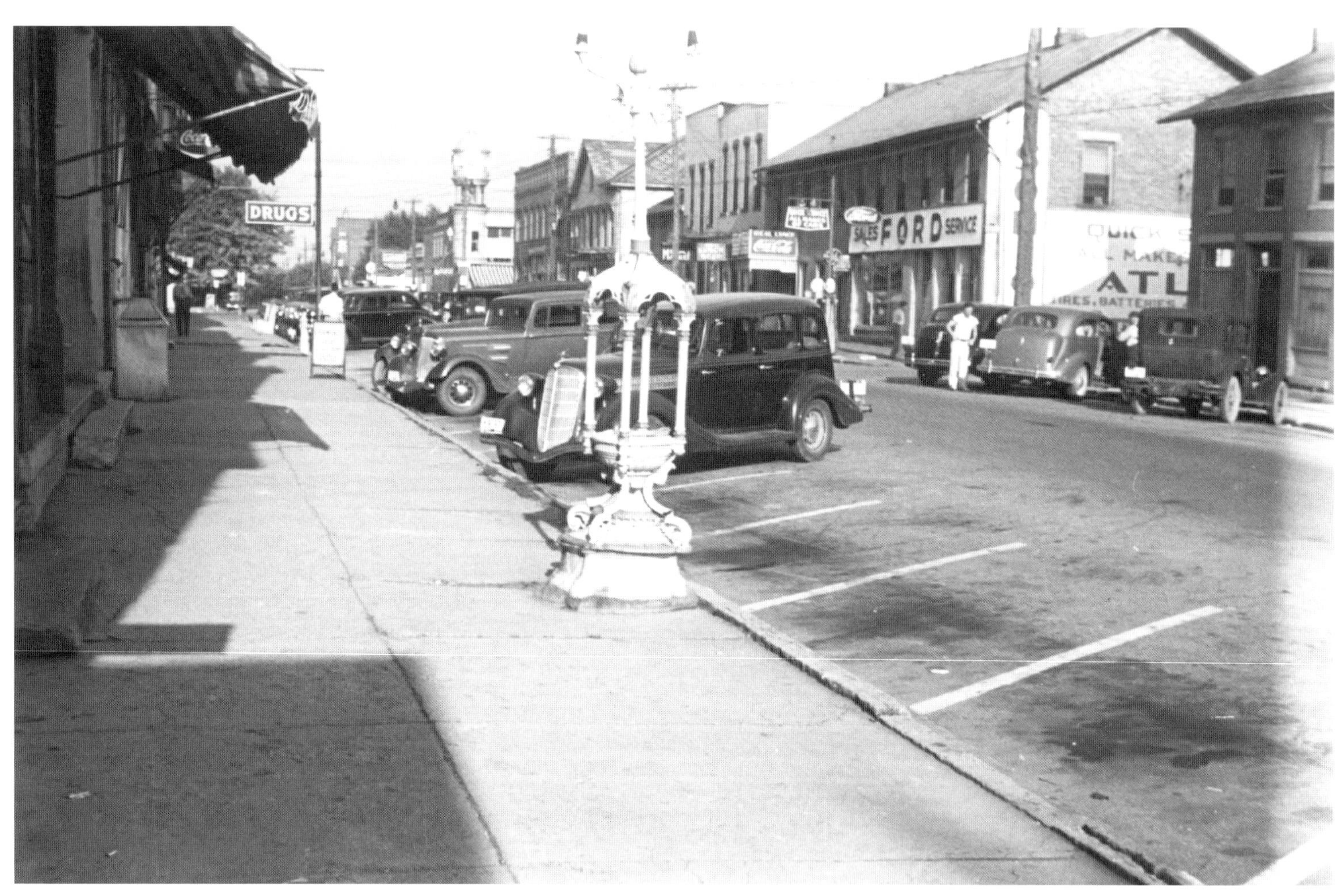

FIG 38 Plain City, Ohio, Main street

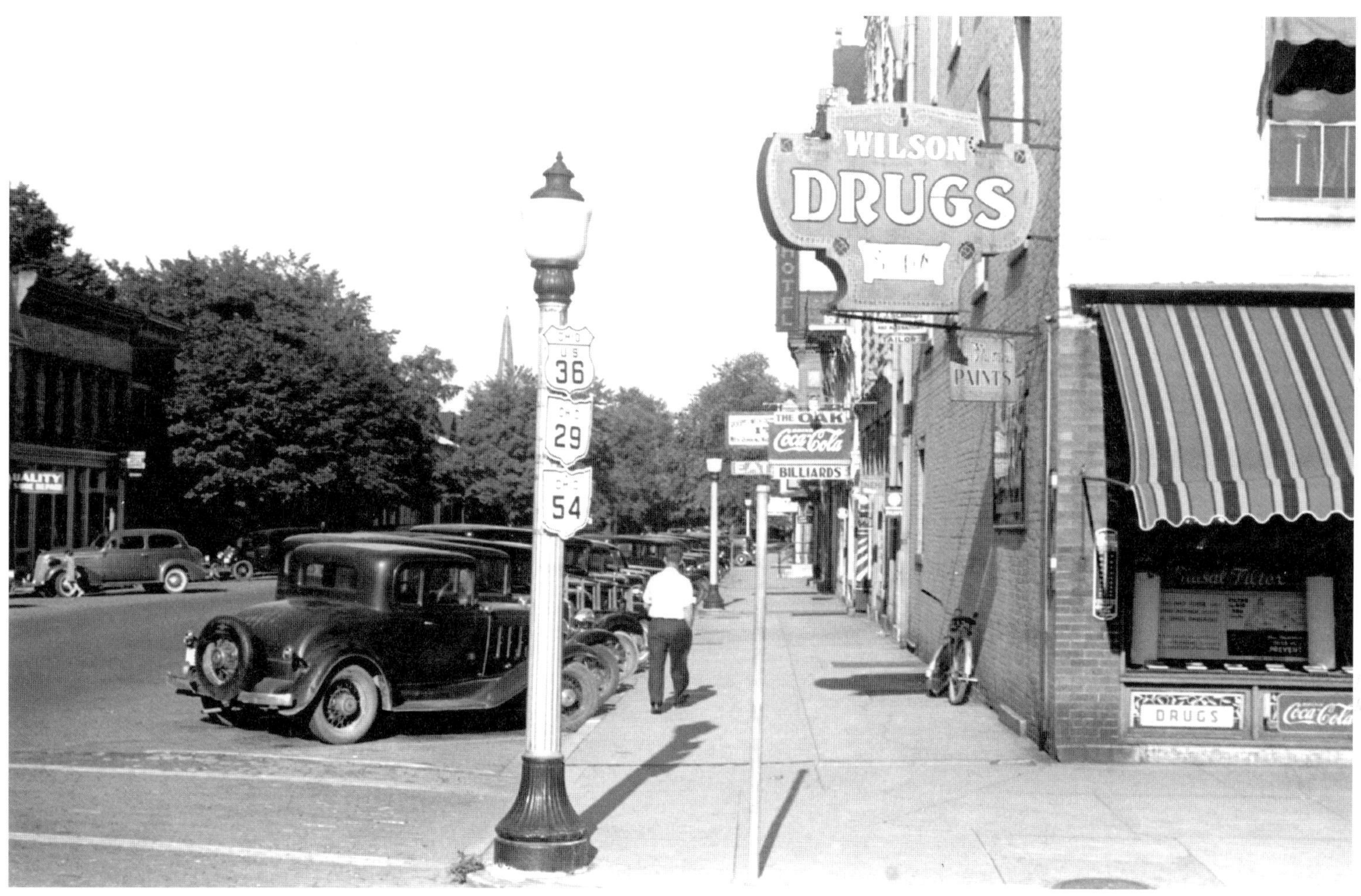

FIG 39 Street scene, Washington Court House, Ohio

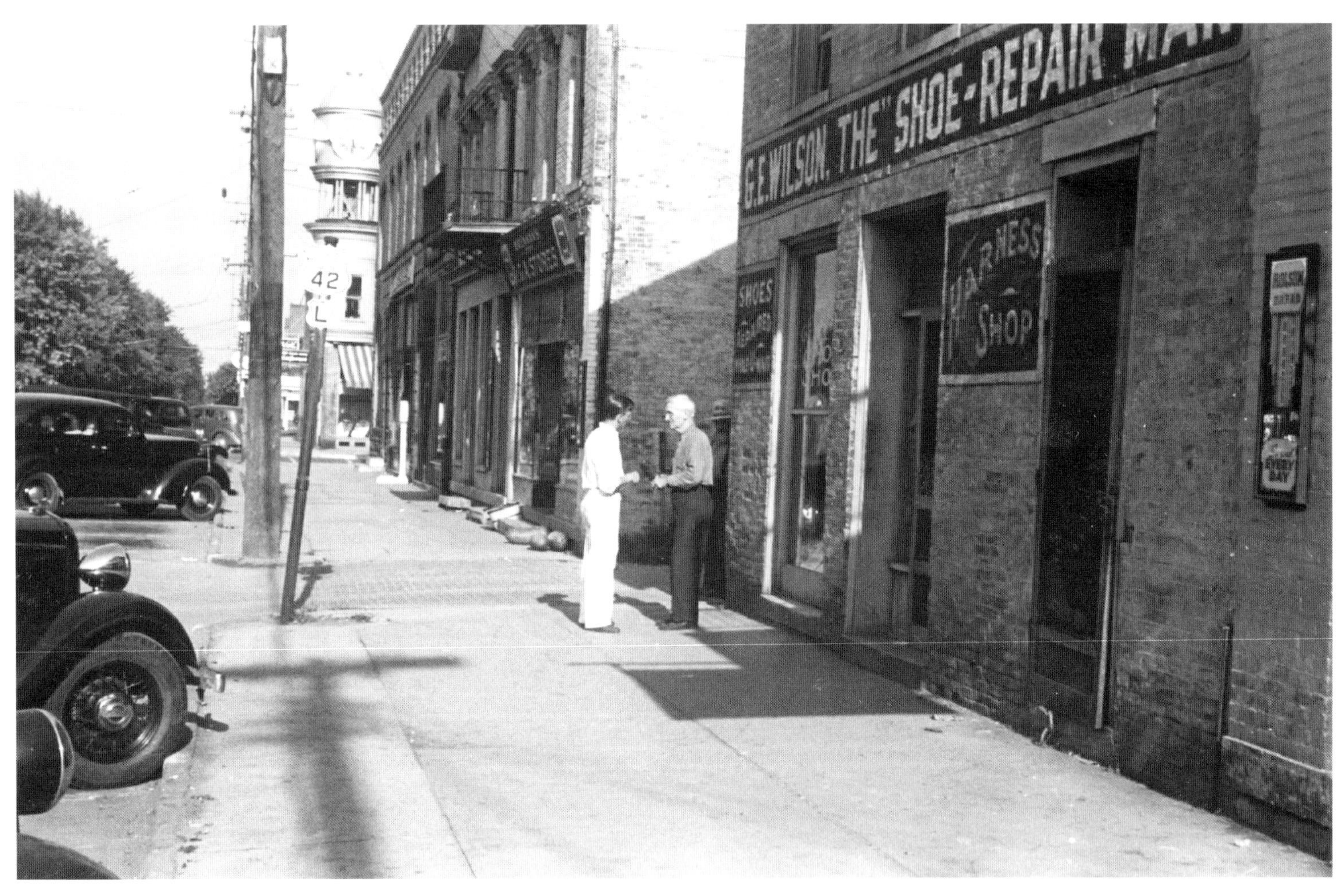

FIG 40 Street scene, Plain City, Ohio

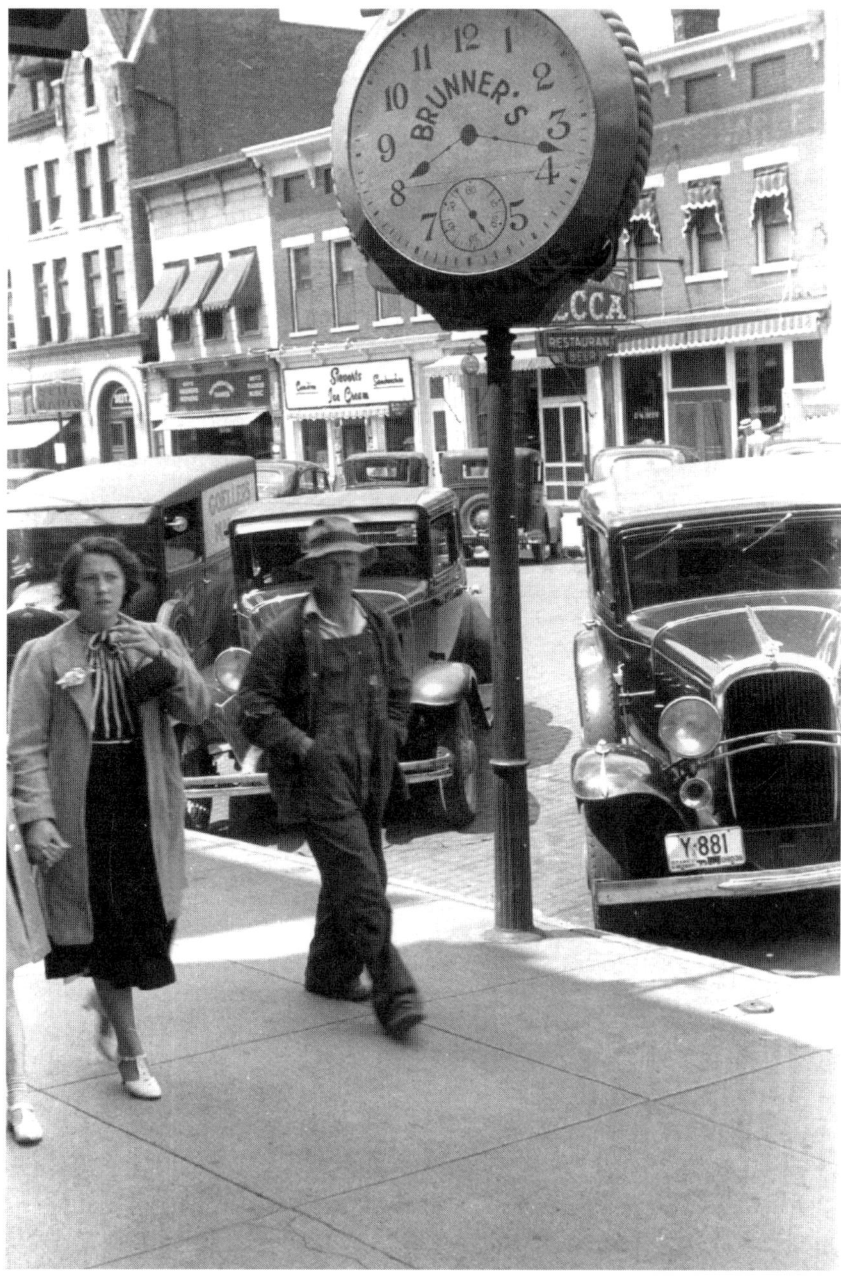

FIG 41 Main and Court Streets, Circleville, Ohio

The point of view of his close-in study of an elderly Circleville woman looking intently into the window of a clothing store is more typical. Her pince-nez, shapeless lace-collared dress, and prim hat mark her as especially old-fashioned. He slightly angled his lens toward the plate glass so that the parked cars and the row of buildings opposite would be reflected along with the window shopper herself, these reflections obscuring the goods she is peering at. The effect is to saturate the picture's left side with visual stimuli—a montage of the doubled woman, reflected cars and buildings, and shadowy merchandise—making the blankness of the sidewalk all the more pronounced as it recedes into the distance with but a lone pedestrian on it (fig. 42).

Because the lens takes in everything in front of it and makes most photographs dense with visual information, they rarely evoke a singular meaning, and that is true of Shahn's sidewalk photographs. While almost always including at least one individual whose demeanor and clothing establish him or her as representing a particular category of citizen, they also incorporate numerous other aspects of the streetscape such as directional and advertising signs, shop fronts, street furniture, and parked automobiles, the sum of which helps define the community's atmosphere. But while these photographs of receding, little-used sidewalks inevitably emit multiple messages, intimating the towns' enervation is their most consistent one.

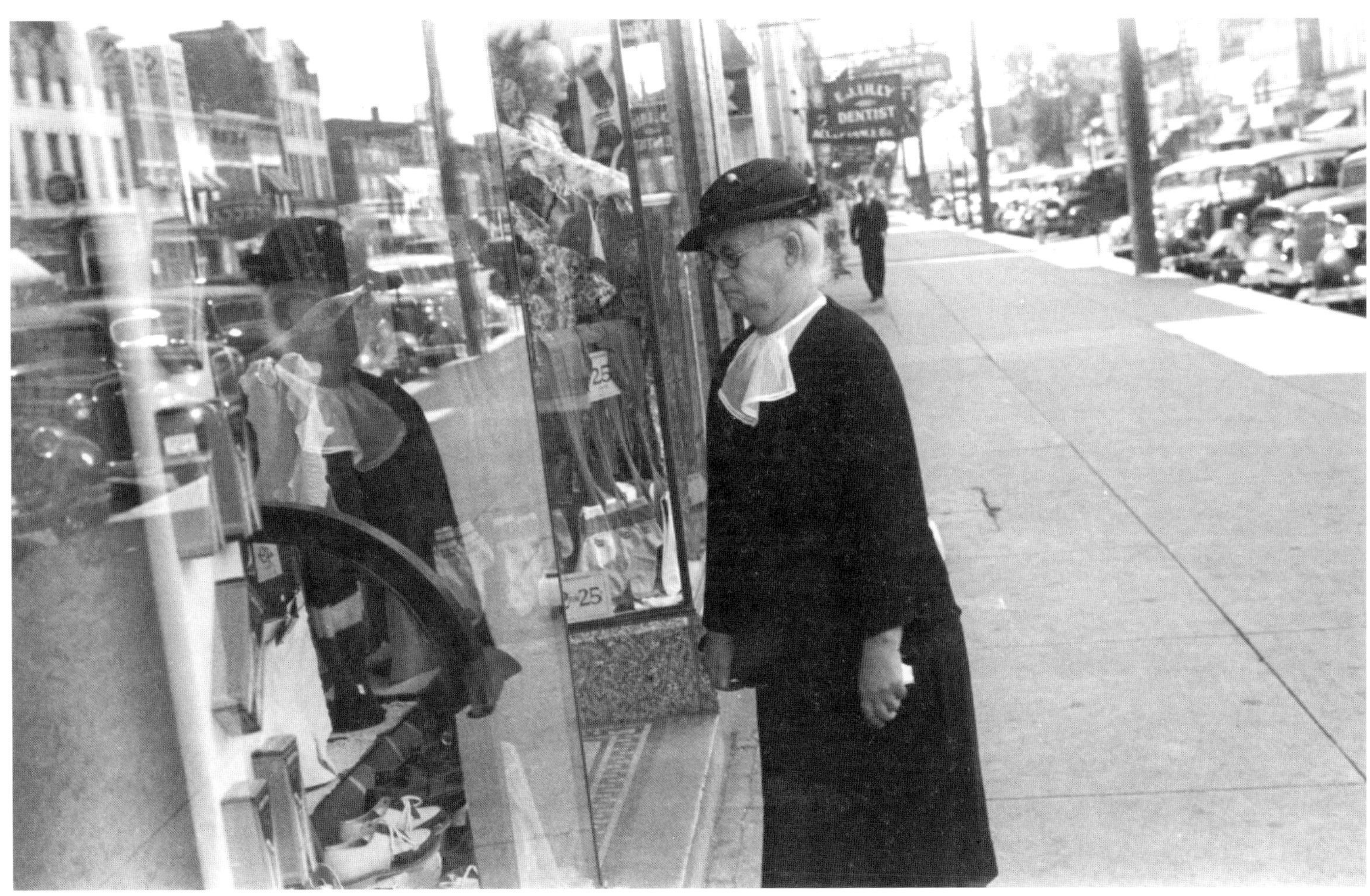

FIG 42 Street scene, Circleville, Ohio

ONE OF CIRCLEVILLE'S notable buildings was the nineteenth-century Pickaway County Courthouse, located a block south of the commercial center at Main and Court. Neither of Shahn's shots of it is very successful, and this may account for why it was the only courthouse he photographed in the eight county seats. In one picture a farmer in overalls is dwarfed by its entrance, a monumental Romanesque arch enclosed by pilasters and a pediment, and the mid-distance asymmetrical composition rather pointlessly emphasizes the structure's repeating stained-glass windows and heavy masonry arches. In the other, from a greater distance, the symmetry of two diagonally parked cars spanning the foreground contributes to making the eclectic courthouse and its clock tower appear especially inharmonious and disjointed, and despite the vertical format, the frame awkwardly cuts off most of the tower's extension. The courthouse is substantial but ponderous, and in these photographs its symbolic overtones are obscure, in contrast to Shahn's studies of the central squares in Urbana and Somerset (fig. 43).

Shahn also neglected other public institutions. He depicted no schools or libraries, police stations or jails, and only one fire department and post office, although pictures of all had been requested in Stryker's script. A relief office and town hall represented municipal institutions, and his photographs of both served only as contextual touchstones for his exposure of the indignities local officials visited on recipients of relief. These omissions reflected the difficulty of making studies of public institutions visually compelling, but also Shahn's intention to center on average citizens and his conviction that their interactions with one another and their built environment would better reveal the towns' atmosphere.

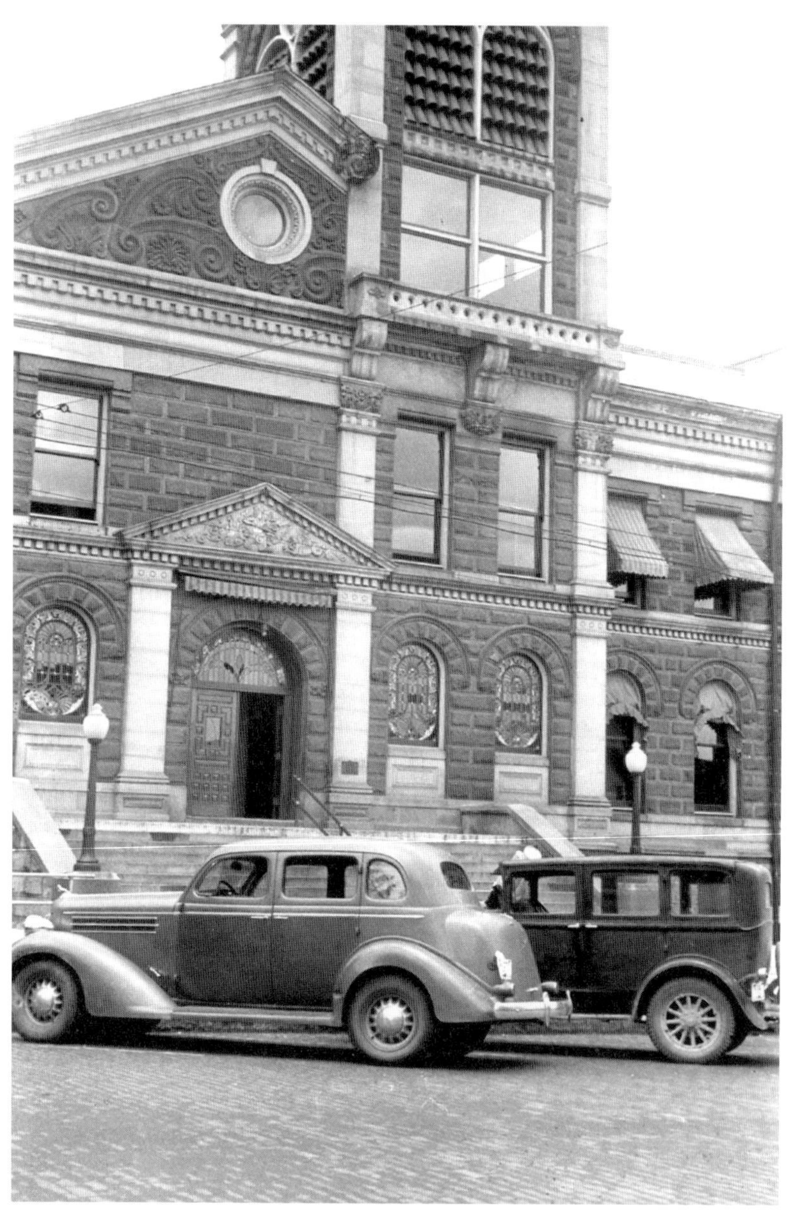

FIG 43 County courthouse, Circleville, Ohio

Stryker's script also unsurprisingly designated churches as among a small town's key institutions and requested pictures of them and of congregants participating in church activities. Shahn complied with more than twenty photographs: a few centered on architecture, but most depicted worshippers departing services. Methodists were the single denomination represented except for the African American gospel church in London, and the overwhelming majority of these pictures he made in Linworth and Unionville Center, hamlets otherwise absent from his survey. In Urbana he made his only studies of town churches, the facade of the small and nondescript Treacles Creek Methodist Church, even more humble than the hamlets' chapels, and a close-up of the First Methodist Church's exterior announcement board, commemorating the Fourth of July with an exhortation by popular nineteenth-century moralist Josiah Gilbert Holland proclaiming the need for sturdy men in difficult times. Visible next to that secular announcement is the church's cornerstone, memorializing its 1836 founding date and the erection of its present building in 1900, but otherwise the view provides no sense of the edifice or of the church's significance in town life.

Church membership in Ohio was substantial, and impressive stone or brick churches were common sights in its towns: it ranked fourth among all states in its number of congregants and the capital worth of its religious structures. It also hosted some one hundred denominations, and according to *The Ohio Guide,* at least ten were represented in "practically every community in the State."[1] Shahn's coverage neglected the variety of religious practice and avoided entirely churches that would be among the most imposing structures of county seats, landmarks signifying their symbolic importance in community life. Moreover, a number of the photographs that he did make of the Linworth and Unionville Center chapels have a creative flat-footedness that was rare in his work that summer. Some are oddly composed, with the buildings awkwardly bisected, and in others the relationship of a picture's elements—departing parishioners and church design—seems merely arbitrary (figs. 44–45).

The most obvious explanation for these insufficiencies is that he could devise no satisfactory photographic strategy for making visually compelling the role of religion in community life, which, unlike, say, that of commerce as revealed on downtown streets, was relatively abstract, and which studies of church exteriors could only faintly intimate. As a secular Jew, he had little interest in formal religion, and even less knowledge of the numerous varieties of Christianity that were practiced in central Ohio. He likely made these church pictures only

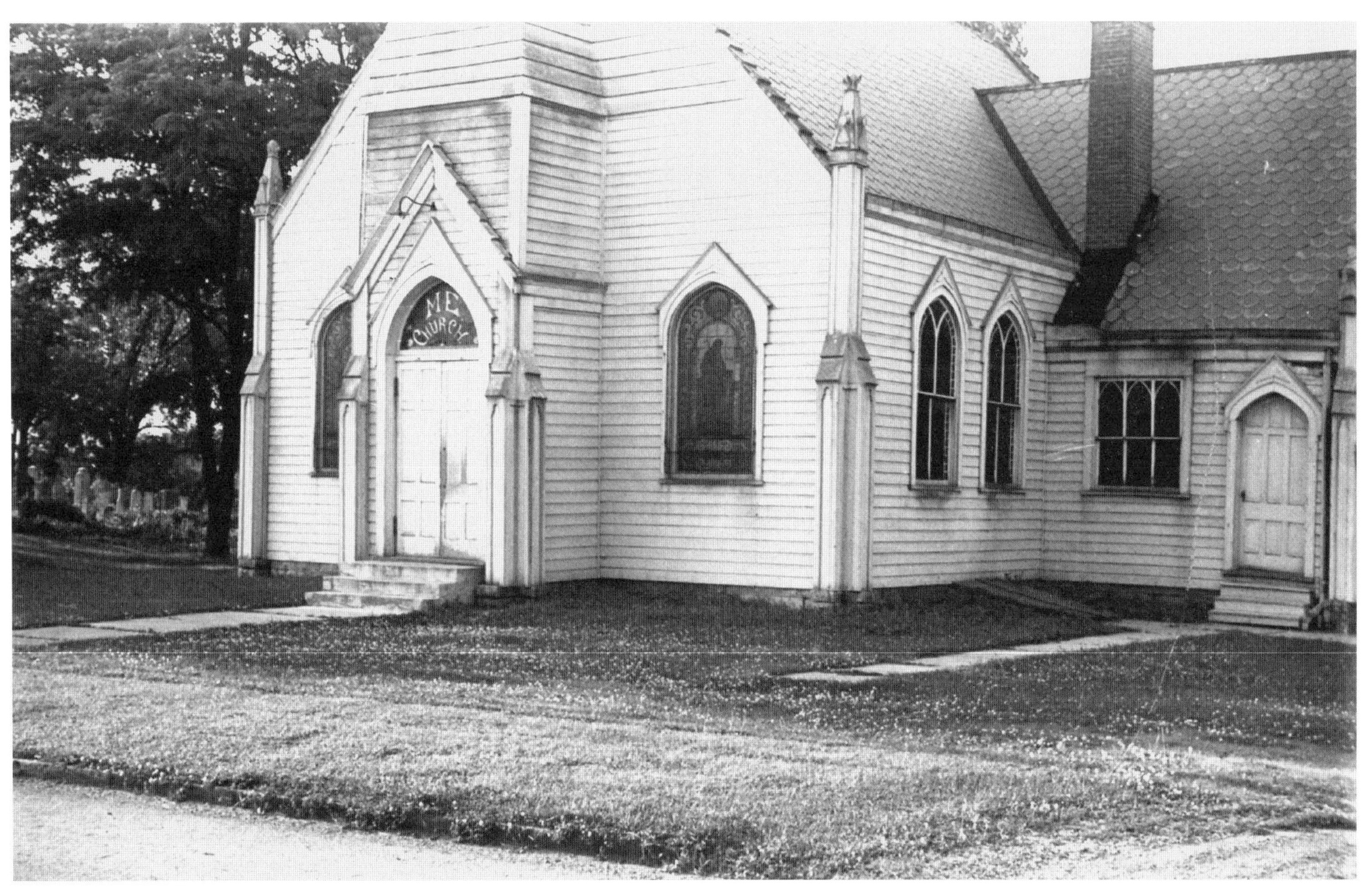

FIG 44 Methodist church, Unionville Center, Ohio

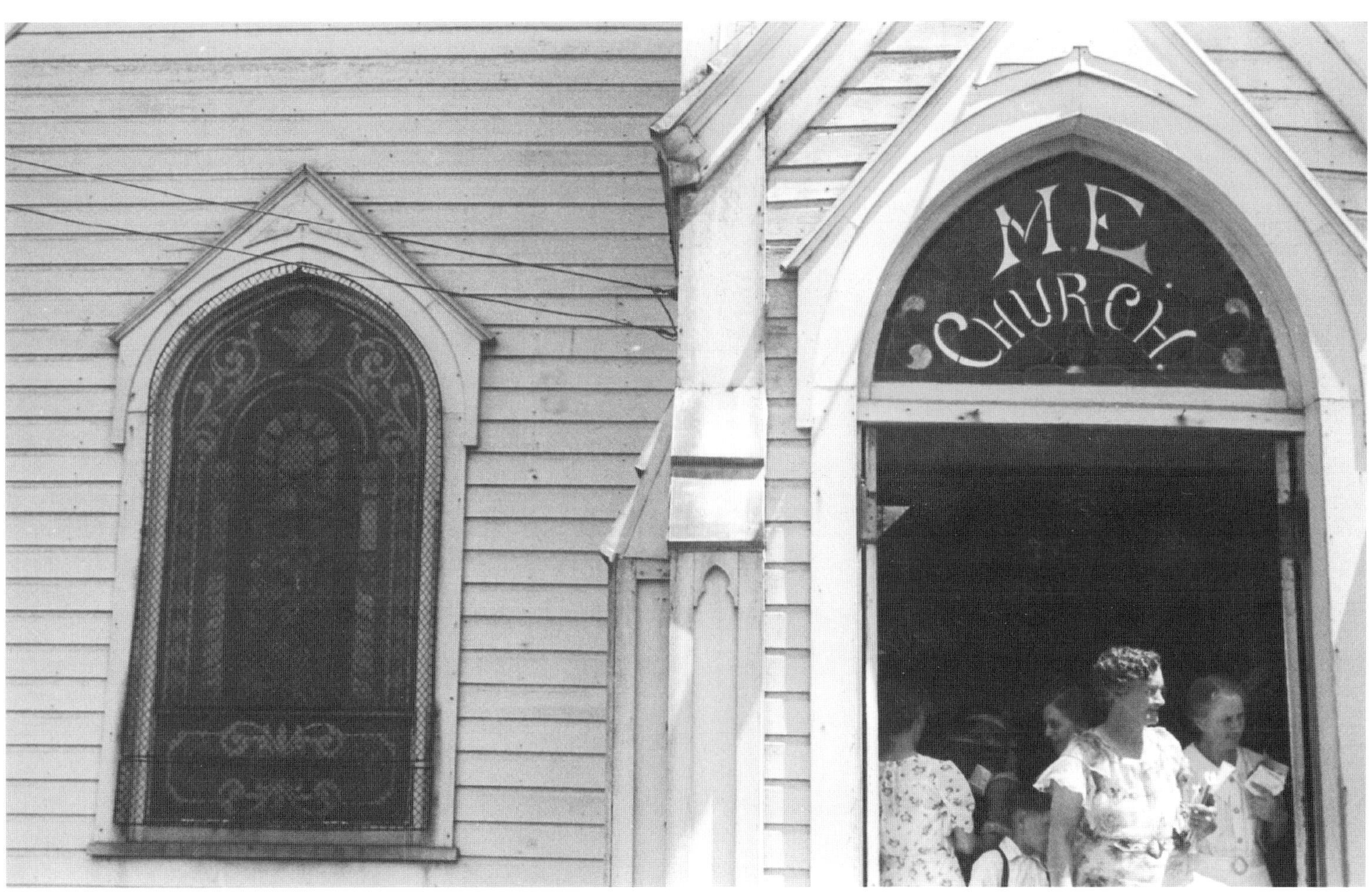

FIG 45 Methodist church, Unionville Center, Ohio

to oblige Stryker. Linworth's and Unionville Center's modest frame chapels more than the towns' monumental churches may also have fitted his preconception of what small-town religious structures ought to look like from his earlier photographic trips to the rural South and his summers in Truro, Massachusetts. Even more, the chapels' cozy proportions symbolized better than the towns' imposing structures the communal intimacy that Stryker believed to be characteristic of small-town life.

Shahn apparently shared this perception, and it accounts for why so much of his church coverage—three-quarters of it—repetitiously concentrated on worshippers after services were over, people filing out to greet the pastor at the door and then clustering on the steps and lawn to chat. Such sociable gatherings perhaps were an extension of the spiritual fellowship experienced inside, but since no tokens of it otherwise appeared, these pictures functioned more in his survey as the Sunday manifestations of the weekday camaraderie he had observed on downtown sidewalks. With the participants all attired in their churchgoing best, photographs of these groups could not dramatize how an egalitarian ethos leveled social distinctions, but otherwise they corresponded with the fraction of his work that celebrated the small town's neighborly and democratic atmosphere (fig. 46).

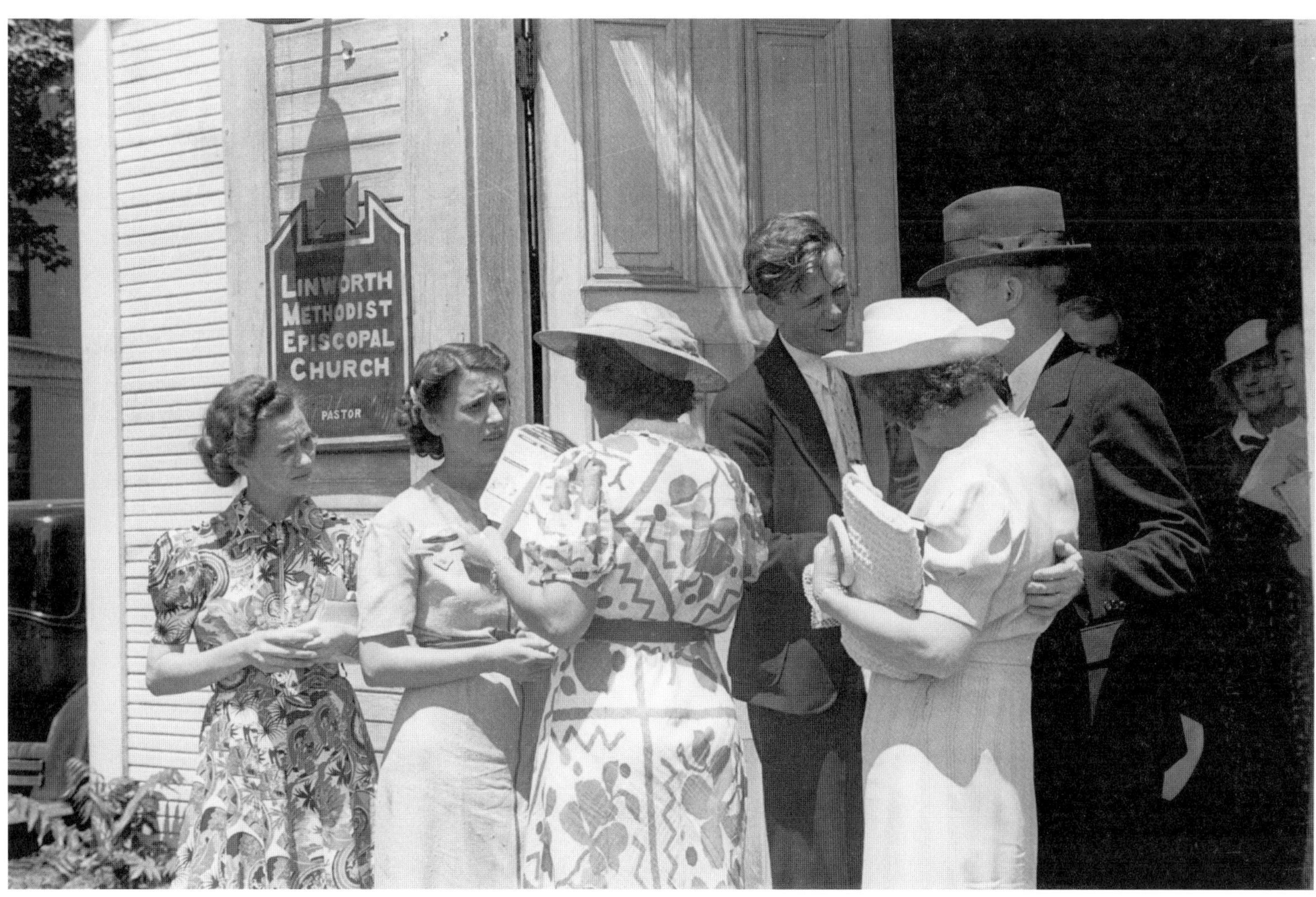

FIG 46 Leaving church, Linworth, Ohio

IN THE PREAMBLE to his script, Stryker defined small towns as "the contact point where men of the land keep in touch with a civilization based on mass-produced, city-made gadgets, machines, canned movies and canned beef." That scoffing characterization of urban civilization reflected his conviction that only a thin veneer of modernity overlay the towns' traditional culture, leaving them fundamentally unaltered. Among the two hundred or so topics the script singled out for photographic treatment, no more than a small fraction referenced twentieth-century technology, consumerism, or mass culture. While Stryker suggested pictures of cars, movie theaters, shop windows, and advertising posters, he much more copiously urged the photographers to concentrate on such time-honored rituals as picnics, town meetings, and sidewalk gatherings, and traditional sites like barbershops, fraternal lodges, and ice cream parlors.

Shahn was more equivocal about the degree to which modernity had infiltrated Ohio's towns. A good number of his photographs emphasize the automobile's ubiquity and trace transformations in the rhythm and even the structure of community life that increased mobility was abetting, changes unacknowledged by the script. But they give only limited attention to other features of modernity, with a surprisingly small number indicating that either mass communications and popular culture or the most coveted consumer goods other than cars featured significantly in residents' daily experience, which other contemporary sources indicate they in fact did. He was apparently reluctant to include too many instances of modernity's incursions because they threatened to compromise the American small town's reputation as a traditional *Gemeinschaft* community, although a handful of his photographs do make these developments more apparent than did the script. His survey thus puts forward an ambivalent assessment of how pervasive the impact of modernity actually was.

He left little doubt, though, that changes brought about by universal reliance on the automobile had permeated town life, from the way public space was organized to how increased mobility encouraged residents to expand their horizons, spatial and psychological, beyond the borders of the local community. Responding to the fact that so many potential customers were behind the wheel, merchants installed perpendicular signs and larger expanses of plate glass to catch drivers' attention, and these embellishments signified the degree to which motorists had supplanted pedestrians as downtown's primary users (fig. 24).[1] To accommodate the press of automobiles, streets needed to be tightly configured to maximize parking, and even dignified squares that had once served as civic ornaments were turned into parking zones (figs. 17, 19). Space was at such a premium that parking became a contentious public issue. Circleville imposed a two-hour limit downtown in 1937, but a new mayor then suspended the restriction except on Saturdays. That made merchants unhappy. They complained that drivers were leaving their cars all day, which hurt trade, and they urged police to be tolerant of customers who double-parked to pick up packages. Chastened by the merchants' disquiet, the mayor reinstituted the two-hour limit and promised a vigorous campaign against motorists who flouted it.[2]

"Cars line streets of Plain City, Ohio" is one among many photographs depicting such phalanxes wedged into parking spaces. Shooting from near the curb to take in the serrated line of cars, Shahn composed to feature as well another instance of a nearly empty sidewalk receding into the distance. His juxtaposition of these parallel elements implies a cause-and-effect relationship—the sidewalk is little used because pedestrians have become motorists, which has diminished opportunities for spontaneous sociability—and it makes his title ironic. Emphasizing the cars' ubiquity calls doleful attention to the sparse human presence (fig. 47).

A Circleville vista featuring a streamlined car—the epitome in the thirties of up-to-the-minute modernity—locates these changes within a broader historical perspective. Shahn aimed diagonally across a downtown intersection toward the block angling away opposite, dominated by a hulking three-story edifice adjoining several lower, less demonstrative structures. His camera position foregrounds an everyday occurrence in the intersection that unifies the picture's several elements. The streamlined car is stopped to allow pedestrians to cross, and the close-in, truncated view of it highlights the sleek modernity of its chromium teardrop

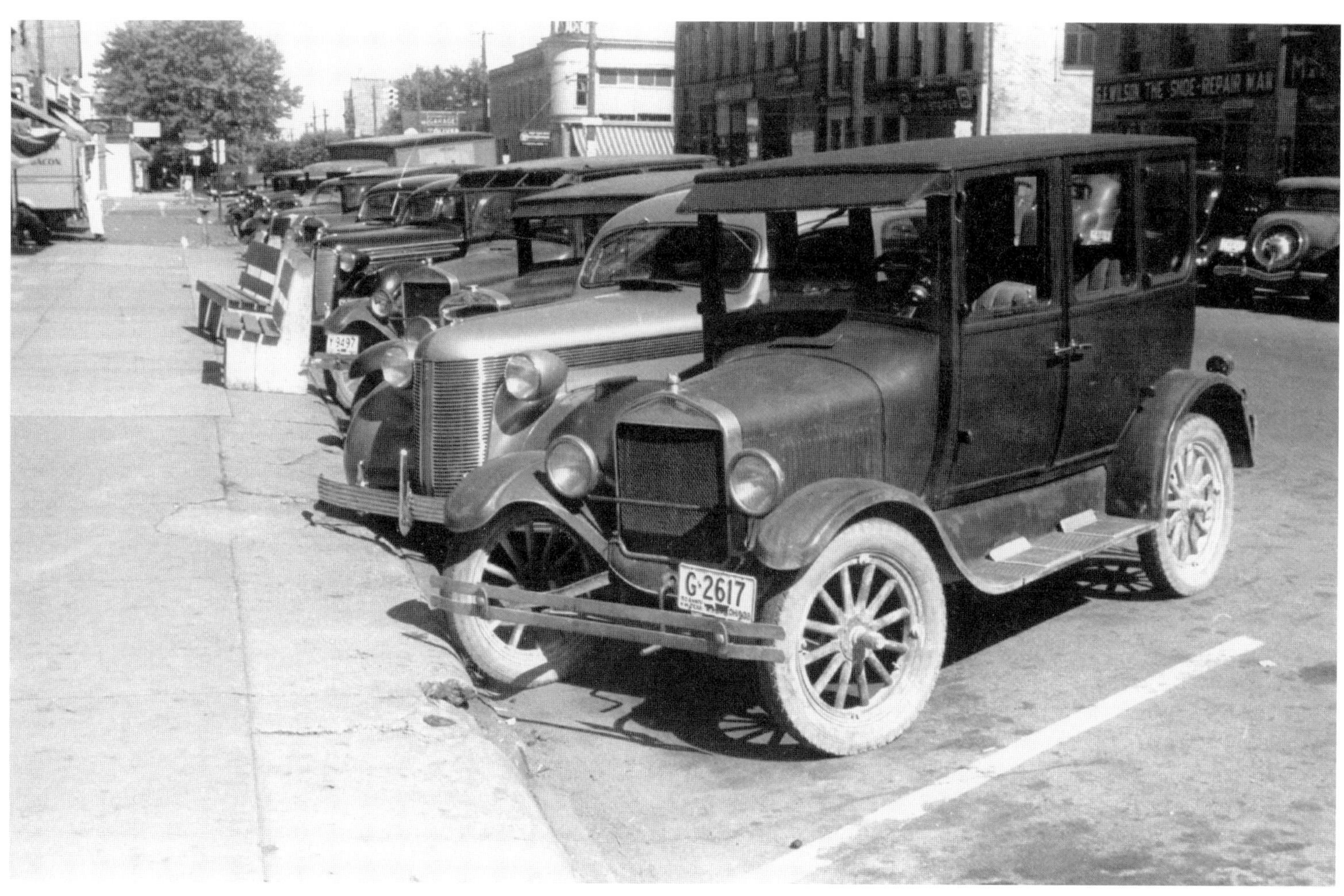

FIG 47 Cars line streets of Plain City, Ohio

headlamp and detailing, aerodynamic design, and dynamic hood ornament. Cater-corner is an enclosed delivery wagon, the only horse-drawn vehicle in all of Shahn's downtown pictures save the special case of Amish buggies in Plain City. In a "general caption" characterizing Circleville, he maintained that "because of its non-industrial surroundings, [the town] retains much of old-time flavor," and the anachronistic wagon is as unmistakable an emblem of that as the stylish automobile is of modernity.

The contrast of streamlined car and boxy wagon is the busy vista's most insistent subject and suggests Shahn's perception of a sea change transforming Ohio's towns. The radical foregrounding of the car brings into bolder relief the files of parked vehicles lining the street, as the ancient wagon does the ponderous nineteenth-century buildings behind it as remnants of the horse-and-buggy era. The human figures also contribute to the contrast of past and present, the contemporary stylishness of the man and woman briskly crossing in front of the sleek car wholly dissimilar to the old-fashioned rustic garb of two idlers passing time on the opposite corner (fig. 48).

Simmering beneath Circleville's stolid ways is a conflict between tradition and modernity, the more autonomous insularity of its past versus the centrifugal forces of contemporary culture that have their origins outside of the local community and are reshaping it. The universally embraced automobile is the most apparent sign of these developments. It is a Trojan horse that would be among the causes for the small town's decline, diluting its atmosphere of sociable self-sufficiency and supplying a ready means for residents to escape it for the alluring attractions of formerly less accessible urban centers.

Such an abstract cultural process was impossible to represent visually, but Shahn discovered an objective correlative for it in two murals adorning gasoline stations serving motorists in Plain City and Marysville. Nominally welcoming tourists passing through, the Plain City mural depicts a rustic log house beside a turbulent western river fed by a stream rushing down from the background mountains; and parallel with a two-story advertisement for "Hi Speed Gas," the Marysville mural features a fast mountain stream arched by towering trees with a fisherman casting his line into it. While the incongruity of these untamed landscapes with the nearby Ohio countryside made for an irony that Shahn could not have failed to notice, satire was not part of his agenda. He believed "it was a curse to make [invidious] distinctions" between fine art and more humble forms of visual expression, and one reason for photograph-

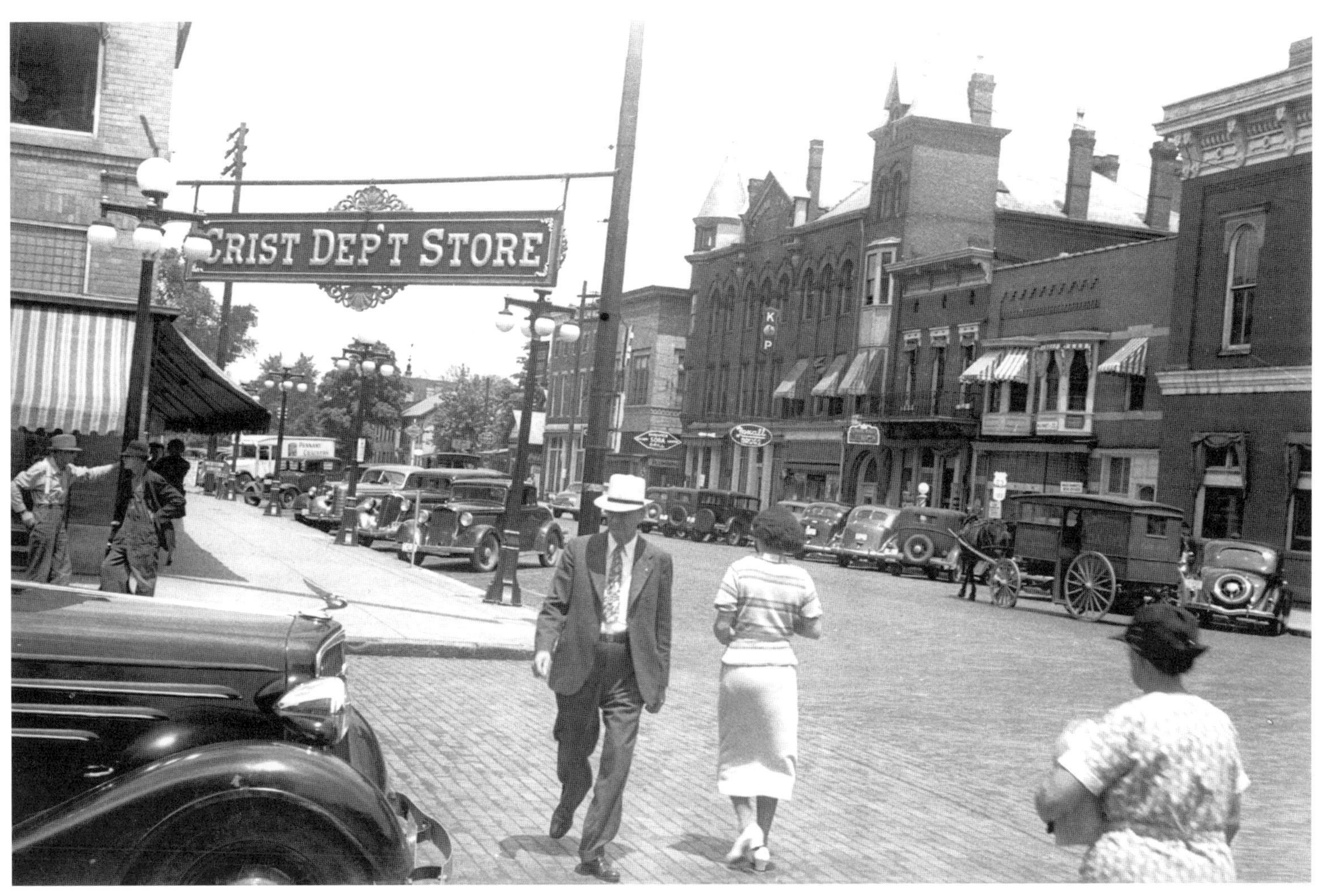

FIG 48 Main and Court Streets, Circleville, Ohio

ing the paintings was to document the visual piquancy they contributed to the townscape.[3] But he was careful to compose so that their unlikely venues were also evident, and he titled both pictures "Filling station" or "Gasoline station" without mention of the murals, suggesting that their location was as significant to him as the art (figs. 49–50).

The murals had been installed to dramatize the expanded opportunities for recreational motoring that modern highways made possible. Their purpose was not so much to encourage tourists to gas up there, or to inspire Ohioans to head for far-off mountains, as to promote gasoline sales in general by reminding locals of the widened horizons that increased mobility offered them. Car ownership meant their experience no longer needed to center so exclusively in the local community, and if mountain travel was unlikely for most, driving to less distant attractions, urban or recreational, had become convenient and inviting.[4] Motorists, of course, were not unaware of the greater freedom their automobiles provided, and the murals were intended to intensify that feeling. The design of the Marysville station also alluded to it. Shahn shot from a great enough distance to highlight the Hi Speed station's Southwestern architecture, so exotically unlike the usual building styles of central Ohio, and another reminder of widened horizons.

Automobiles were the most conspicuous symbol of a nationwide consumer culture that, having taken off in the 1920s, had striven to transform previously nonessential, discretionary goods into basic needs and introduced a plethora of new products, some technological, promising to enhance their purchasers' well-being. Just the year before Shahn photographed in Ohio, Robert S. and Helen Merrell Lynd had updated *Middletown,* their 1929 study of another Midwestern community, Muncie, Indiana, to determine how the Depression had affected it. In *Middletown in Transition* they characterized residents as "hypnotized by the gorged stream of new things to buy—automobiles, electrical equipment for the home, radios, automatic refrigerators, and all the automatic ways to live," and the town's atmosphere as one "in which private business tempts the population in its every waking minute with adroitly phrased invitations to apply the solvent remedy of more and newer possessions and socially distinguishing goods and comforts to all that flesh is heir to."[5] The Depression had reduced many people's ability to purchase such desirable commodities, but not their desire to do so, which continued to be stoked by aggressive print and radio advertising campaigns coordinated with local retailers' promotional efforts.

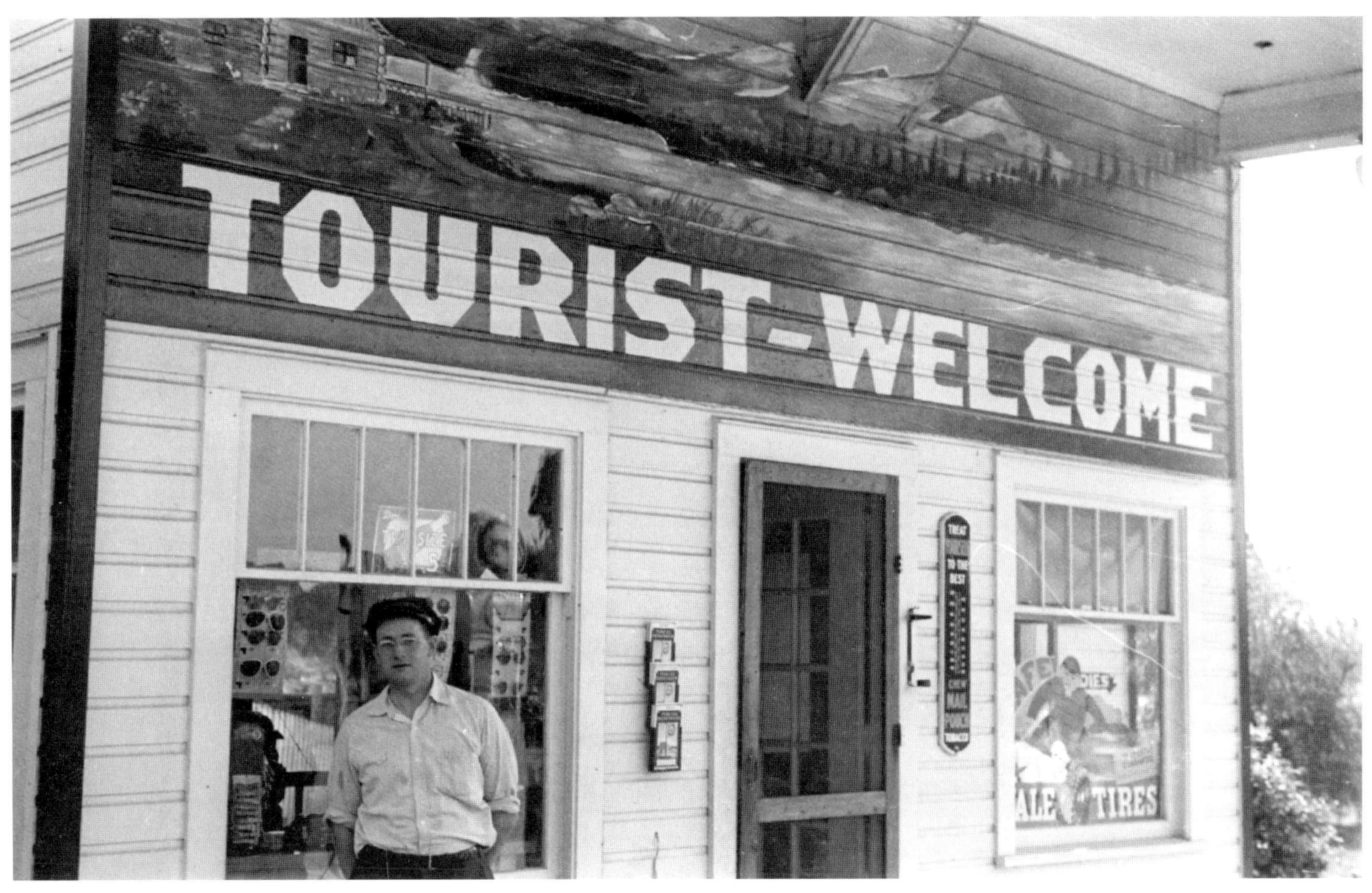

FIG 49 Filling station, Plain City, Ohio

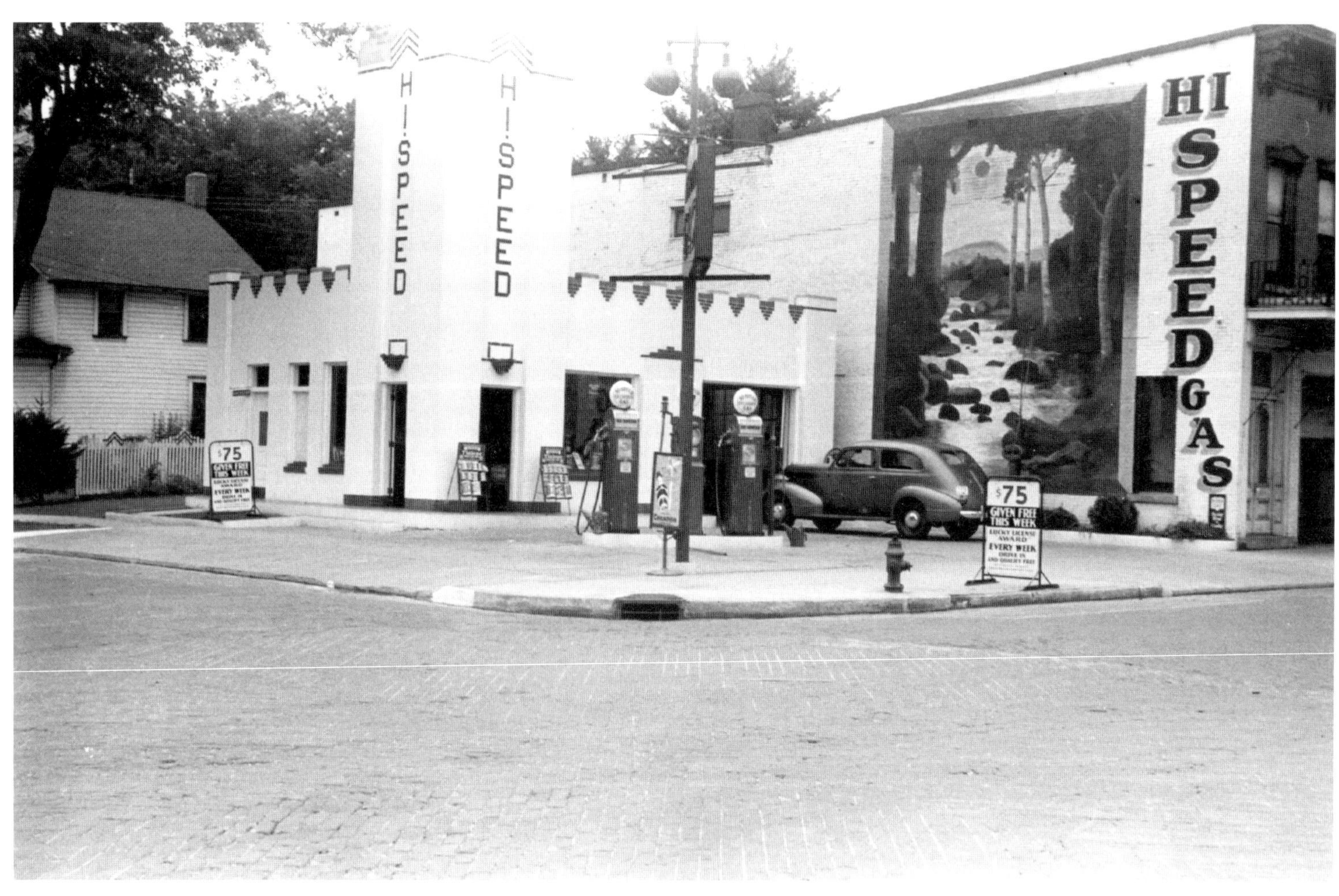

FIG 50 Gasoline station, Marysville, Ohio

Shahn neglected most sites where manifestations of that hypnosis would be especially palpable. While his survey included three used-car lots, he excluded new-car dealers' more upscale showrooms even though the county seats all had three or more such enterprises. He made fifteen photographs of the goods offered by secondhand concerns (fig. 51), but none depicting the more desirable wares in the windows of department stores. In a shot that did include a men's store displaying stylish haberdashery, he composed asymmetrically to give prominence to two individuals in workingmen's garb, subordinating consumer culture to a secondary role in a study of class distinctions (fig. 52). More typical of his storefronts was a modest concern purveying cheap work shoes and humble everyday apparel; its goods and their haphazard display were more redolent of the nineteenth than the twentieth century (fig. 53).

Electrical home appliances—especially refrigerators, ranges, washing machines, and radios—ranked among the most advertised and coveted consumer goods in the thirties. A sign of the preeminence they had attained in consumers' aspirations was that a few weeks before Shahn's visit, London's newspaper published a "Home Appliance Edition" dedicated to offering "suggestions for home improvement and home comfort" inspired by the "many, many new home appliances" available; the special edition assured readers that, thanks to the economies of mass production, these modern marvels were now "within easy reach of a majority of our homes." Complementing the fulsome editorial commentary, display advertisements by eight local firms (and an ice dealer, touting the superiority of iceboxes that never needed repair) urged Londoners to visit their showrooms to inspect these technological wonders.[6] That a community of fewer than 5,000 had so many appliance dealers suggests the extraordinary popular preoccupation with these goods and the degree to which modernity pervaded Ohio's small towns.

Home appliances do appear in a handful of Shahn's photographs—if less often than might be expected given the number of firms offering them—although some of these devices are merely peripheral in compositions centering on something else, as in his picture of a man lounging near the Somerset firehouse (fig. 54). But even though a washing machine is more conspicuous in his study of a hardware store, his shooting strategy militated against viewers' identification of it as a symbol of the diffusion of modernity. Centered in the store's entrance, a white-haired man with an old-fashioned beard addresses the camera; presumably he is its proprietor, W. J. Guy, his prominence heightened by the doorway framing his body and the tonal contrast of

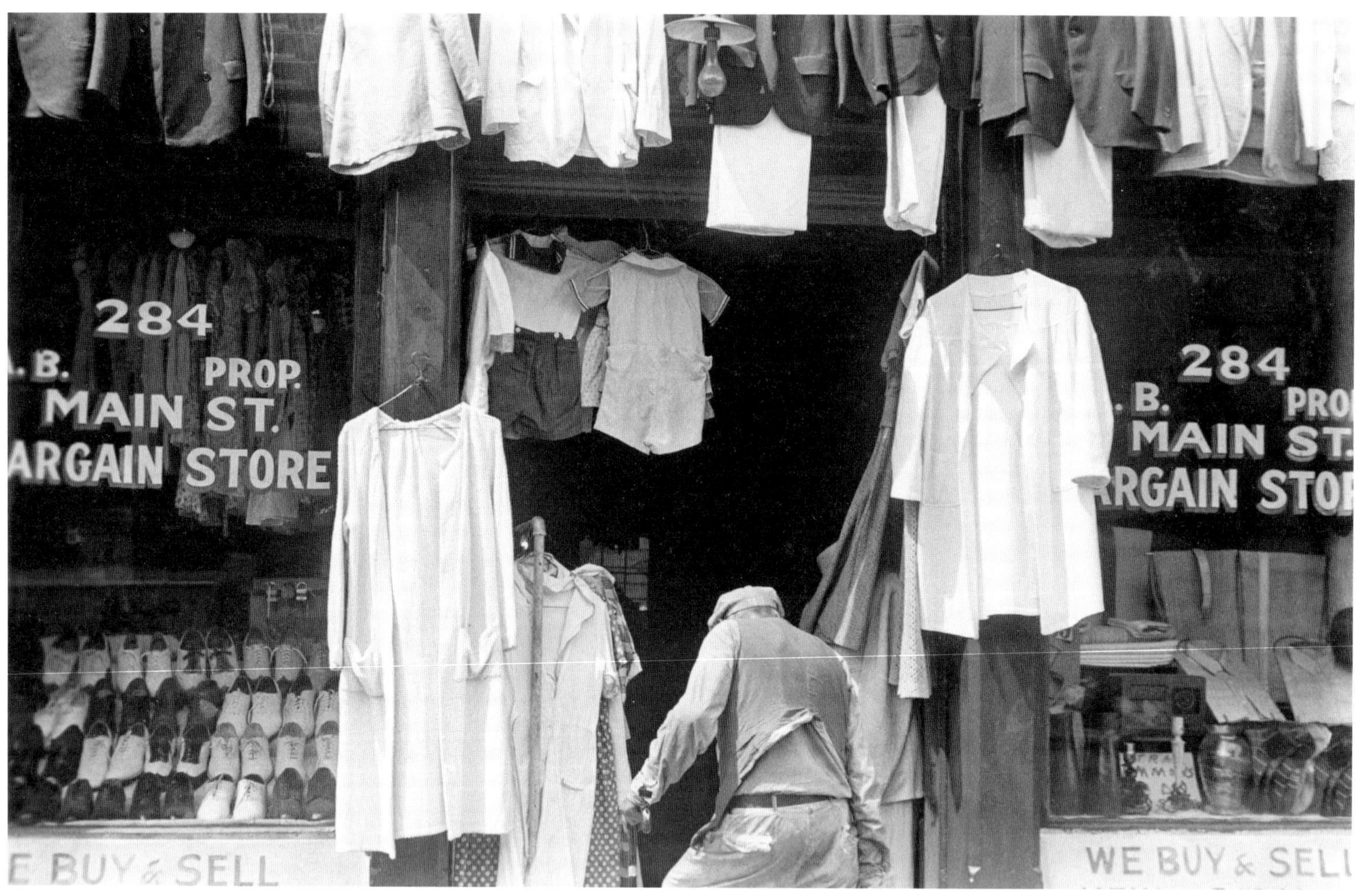

FIG 51 Secondhand clothing store, Columbus, Ohio

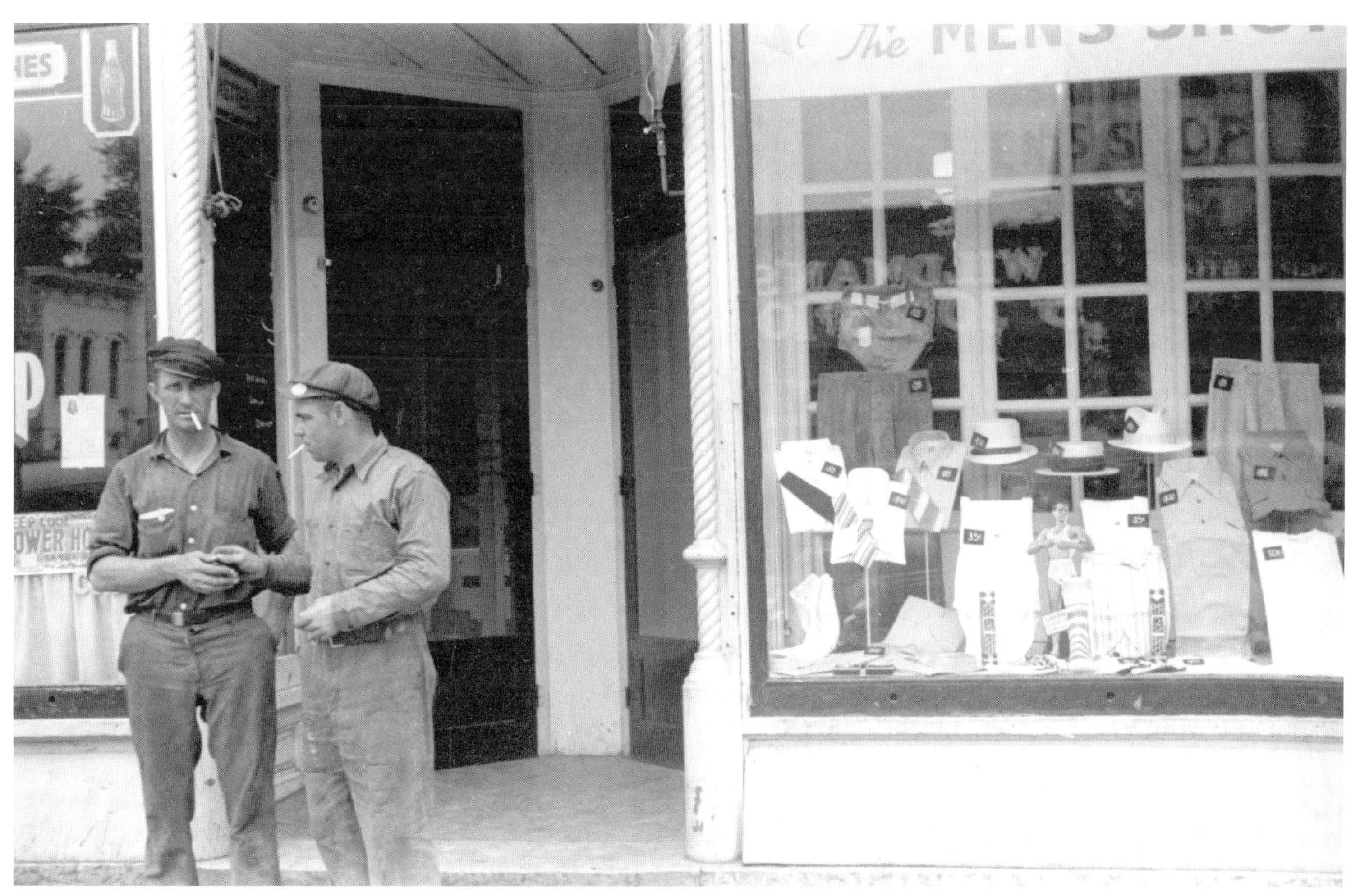

FIG 52 Street scene, Washington Court House, Ohio

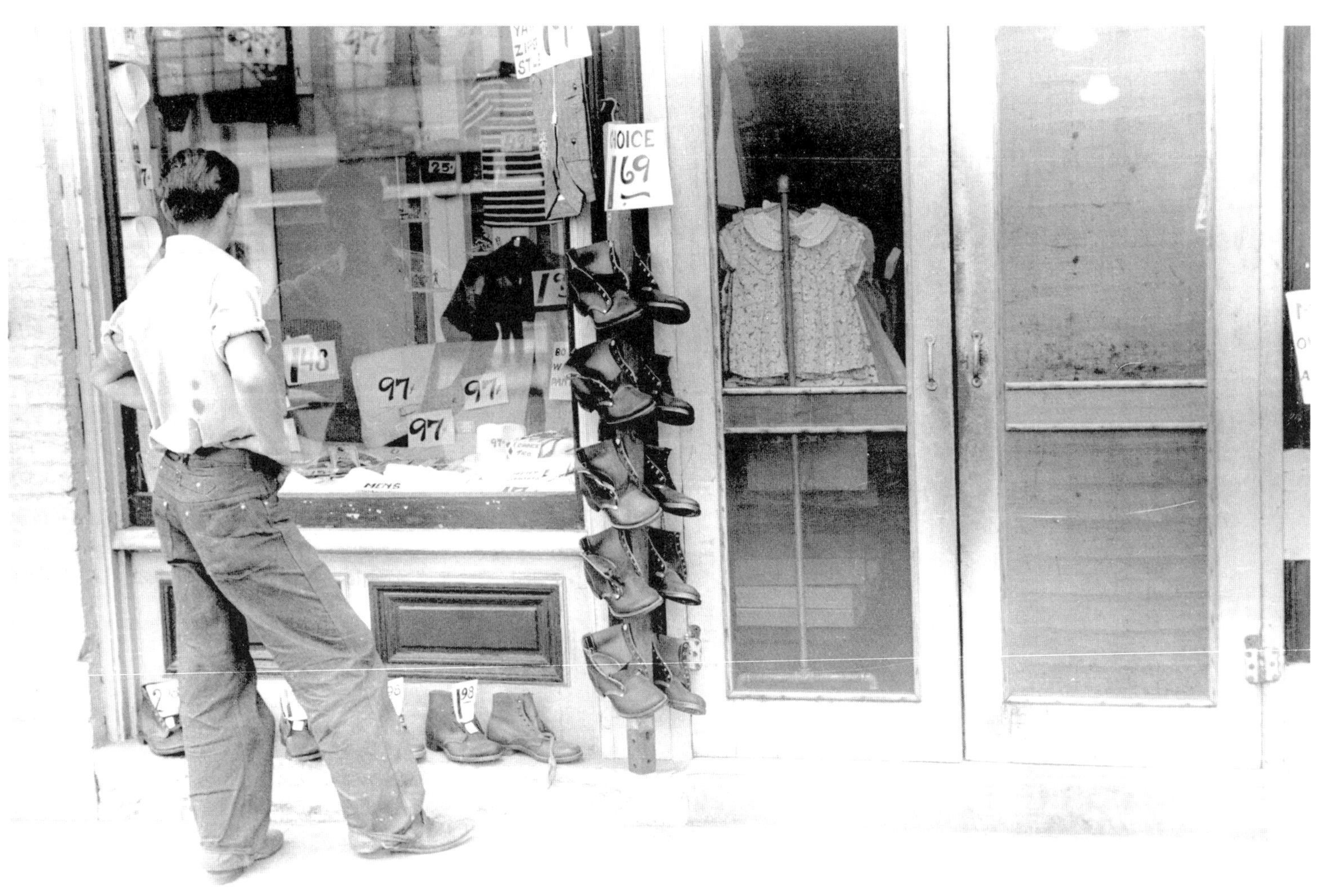

FIG 53 Street scene, Washington Court House, Ohio

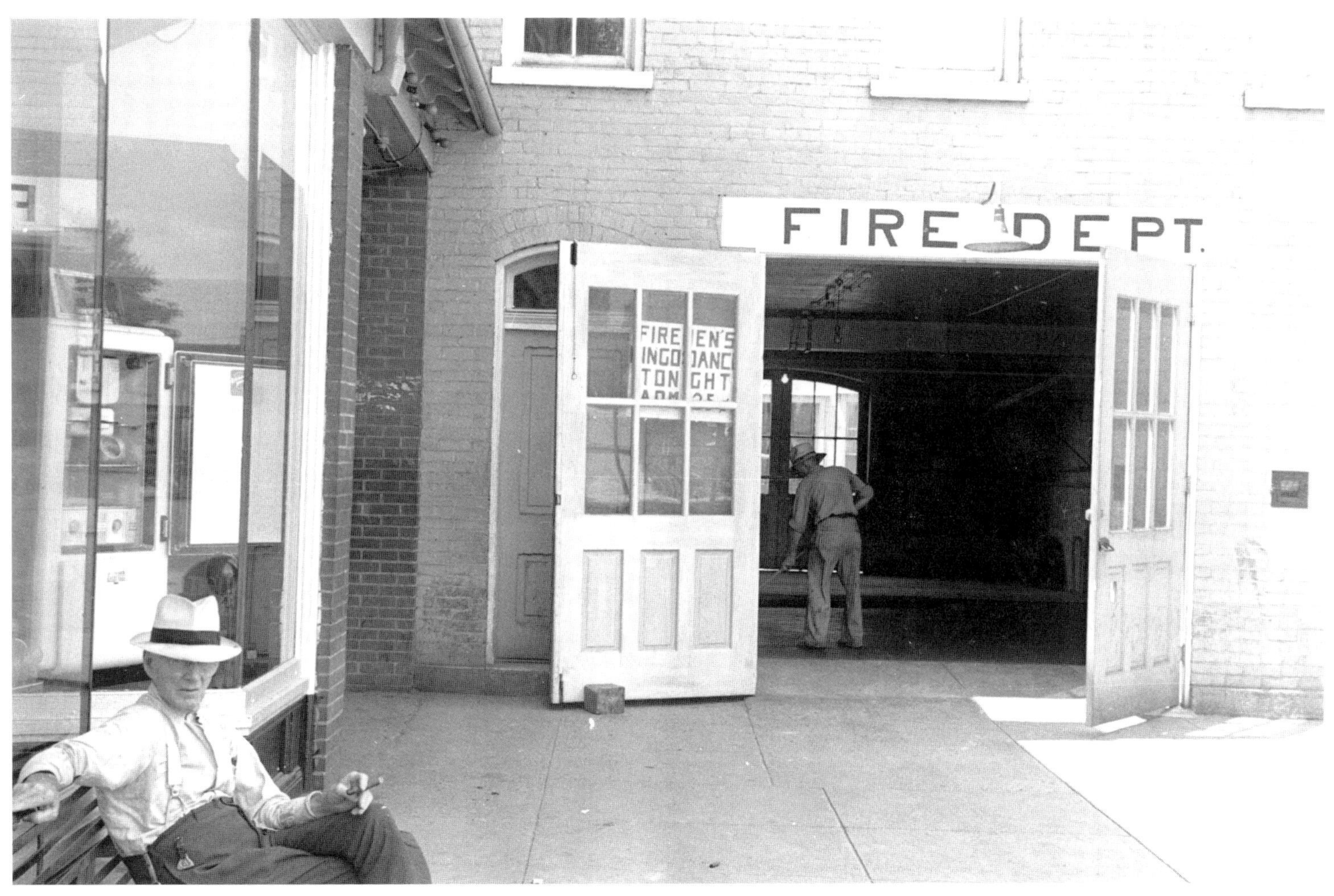

FIG 54 Fire department, Somerset, Ohio

his white hair and light clothing against the store's dark interior. Next to him are a horse collar and harness dangling from the door jambs, and that juxtaposition proposes a correspondence between them, the aged Mr. Guy and the tack both quaint remnants of a bygone era. Because the formal organization of the composition so directs attention to Mr. Guy, the implications of the contrast of traditional and new technologies—the antiquated equine apparatus versus the modern washing machine—are muffled, as a viewer realizes by imagining what different valences the photograph would have if Shahn had shot it without the proprietor, as he easily might have done. Reading the photograph in that way is not to suggest its inadequacy—it is among his most visually compelling—but rather to understand his priorities, which did not include emphasizing the pervasiveness of consumer culture (fig. 55).

But if the hardware store photograph downplayed modernity's allurements, another of a firm specializing in home appliances and farm equipment acknowledges more schematically that Ohio's towns were not immune to them. Locating himself close in, Shahn aimed at a column separating the store's street window from another leading to its recessed entrance; to the column's left are a draped harness and a Goodyear advertisement, and to its right, in the salesroom behind a decal advertising RCA radio equipment, is an appliance, probably a range, but in any case "white goods." Like the hardware store picture, it contrasts symbols of traditional and modern ways of life, but more insistently calls attention to the cultural dispositions they represent, owing in part to its vertical format, which narrows attention to these symbolic objects. His careful juxtaposition of them indicates his perception that small towns had entered a phase in which cultural developments originating elsewhere were exercising an increasingly greater influence in their daily life. The Goodyear and RCA advertisements signify it as well, these corporate entities and their aggressively promoted products universally recognized as integral to consumer culture (fig. 56).

But his disinclination to lay particular stress on the penetration of consumer culture is suggested by a second picture of the firm, taken from a greater distance to feature an old-fashioned reaper and farm wagon displayed on its sidewalk. Although the home appliance is no longer visible, the harness and Goodyear sign are, and so is a small placard advertising Maytag appliances. Had he composed the closer-in shot to include it with the showroom display, the hegemony that consumer culture was assuming would have become more evident (fig. 57).

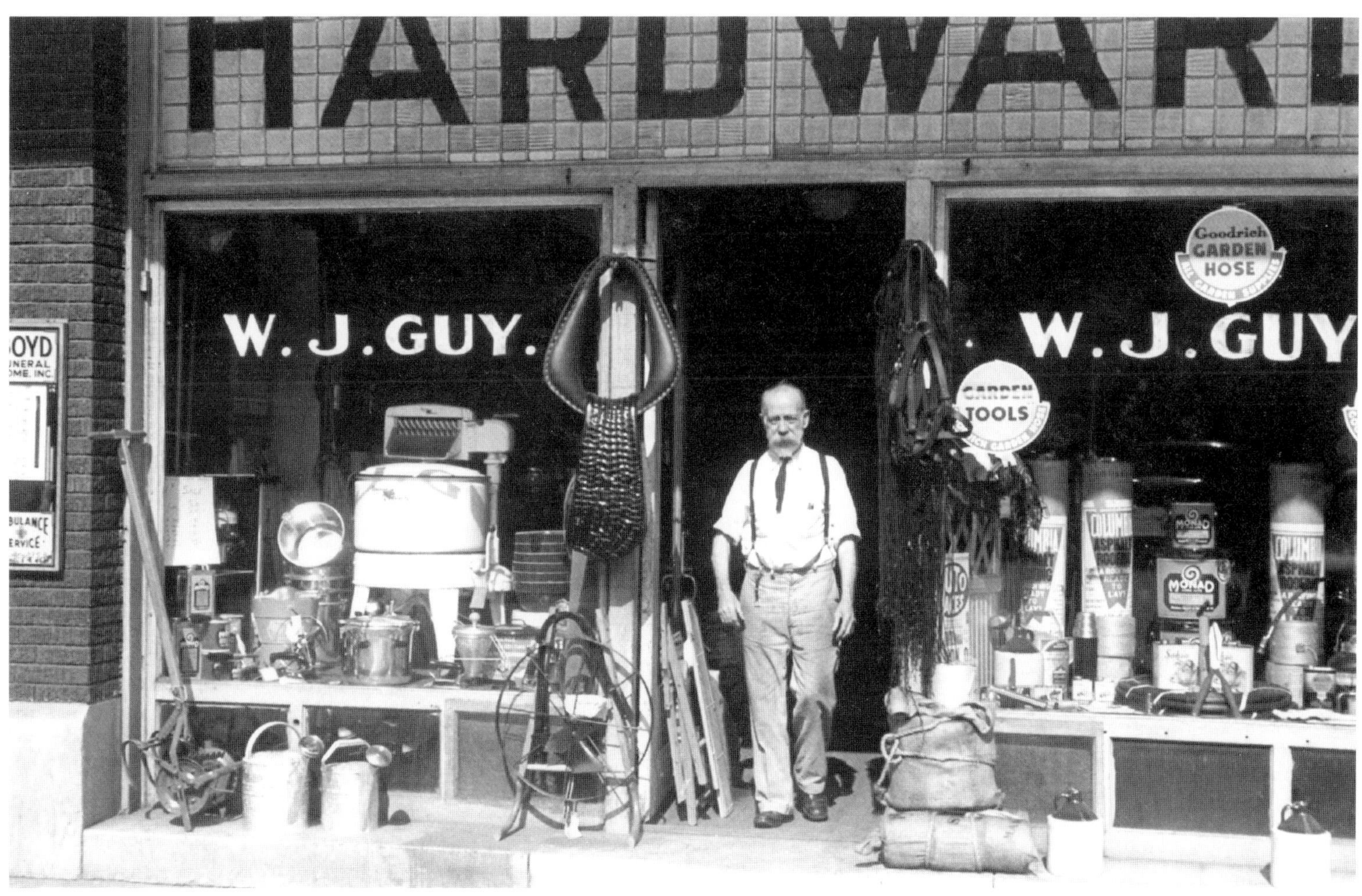

FIG 55 Hardware store, Marion, Ohio

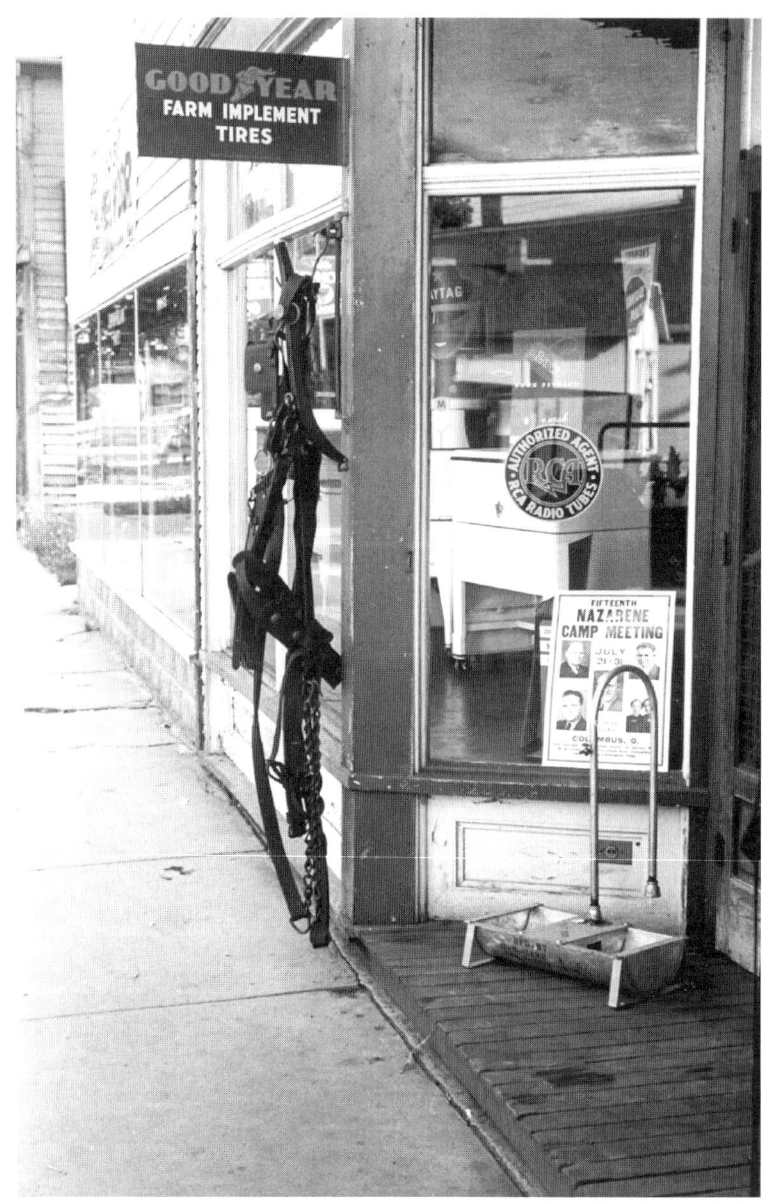

FIG 56 Store in Canal Winchester, Ohio

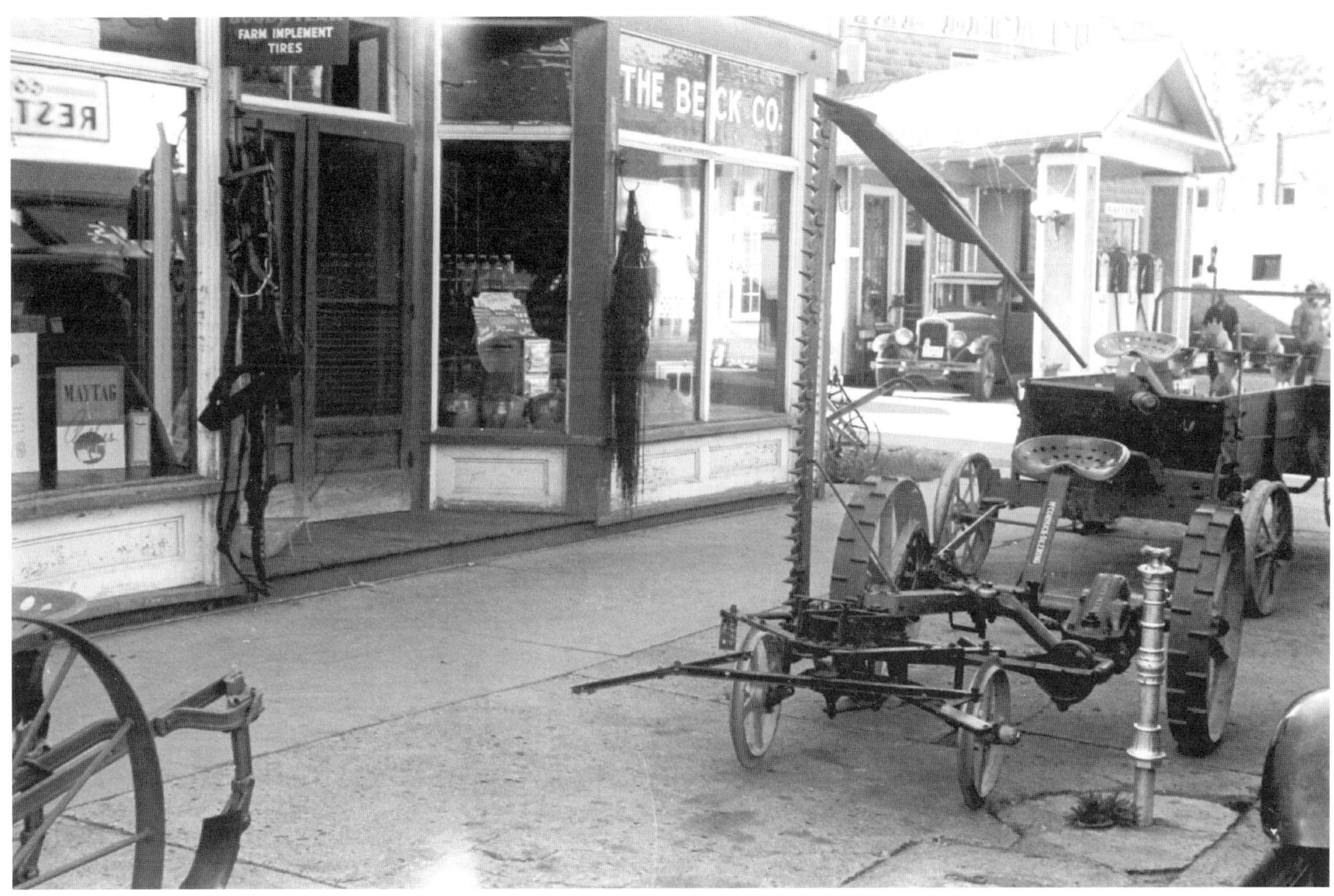

FIG 57 Farm implements outside store, Canal Winchester, Ohio

Many of the storefronts Shahn photographed were of businesses purveying basic commodities or personal services—hardware, shoe repair, garment pressing, and the like—and locally owned; a few specialized in farming needs. Less conspicuous in his coverage were the national or regional retailers that had established a substantial commercial presence in the years following World War I, such as variety, grocery, and drug chains and the general merchandise giants Sears, Roebuck and J. C. Penney. Only a single photograph includes an identifiable chain variety store—the G. C. Murphy outlet in Circleville (fig. 25)—although the firm traded in five of his eight county seats, and W. T. Grant, S. S. Kresge, or F. W. Woolworth five-and-dime stores were also represented in most towns. None of his pictures from Lancaster and Newark included their J. C. Penney or Sears, Roebuck outlets, and he photographed just one Rexall drugstore. Grocery chains were only slightly less obscure in his coverage, A&P markets in two towns and a Kroger store in another.[7]

Local merchants resented and felt threatened by the chains, which violated "a cherished small-town tradition that business by right belonged to locally owned and locally managed stores," and they attempted without much success to persuade townspeople that such stores controlled by outsiders were a menace to the community.[8] These organizations could undersell local firms owing to the discounts they demanded from suppliers for buying in quantity as well as their more efficiently organized purchasing and distribution systems, and their advertising budgets and promotional expertise far surpassed those of independent businesses. The chains rationalized retailing practices, and in that sense they represented a development parallel to and congenial with the mass production techniques utilized by manufacturers to supply a burgeoning consumer culture. The visible signs of these developments were the uniform appearance of the chain stores, the standardized line of goods they offered, and the prominence of their corporate trademarks, on storefronts as in advertising campaigns.

The uniformity they strove for was likely one reason why chain stores appear so infrequently in Shahn's photographs despite their presence on town streets. One outlet could represent all its siblings, while the varied fronts of independently owned firms offered a richer array of visual perceptions. But the standardized signage with which the chains promoted themselves deterred him even more. His eye was drawn instead to the unique signs painted by anonymous craftsmen identifying local firms—as a young man, he had himself been a Coney Island sign painter—and his photographs highlight numerous examples of that species of vernacular art. Even twenty-five years after he worked in Ohio, he remembered how ardently he had responded to the idiosyncratic signage he photographed there: "Here was a folk art of great quality. . . . In those days the slogans were not yet supplied by printing houses. The lettering was laborious and of an impressive quality."[9]

Such signage might be as flamboyant as that covering the facade of a derelict Plain City quick lunch stand (fig. 58), or as restrained as the sash window of a blacksmith's shop advertising its sharpening services with an eclectic combination of Art Deco and trompe l'oeil shadowed Roman lettering enclosing a representation that could signify both a horse's hoof and a plow's shears (fig. 59). His composition portraying a nonchalant young man, his light clothing making him blend into the wall he leans against, draws stronger attention to the window of the Davis Seed Service, with its arresting combination of cursive Italic and stylized block lettering against its dark interior (fig. 60). Two photographs depict the windows of a meat market, one featuring a painted steer's head, the other a pair of piglets peeking over a fence; above the piglets, the shop's name in shadowed letters ingeniously shares oversized capitals. He titled only the close-in shot "Folk art," perhaps because the more distant view of the piglets contrasts the window's handmade artwork with the mechanically reproduced lettering of a poster and a Mail Pouch thermometer (figs. 61–62).

The rich and varied distinctiveness of these expressions of an indigenous folk art distinguished local firms from the chain stores, which relied on mass-produced signage supplied by corporate headquarters to coordinate with regional and national advertising campaigns and to reinforce the perception of their outlets' uniformity. A repetitive, standardized typeface proclaimed the orderly predictability and systematic efficiency that made the chains' operations so modern and distinguished them from local firms, whose more motley visual presentation suggested an earlier, anachronistic business model. A chain's logo also did more than identify the store: trading on consumers' familiarity with it from advertising, it reminded them that the formidable resources of a national corporation stood behind its local outpost. In Shahn's coverage of the towns' business districts, his few photographs of chain stores made them symbolic of the cultural homogenization that was integral to modernity's transformative energies.

His studies of chain stores gave special emphasis to the uniformity of their signage, and that he made many fewer pictures of them than of local firms reflected not only an esthetic preference, but also his perception that too much attention to the chains would subvert his

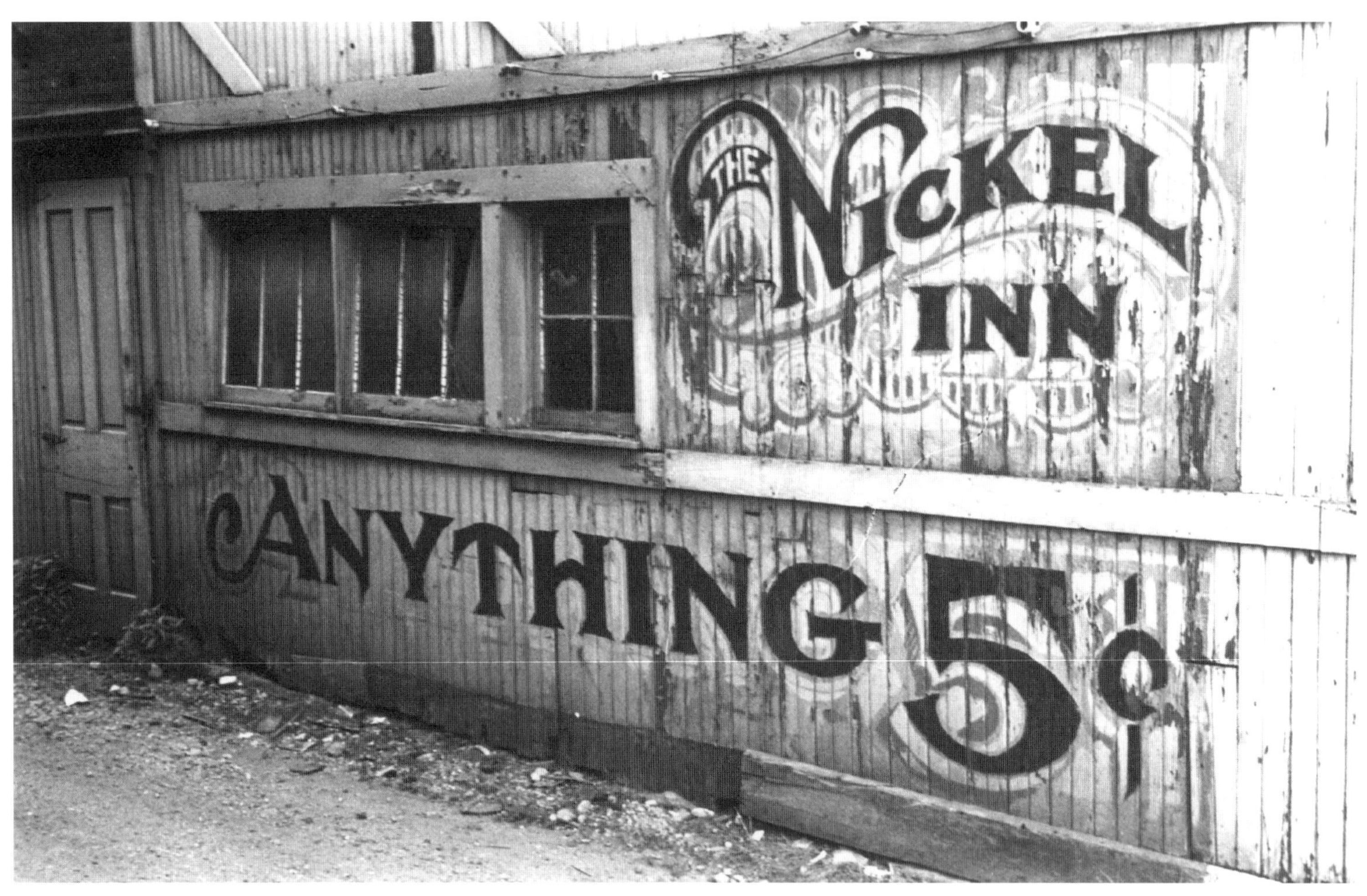

FIG 58 Quick lunch stand, Plain City, Ohio

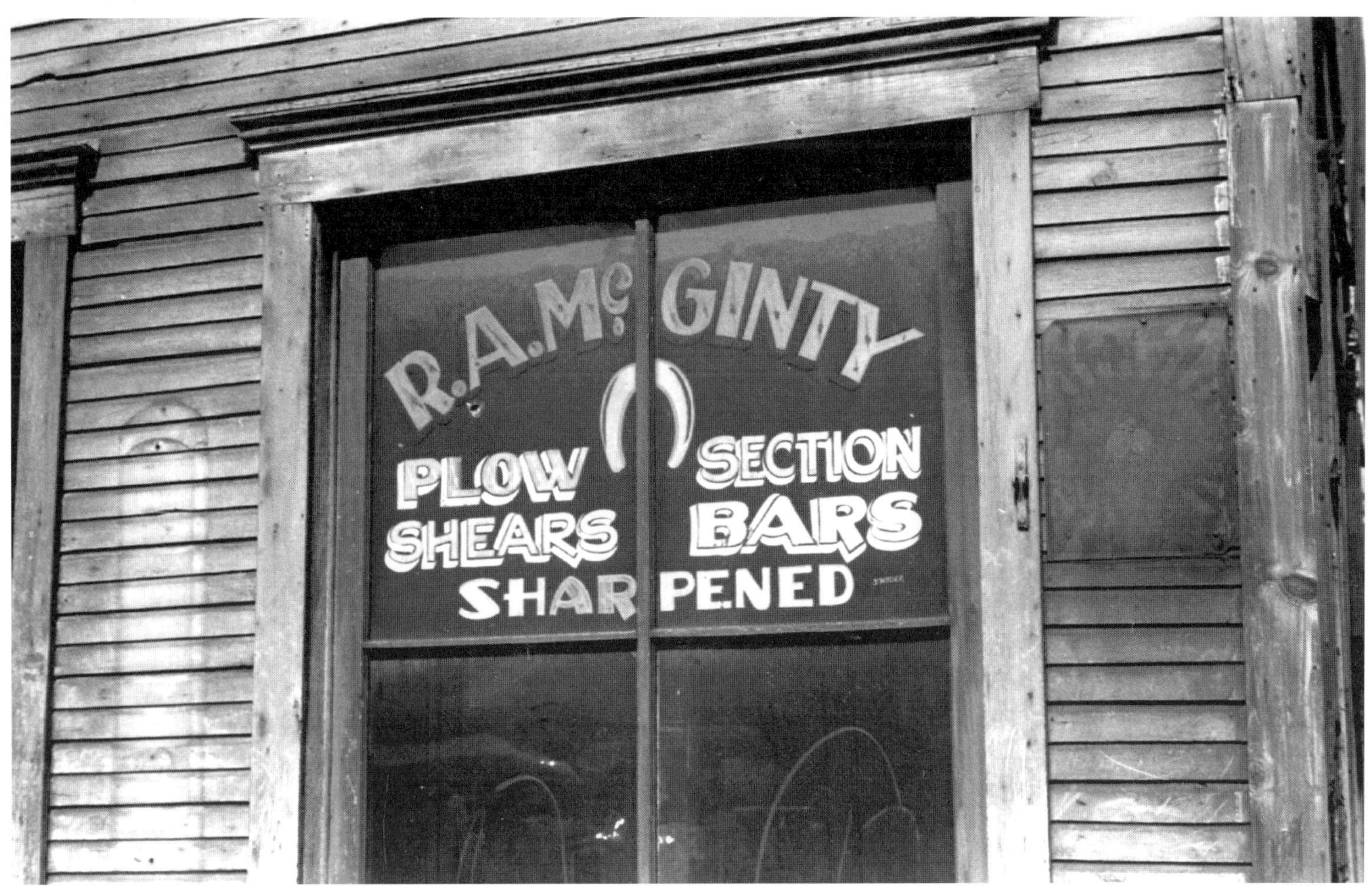

FIG 59 Sharpener's sign, Marion, Ohio

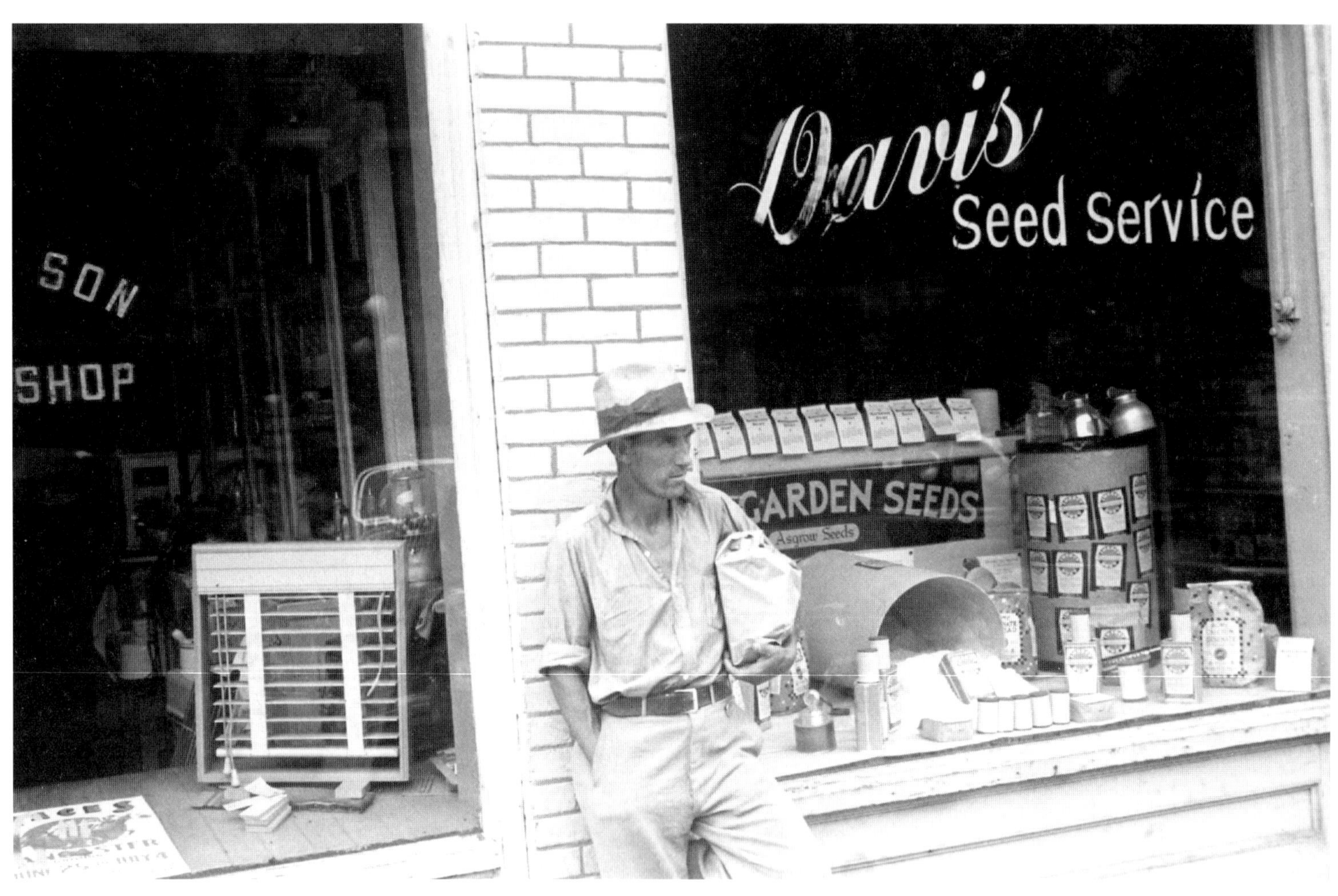

FIG 60 Street scene, Washington Court House, Ohio

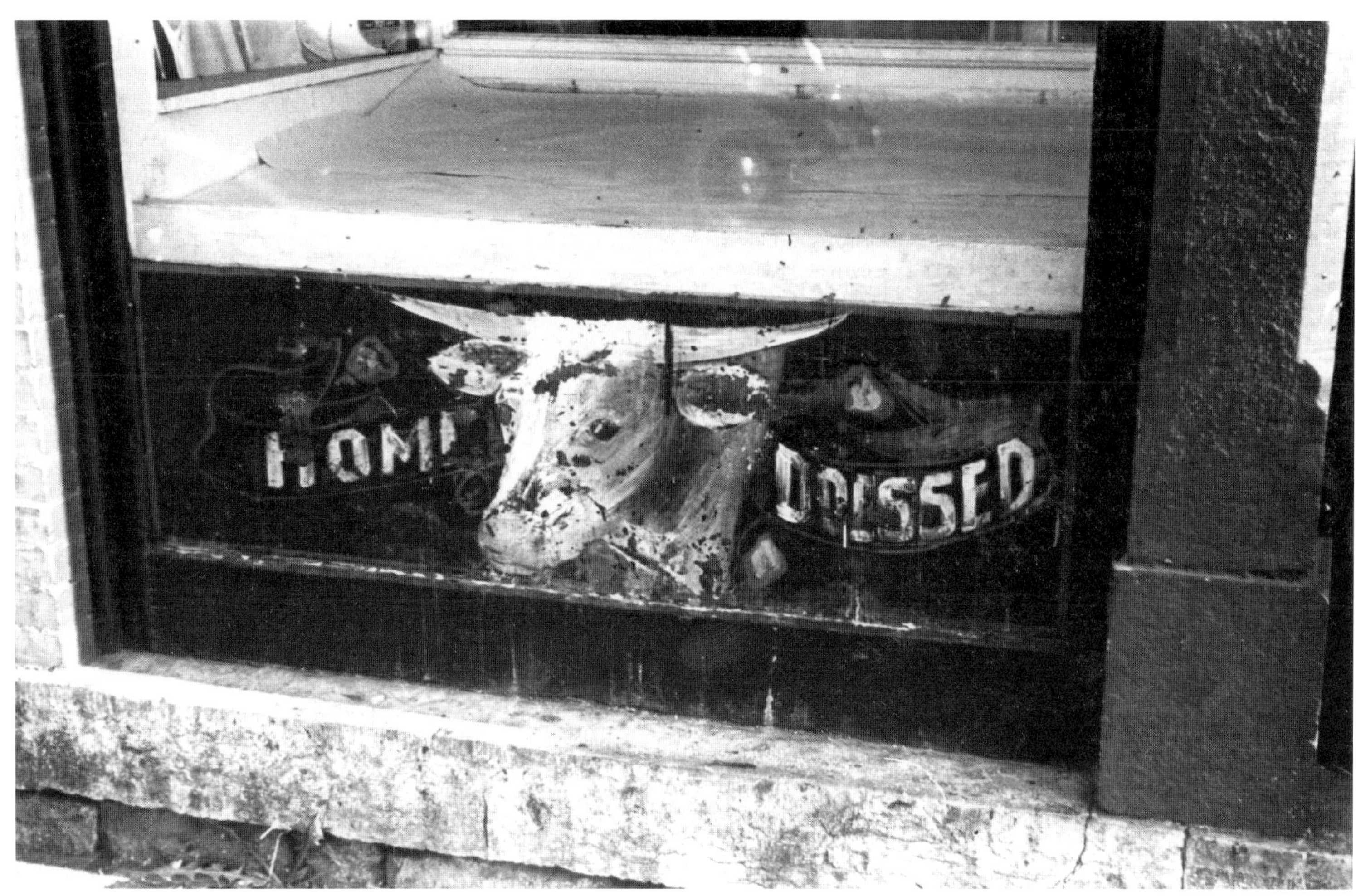

FIG 61 Folk art, Plain City, Ohio

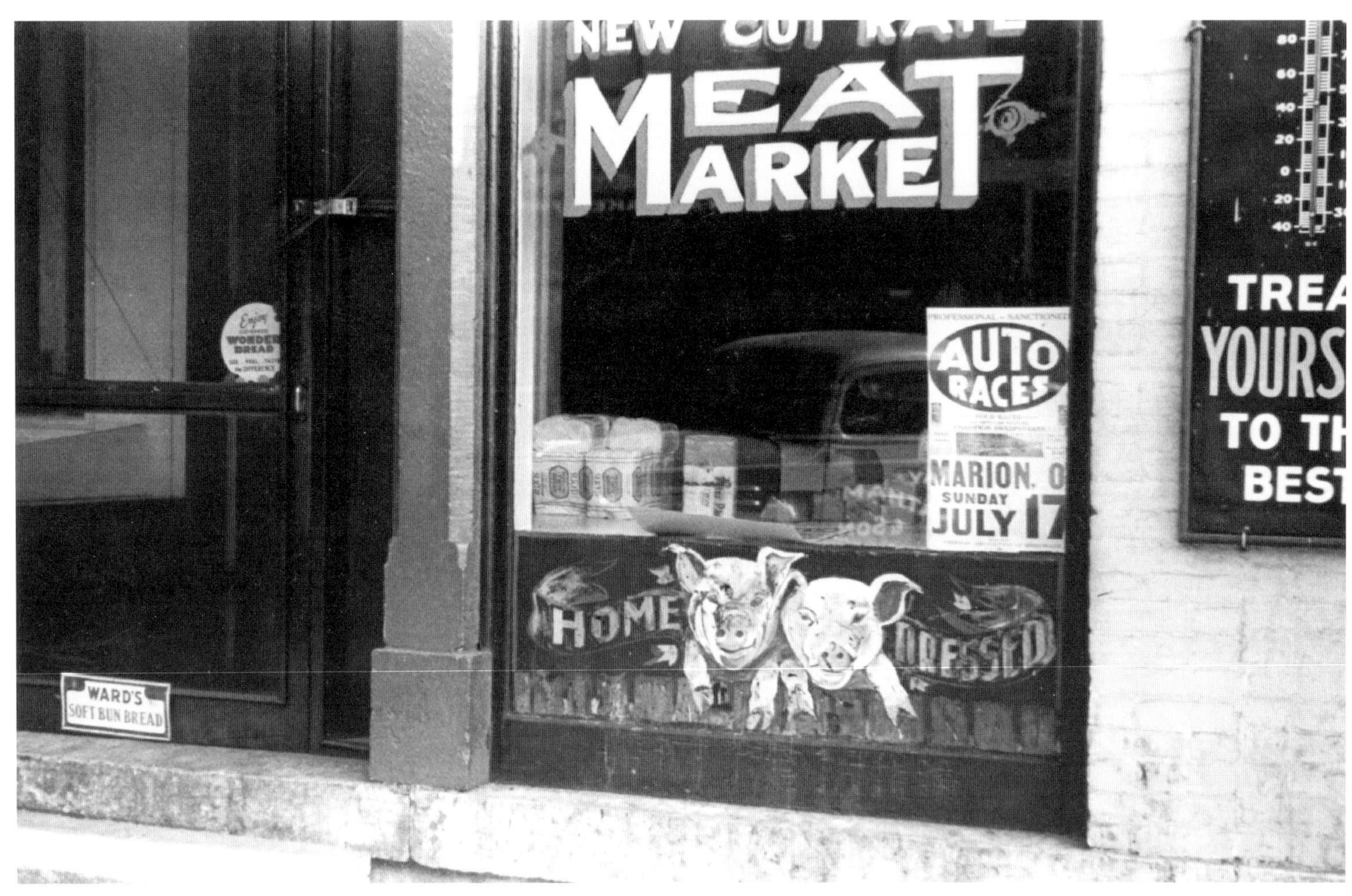

FIG 62 Meat market, Plain City, Ohio

effort to lay stress on the towns' self-contained traditionalism. His compositions indicate his awareness of that hazard: while all include a human presence, repetition of the symbolically potent standardized signage is their most assertive graphic element. The two pairs of human figures in front of an A&P outlet—a clerk speaking to a customer, and two girls absorbed in something beyond the frame—are portrayed with animated individuality, but located near opposite edges of the frame, they are visually subordinate to the store's signs, the standardization and repetitiveness of which are echoed by the methodically arranged goods displayed on the sidewalk and in its window (fig. 63). Three kibitzers outside a drugstore are also at the frame's edge, and the picture's dominant feature is the uniformity of advertisements for brand-name products that span its facade (fig. 64). Rexall drugstores were franchises rather than part of a chain, but they exploited the same business methods, including central purchasing and distribution, a standardized product line, and national advertising and promotional campaigns. Beneath the franchise's logo, some fifty advertisements covering a Rexall store's window advertise a "lowest prices in town SALE"; the forward motion of two passersby underscores the signage's monotonous uniformity (fig. 65).

In his 1975 novel *Ragtime*, E. L. Doctorow proposes that the "duplicated event" was fundamental to modernity's transformation of American culture in the early twentieth century. A duplicated event is one that may be infinitely repeated in precisely the same form and which thus permits many thousands or millions of people separated by space or time to experience it identically. Because it may be diffused so universally, it encourages the standardization of experience and fosters the coalescence of a uniform and homogeneous national culture that was unattainable before new technologies made it possible to address a mass audience and do so reiteratively. Henry Ford's rationalization of the assembly line, and the identical automobiles it produced, provided the model for the duplicated event, which manifested itself in innumerable forms. The photograph itself was a precursor, and in the twentieth century, phonograph records, the movies, radio programming, national advertising campaigns, and chain stores' merchandising strategies such as were represented by the signs in the A&P and Rexall windows all exemplified the duplicated event.[10]

As was true of Shahn's only sketchy attention to the inroads made by the chains, his Ohio coverage as a whole minimized the pervasiveness of the duplicated event, and that avoidance was most evident in how rarely he photographed its two most photogenic manifestations,

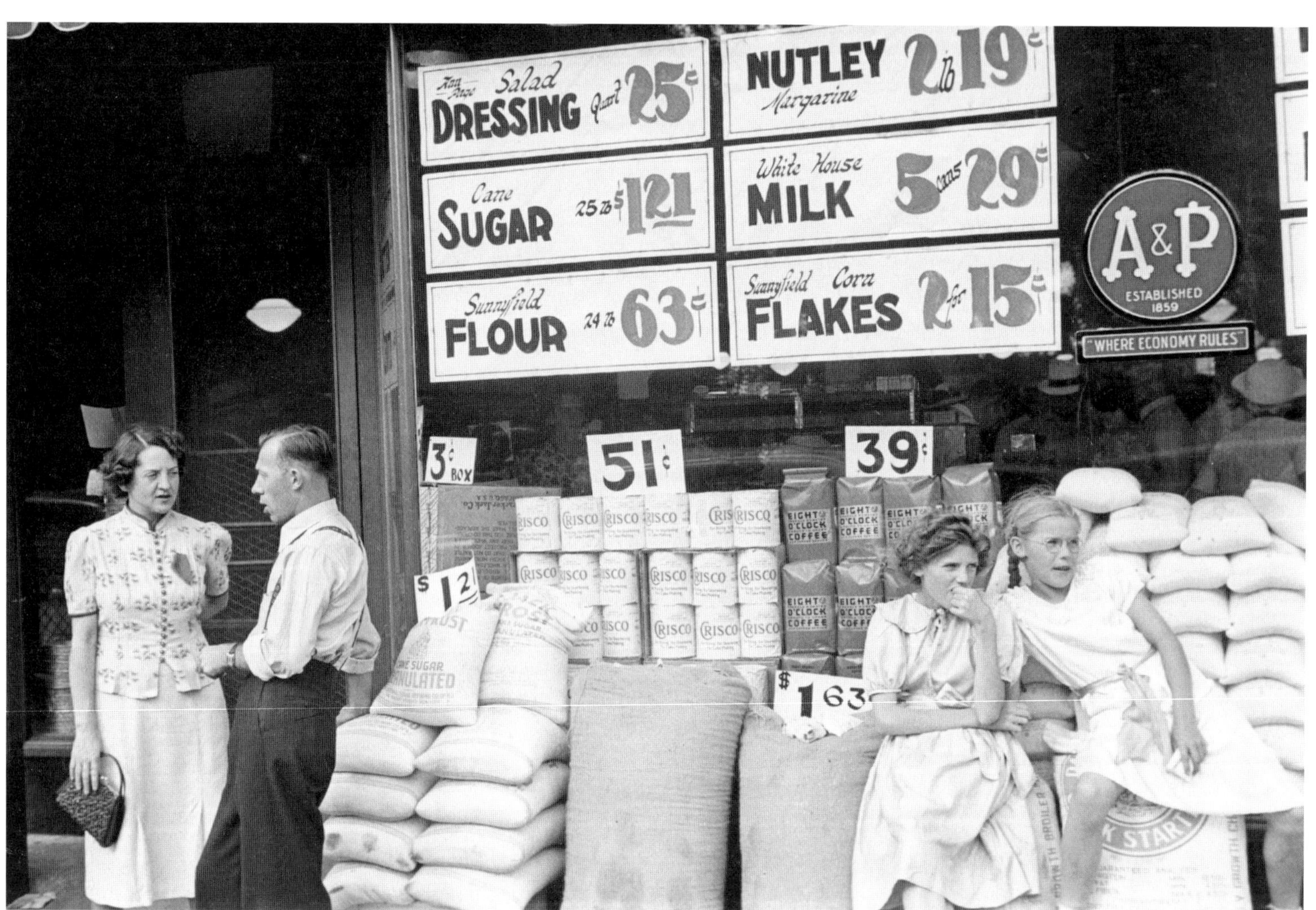

FIG 63 A&P store in Somerset, Ohio

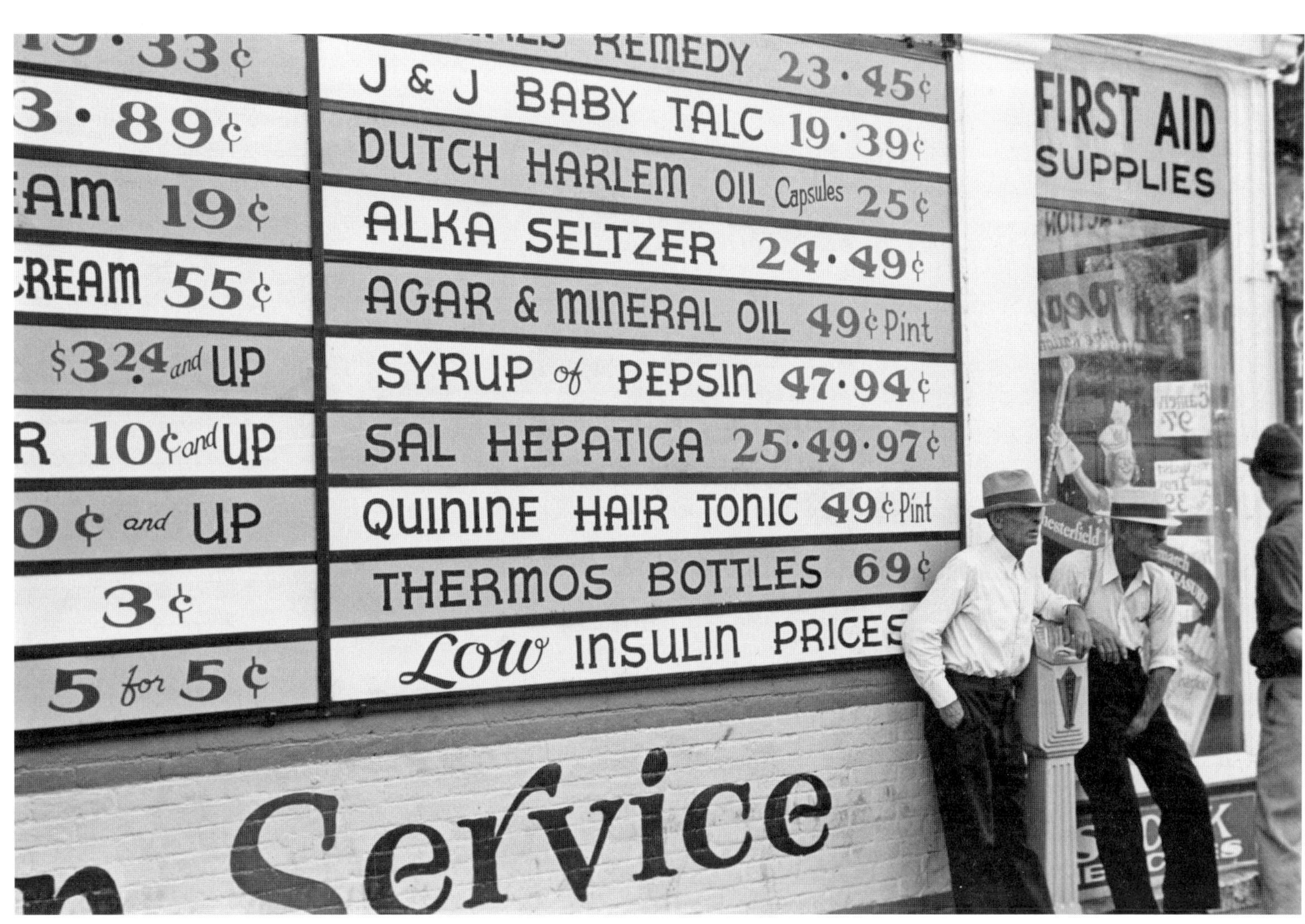

FIG 64 Sign on drugstore, Newark, Ohio

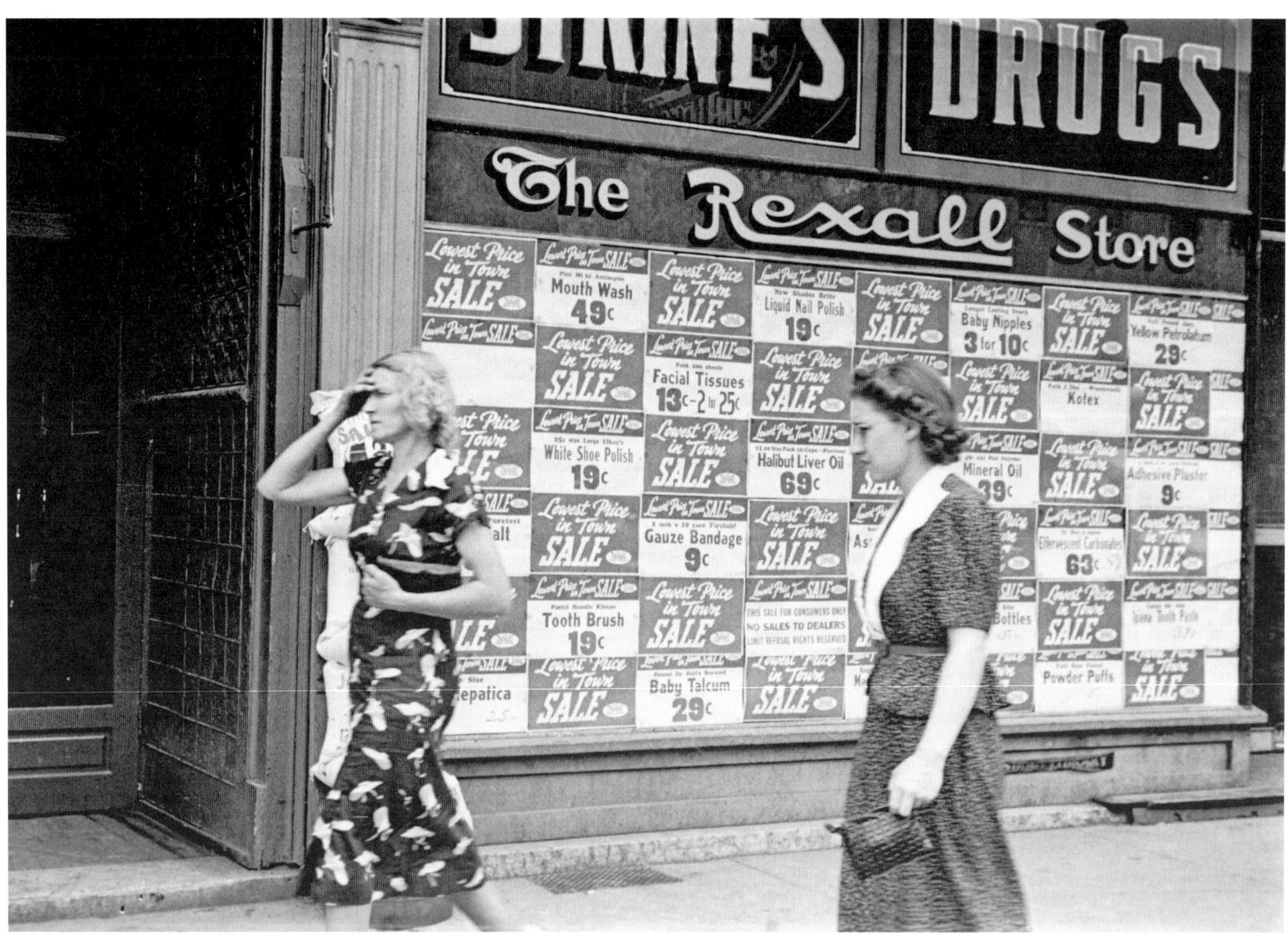

FIG 65 Drugstore window, Newark, Ohio

the newsstand and the movie theater. His FSA colleagues made close-in views of newsstands almost a staple, with Arthur Rothstein, John Vachon, and Russell Lee producing numerous such images.[11] The repetition of magazine covers within a newsstand's array of periodicals made for strong visual design, and these studies also signified that smaller and larger communities alike participated in the mass culture that was among the twentieth century's most conspicuous developments. Shahn photographed the building exteriors of the daily *Marysville Tribune* and weekly *Plain City Advocate*, in the most literal sense documenting these local channels of communication, but his only hint of Ohioans' exposure to national media is in two pictures of a Lancaster newsstand that make it secondary to the compositions' most arresting element, a near-life-sized representation of a newsboy hawking the *Columbus Citizen*. In a caption balloon he implores passersby, "Don't forget your CITIZEN," and he proffers the paper's latest edition, its banner headline reporting the adjournment of the state's legislature: "Kill Ohio Relief Plan, Go Home."

In one of these pictures, three teenage males have come abreast of the newsboy, and the nearest seems about to make a rude gesture, although probably he is only biting his fingernail. The humor in the image depends on the contrast between the teenagers' swagger and the newsboy's decorous air and ingratiating smile. Most of the newsstand's sign is visible, as is a Coca-Cola advertisement, and so are racks displaying periodicals (fig. 66). The tone of the second picture is even more ironic. Having passed by the newsboy and with their backs to him, a father and two daughters momentarily pause on the sidewalk, the girls' dresses elaborately frilly and their white shoes dressy, their father natty and also in whites. The family is self-evidently too prosperous to be affected by the legislative neglect of relief announced in the headline. The newsboy's injunction not to "forget your CITIZEN" thus becomes political. In composing this shot, Shahn moved closer to the newsboy and shifted his camera angle slightly to include less of the sidewalk, reducing the sense that the site is a newsstand: the periodical racks and Coca-Cola sign are eliminated, and the newsstand's sign is less prominent. It is a witty photograph, formally adept and rich in implication, but it indicates little about the presence of mass culture in these Ohio towns (fig. 67).[12]

Movies were the era's duplicated event par excellence, their purveyors having organized an efficient, smoothly integrated system of industrial production, distribution, and exhibition that made possible the screening of new releases nearly simultaneously in most towns and cities

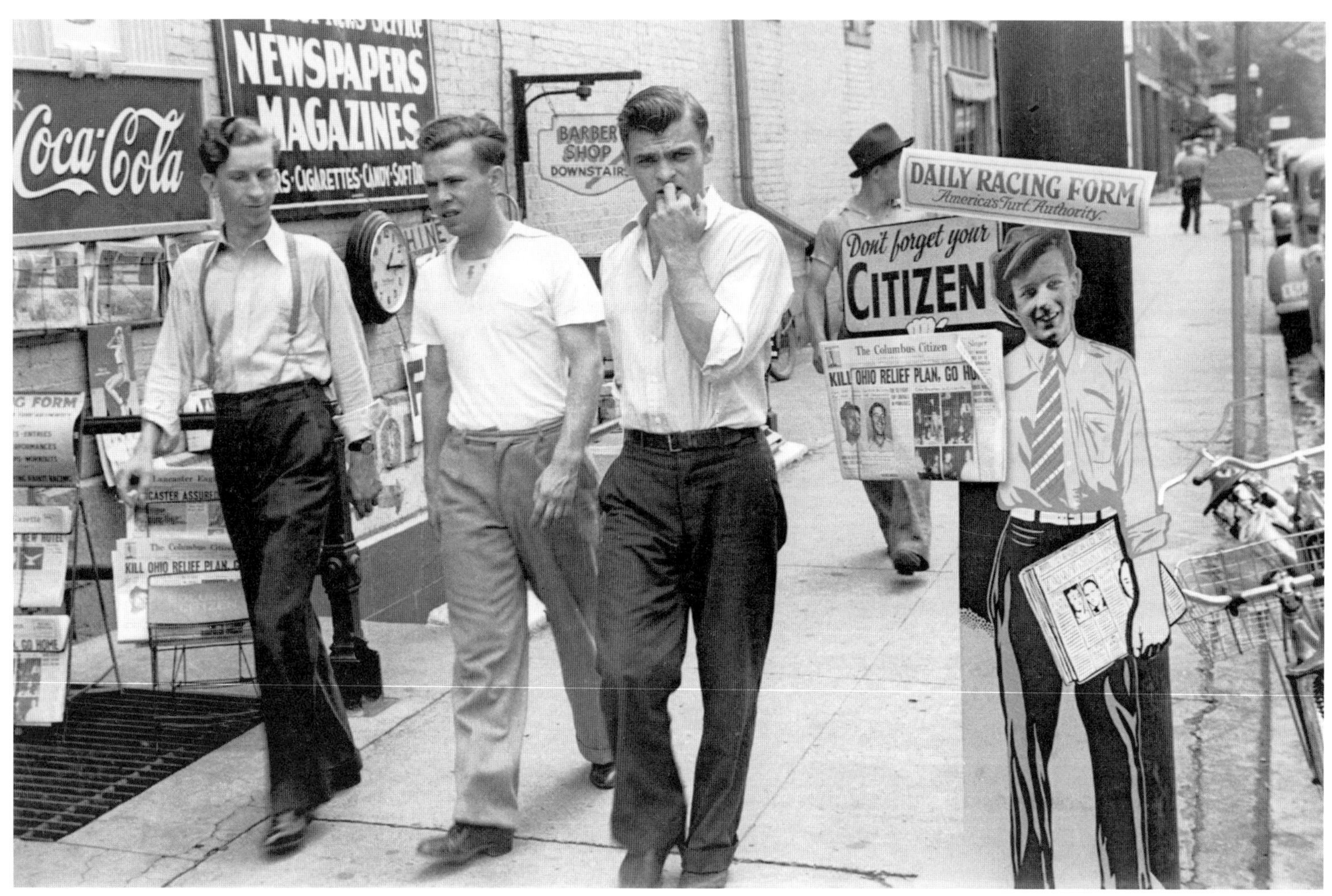

FIG 66 Main street, Lancaster, Ohio

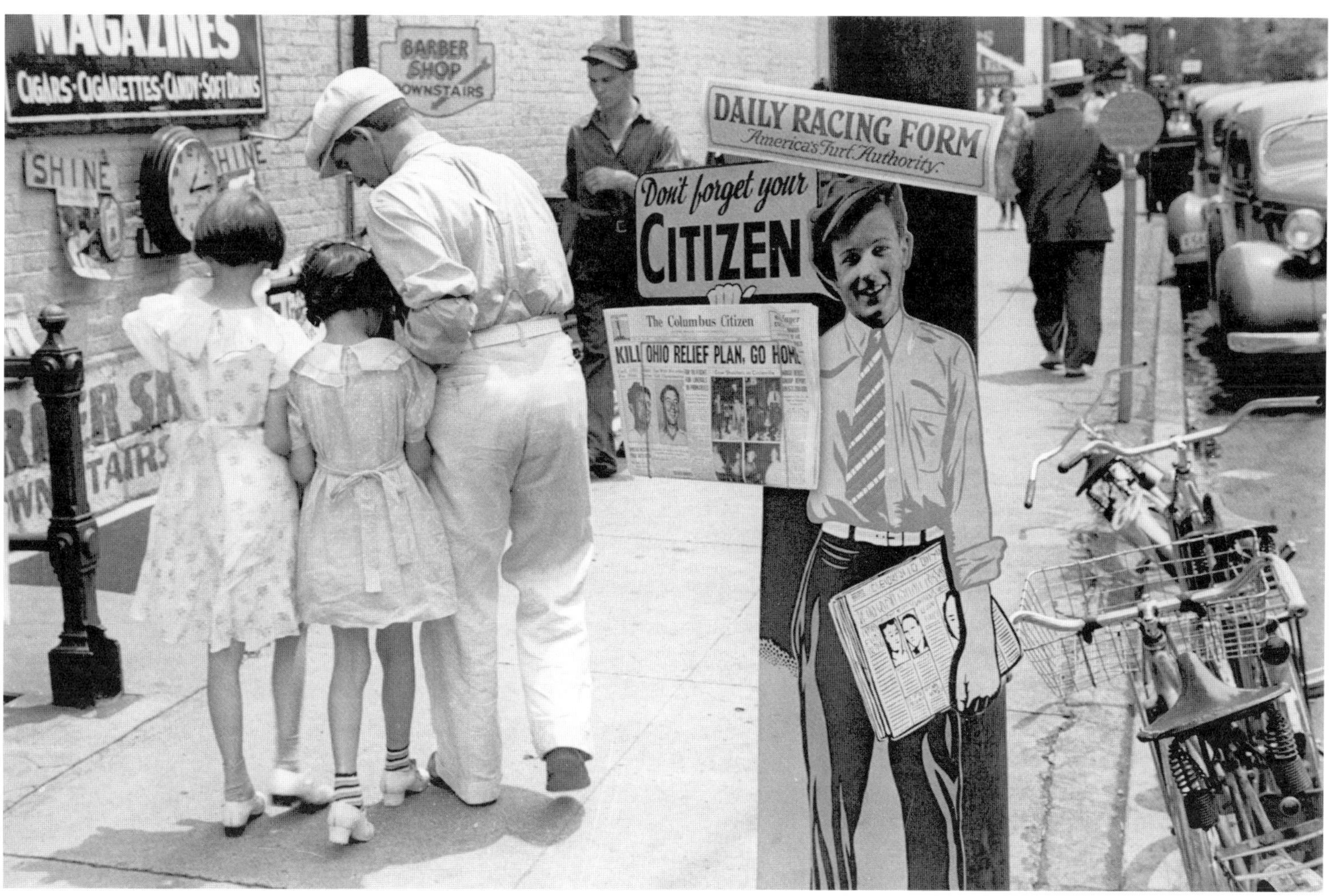

FIG 67 Main street, Lancaster, Ohio

of the United States. By the late thirties, from a national population of 130 million, movie theaters attracted some 85 million ticket buyers every week, and more than 300 correspondents for newspapers, magazines, and radio networks were permanently assigned to Hollywood to keep audiences abreast of ongoing developments there. So transfixed were Americans by the movies that Hollywood ranked behind only Washington and New York as a source for national news stories.[13]

Perhaps because that universal preoccupation made mention of it unavoidable, Stryker's script did propose shots of movie houses and of townspeople inspecting posters trumpeting current attractions. Theaters in many towns, moreover, with their showy neon-lighted marquees, garish posters ("exploitation," in Hollywood parlance), and often sleekly modernized facades, were frequently Main Street's most conspicuous landmark, their fronts' extravagant busyness making them especially inviting for photographic treatment. All of the county seats and most of the smaller towns Shahn worked in had movie theaters downtown. The smallish London had two, as did Circleville; even tiny Plain City had two. In larger towns such as Newark and Lancaster, moviegoers could choose among four theaters. City theaters in Springfield also regularly advertised their offerings in small-town newspapers ("Drive into Springfield—and enjoy a good show"), touting their ample parking, modern lounges, free coat check, and four venues offering nonstop programming from noon until midnight.

But Shahn mostly avoided these popular sites, and the small attention he gave to the pervasiveness of the movies in thirties culture is the most striking lacuna in his Ohio survey. A theater playing *One Wild Night* is his only depiction of a typical movie palace. His shooting angle from next to an adjacent storefront permits a side view of the theater's prominent marquee but eliminates its facade and exploitation paraphernalia, while the conversational group under the marquee seems to be only inadvertently gathered there and indifferent to the theater itself (fig. 68).[14] The Princess Theater in Plain City dated from 1880, before the invention of movies, and shared space with a store and second-floor offices or apartments; its staid, old-fashioned appearance was uncharacteristic, as exhibitors usually strove to make theaters look as up-to-date and conspicuous as possible. Shahn's view of it, obliquely angled from thirty feet across the street, reveals no information about the theater itself, including whether it even showed films, since it lacks a marquee and none of the usual trappings of movie exhibition are visible; nor did his terse title, "Street scene," clarify the ambiguity (fig. 69). A cursory evocation of

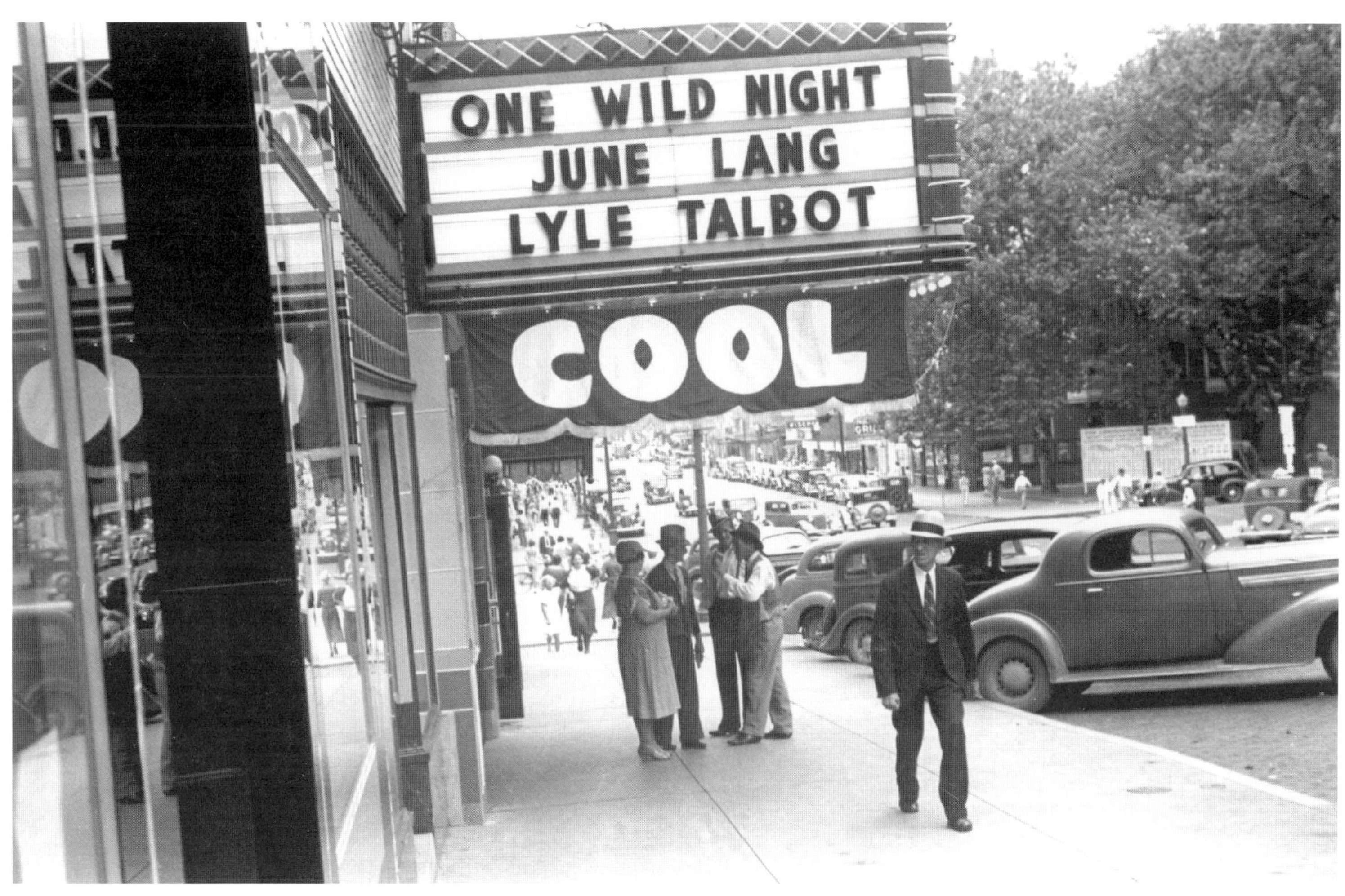

FIG 68 Street scene showing movie theater, probably in the vicinity of Lancaster, Ohio

what prospective moviegoers might experience is his photograph of three adjacent sites of leisure activity: a second-floor pool hall's street entrance, flanked by a theater and ice cream parlor. Shot close-in from an upraised angle, it concentrates on the "London Recreational Hall Pool-Card's" sign above its stairs; and while the Sunlight Ice Cream shop's counter is visible through its window, the theater can be inferred only from "To-Day" on a four-legged placard, a young man leaning on it, and two mostly inscrutable film posters (fig. 70). The pool hall, an old-fashioned holdover from the premodern era of leisure, was one of three that Shahn photographed, the same number as the more widely used and culturally influential movie theaters, even counting Plain City's ambiguous Princess and this barely glimpsed one.

A close-in study of a barbershop offering its services to both men and women did call attention to the influence Hollywood exercised in townspeople's lives. Above a list of twenty hairstyles on offer—bobs, shingles, swirls, and pompadours—its window assured female customers of being coiffed in "The Season's Smartest Styles *from* Hollywood" (fig. 71). But that acknowledgment of the movies' impact on personal behavior reverberated only faintly, because the shot brought forward an effect without a firmly articulated cause inasmuch as the sites where townspeople imbibed this influence were so meagerly represented.

A photograph of a loudspeaker truck with a sign advertising *Birth of a Baby,* "the most talked about picture of the year," seems to address more explicitly the pervasiveness of movie culture. But the film being ballyhooed was so anomalous, and in so many ways, that it did not at all represent the movies audiences usually saw, the kind that encouraged female viewers to emulate the stars' hairstyles. It was a mock documentary rather than a fiction film, featured unknown actors, was characterized by primitive production values, had been made and distributed outside the Hollywood system by a producing company with the spuriously altruistic name the American Committee on Maternal Welfare, Inc., lacked the Production Code seal of approval that virtually all other films playing in local theaters were required to have, and was unabashedly an exploitation film depending solely on its sensational subject matter to attract viewers. The photograph's generalized title, "Amusements," was technically accurate but misleading insofar as it suggested that *Birth of a Baby* typified the glossy Hollywood entertainments customarily enjoyed by moviegoers (fig. 72).

Cinemas in several towns had been remodeled in the thirties with new facades of shiny terra-cotta tile and more prominent, brightly lit marquees, such modernizations reflecting

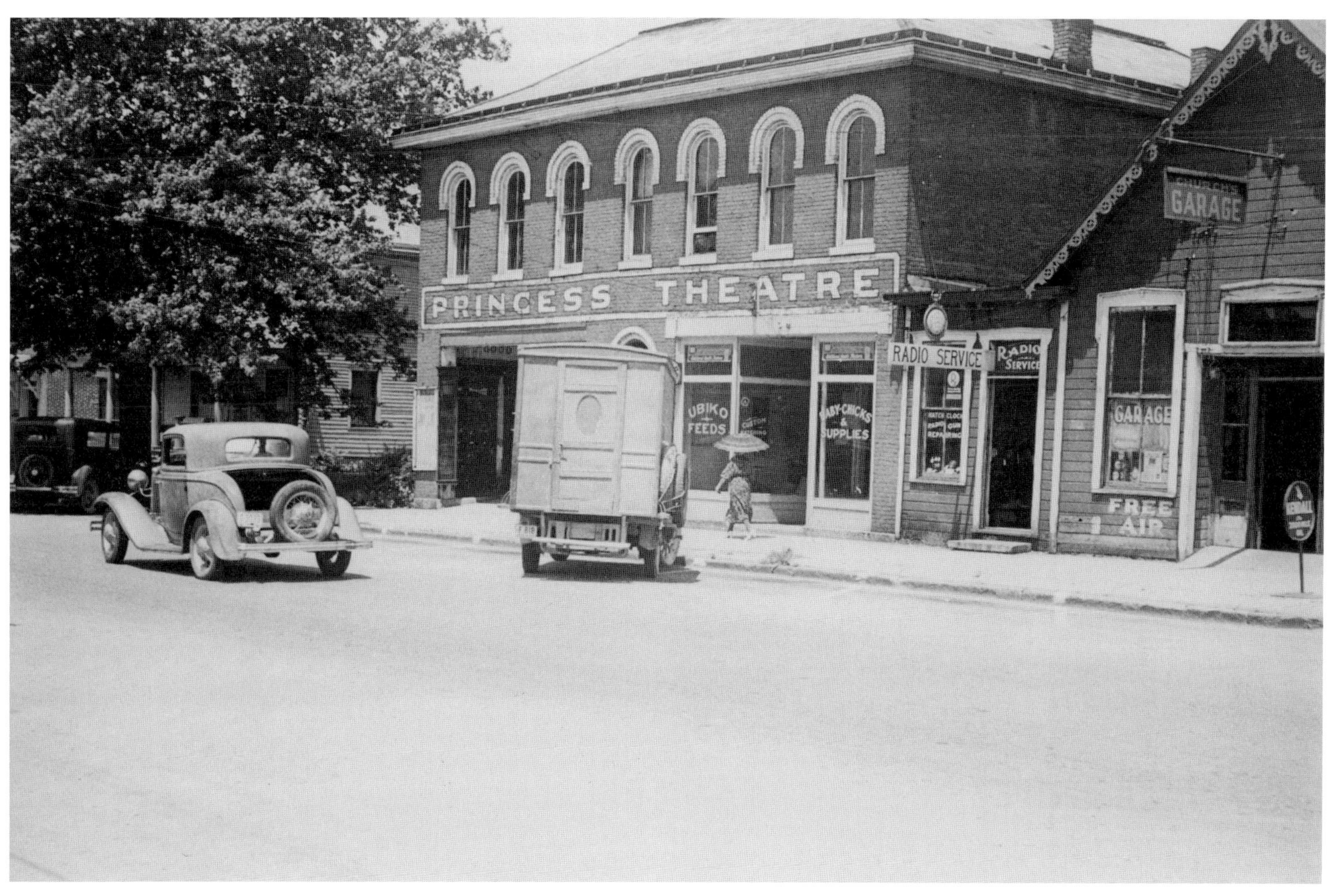

FIG 69 Street scene in Plain City, Ohio

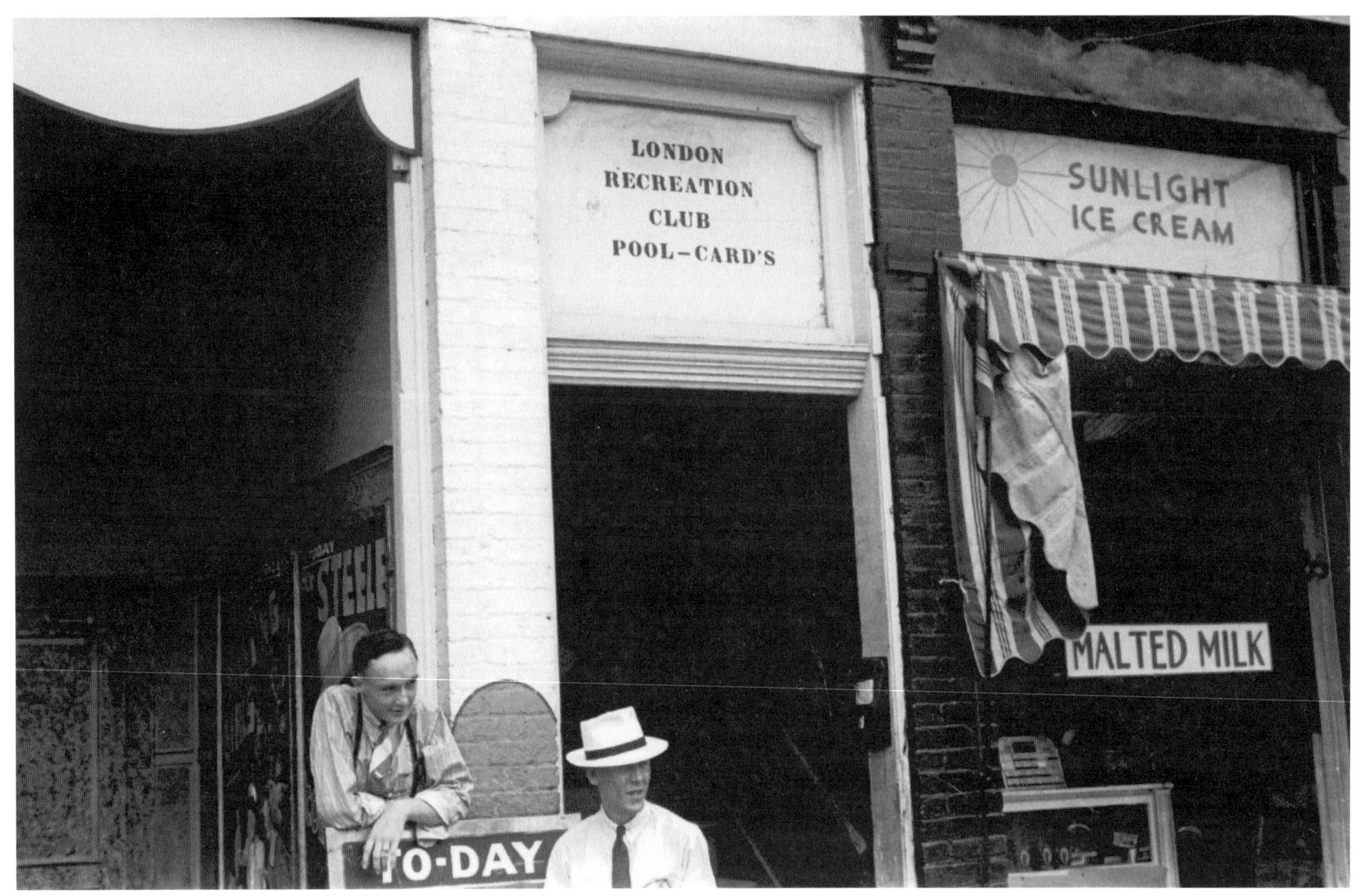

FIG 70 Saturday afternoon in London, Ohio, "the main street"

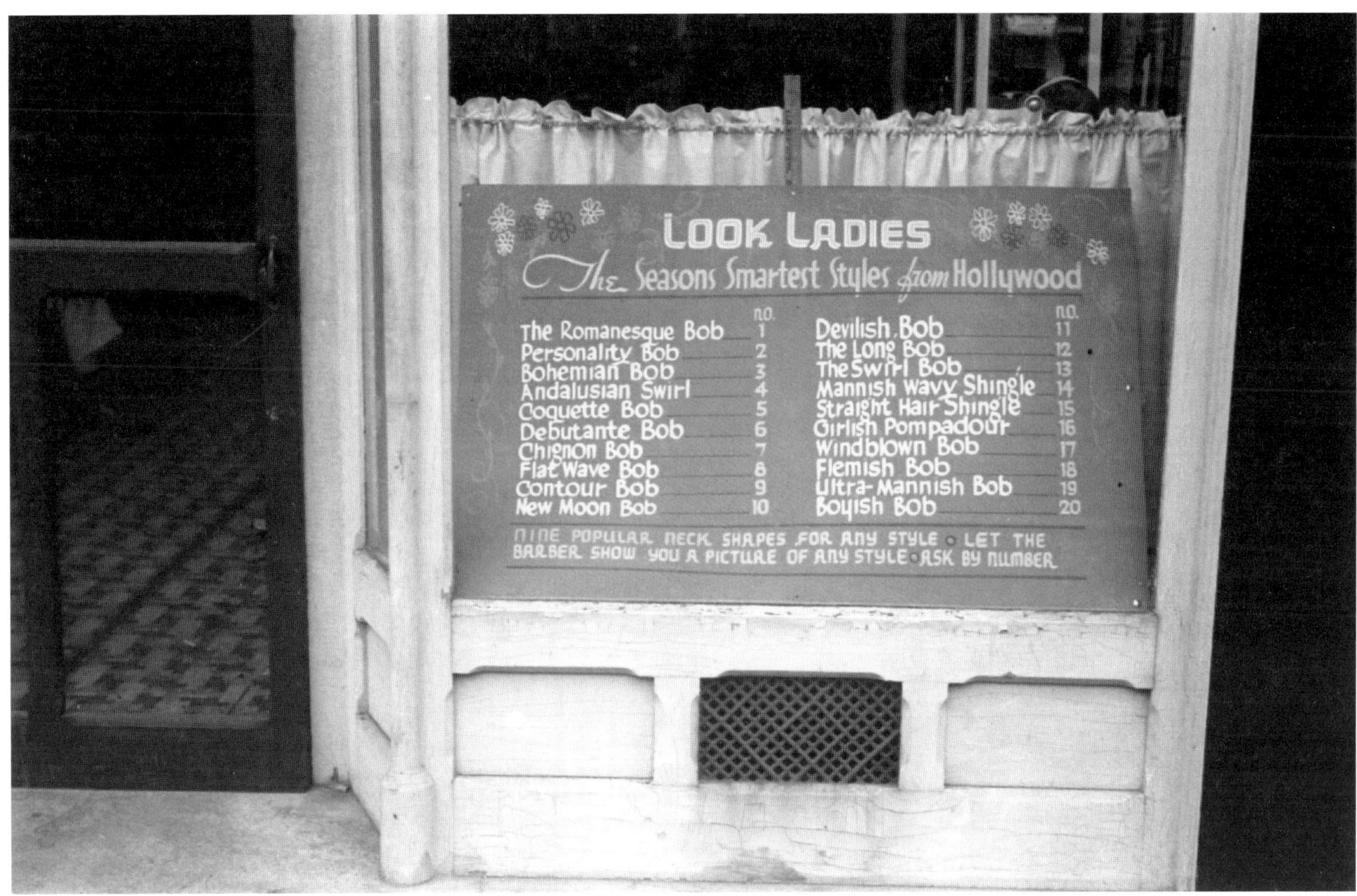

FIG 71 Barbershop sign, Lancaster, Ohio

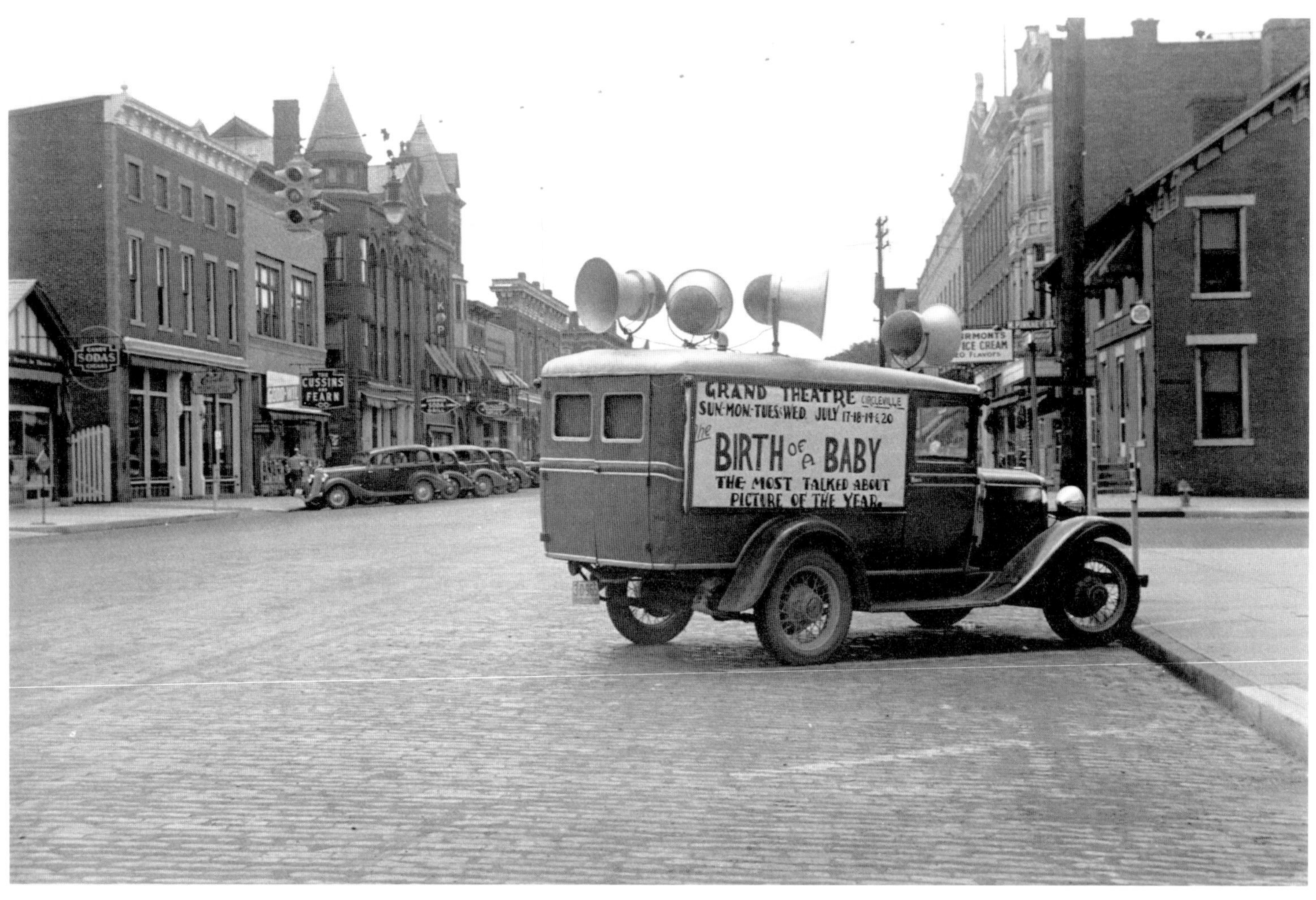

FIG 72 Amusements, Circleville, Ohio

exhibitors' conviction that their establishments needed to project a contemporary aura commensurate with the movies they screened.[15] Shahn's inattention to these theaters paralleled his neglect of the modernized facades of other downtown buildings, frequently emphasized by the WPA's *Ohio Guide.* Worthington's "few blocks of chromium-trimmed stores and service stations and a modernist apartment building or two" do not appear; Plain City does not seem especially "spruce, up to date," nor does Lancaster's business section reveal "smart facades intermingling with the somber brick fronts of the 1890s."[16]

Facade makeovers were so numerous, though, that a few do show up peripherally in downtown vistas, but Shahn made just a single photograph that concentrates on one, of a firm specializing in small loans. Its shiny tiled front and chic Art Deco lettering are vividly emphasized by contrast with the heavy lintels, exposed columns, and plain signage of the adjacent old-fashioned storefront (fig. 73). The loan office was an outgrowth of modernity's transformation of cultural values—its business of extending credit to small borrowers was integral with the spread of consumer culture—but because Shahn's attention to such developments was sparse, his survey underrepresented the degree to which they had penetrated Ohio's towns.

By contrast, the Lynds in *Middletown in Transition* compared modernity's pervasiveness in small communities to a deluge, their tranquil isolation dissipating under "a drenching of movies, radio, and other agencies of sophistication" as well as such equally ubiquitous phenomena as "chain store and nation-wide distribution systems" and "automobile mobility." Townspeople, they reported, were encouraged by that inundation to regard themselves as "essentially indistinguishable from big city folk."[17]

With the notable exception of cars, Shahn's tendency to downplay the artifacts of modernity made Ohio's towns appear to be anachronisms, to be still largely self-contained "island communities," in the words that historian Robert Wiebe used to describe the autonomy small towns experienced in the premodern era. Such local autonomy, says Wiebe, had disappeared in the United States by no later than 1920, as the "bureaucratic web" of modernity imposed "regularity, system, [and] continuity" on most aspects of all communities' social organization and daily experience, making life in small towns not fundamentally different from life in the nation's cities.[18]

If Shahn minimized the impact of modernity, he did not erase it entirely, and as a whole his survey presents an ambivalent assessment of its significance, acknowledging its encroach-

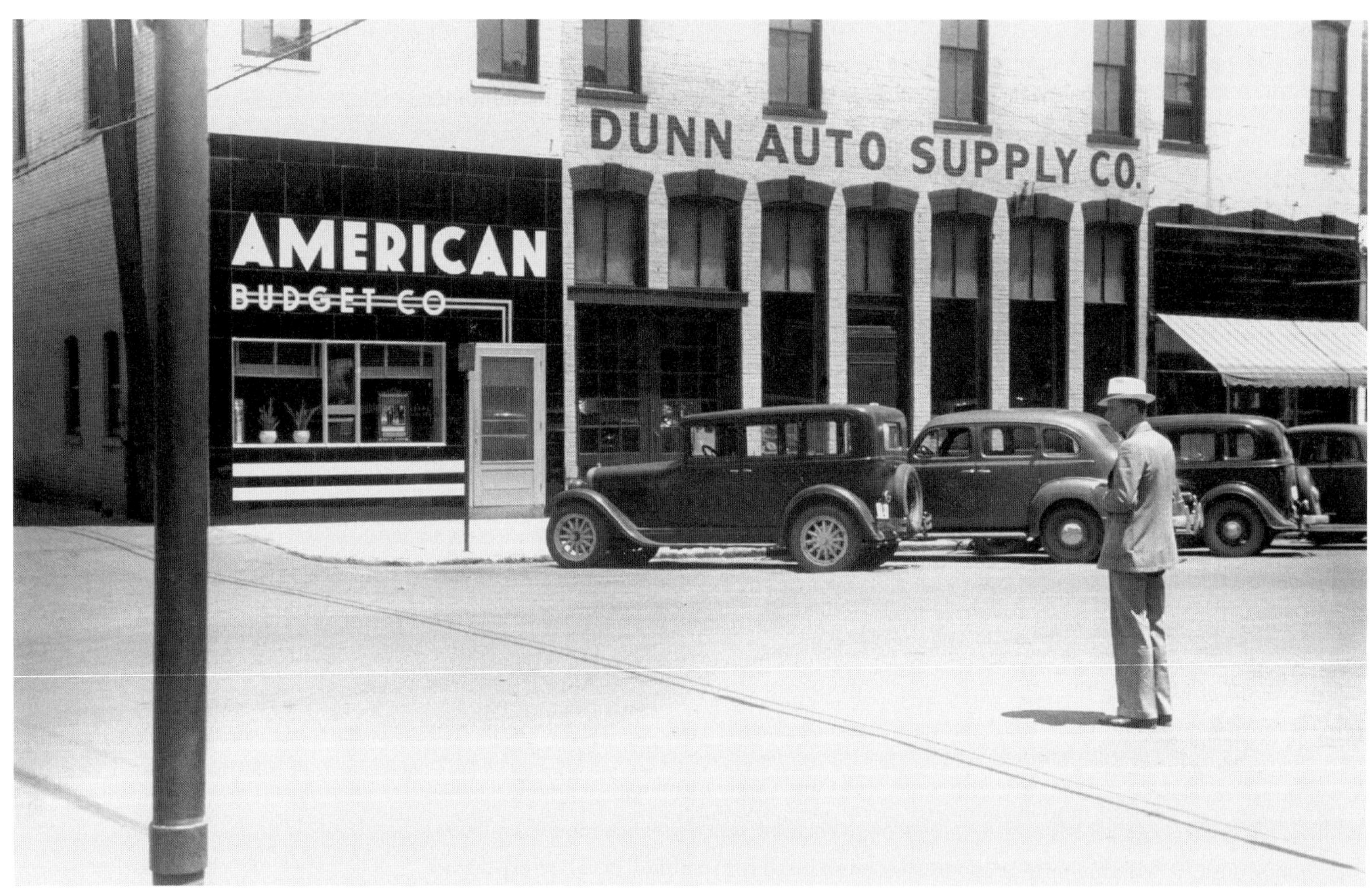

FIG 73 Street scene, Washington Court House, Ohio

ments while conveying the impression that most were largely peripheral. Emphasizing the automobile and its role in altering the physical layout of the towns and how residents related to their environment was probably inescapable given the profusion of cars lining the streets, and he took some care to depict these changes. Other, less omnipresent indications of modernity he abridged in favor of emphasizing more traditional expressions of town life, such as the hand-painted signs on shop windows, or the interplay of solid nineteenth-century buildings with the spacious sidewalks and broad streets fronting them, or groups of conversationalists clustering on those streets. No doubt he found these customary sites and rituals offering richer potential for distinctive visual treatment than the more banal evidence of modernity's incursions, and these representations of tradition comported better with Stryker's script than the innovations of modernity that were changing smaller and larger places alike. If photographs of these communities were to represent the enduring soundness of the American way of life, then that goal pointed toward a stress on stabilities and not more recent developments.

But such an emphasis also aligned with a contrast between civilization and culture that achieved substantial currency in the thirties, and its influence accounts as well for Shahn's ambivalent approach to modernity. "Civilization" became a shorthand term for characterizing the failures of the nation's industrial system, and thus implicitly of modernity, while culture was perceived as civilization's antithesis in laying stress on the fundamental soundness and irrepressible resilience of ordinary people and their traditional ways of life. It was a distinction that Stryker himself employed in his small-town script with his disdainful allusion to civilization's "mass-produced, city-made gadgets, machines, canned movies and canned beef" as a prefatory contrast to his exhaustive itemization of traditional cultural expressions.

Nor was the invidiousness of his contrast surprising, because the dichotomy between civilization and culture was, according to the historian Warren Susman, "a key structural element" in the thirties, one embraced by numerous writers, artists, and cultural critics. For them civilization was represented by the industrial, commercial, and media institutions that had matured in concert with modernity, and it was dedicated to the standardization of experience, a bureaucratic ideal of efficiency, and to measuring the quality of life exclusively in material terms. Culture, as its opposite, was characteristic of smaller social units that preserved an ideal of intimate community interaction, permitted greater variety of experience, and were more attentive to the nonmaterial needs of its members. Unlike civilization, which worshipped the future—its cardinal tenet was a belief in ever-imminent progress—culture found continuity and meaning in the confluence of past and present. It was expressed in "all the things that a group of people inhabiting a common geographical area do, the ways they do things and the ways they think and feel about things, their material tools and their values and symbols," as Robert Lynd summarized its key elements. The thirties' emphasis on the authenticity of cultural experience—indigenous, organic, and honoring tradition—resulted in, observed Susman, "for the first time, frequent references to 'an American way of life.'"[19]

Shahn's intention to concentrate on "the average American"—and his scanting of modernity—indicates that the prevailing disposition among the thirties intelligentsia to celebrate culture resonated with him as well, as it did with Stryker. But despite Shahn's attraction to this view, his fitful attention to the encroachments of civilization exceeded the script's glancing and cursory notice of them, and taken as a whole, his survey brought forward at least some evidence that called into doubt the script's assumption that small towns were a bedrock of stable tradition. Just as a number of his photographs intimated that the vitality of small towns was declining, so did a handful concentrate on the centrifugal forces that were contributing to that trend. These communities might still retain much of their "old time flavor," as he said of Circleville, but the inroads that modernity had opened threatened to denature, even liquidate it. Following Stryker's script, he had started with the assumption that his exposition of small-town life would reveal an enduring, stable culture that would dramatize the strengths of democracy, and a good number of his pictures do suggest that, but in others his unblinking artist's eye could not help but also observe what seemed to be transforming the towns, as they too embraced the modernity that suffused metropolitan centers. Shahn's ambivalence may have disappointed Stryker—although evidence that it did is lacking—but from the point of view of posterity, it is what makes his photographs so richly revealing about the ongoing tensions that were percolating just below the more obvious perturbations brought on by the Depression.

SIGNS OF THE DEPRESSION, though, were nearly invisible on Ohio's Main Streets. They often have an air of indolence, but of the leisurely and not enforced kind, and townspeople do not exhibit the numbed or bewildered look so common in many FSA pictures, including some that Shahn himself had made in the South; nor are they garbed so inadequately as to signal impoverishment and want. Aside from the rundown lunch stand in Plain City, there are no shuttered businesses or decrepit storefronts, and downtown buildings bear no markers of neglect or decay. The cars that line streets vary considerably in age and stylishness, but none resembles the tired jalopies that were a frequent motif in FSA photography, and whatever else they might imply, the sheer number of automobiles thronging the towns connotes an air of modest well-being.

A close-in portrait Shahn made in Columbus of two idle, dispirited males is closer to the conventions of thirties social documentary, and in subject matter and tone it contrasts with his Main Street photographs. Hunkered down in a scrubby and anonymous alleyway, an aging man expresses both wariness and anxiety; his proximity to a second idler appears only inadvertent, and the scene is devoid of the animated sociability of male gatherings in the towns (fig. 74). These residents of the region's metropolitan center were plausibly victims of the Depression, but no one betraying a comparable aura of desolate torpor was to be seen on the sidewalks of smaller communities.

Grim, shabby sidewalk vendors of cheap commodities such as apples or pencils were often featured in thirties photography because the patent incommensurability of their dogged enterprise and the paltry returns they could expect dramatized how disastrously the De-

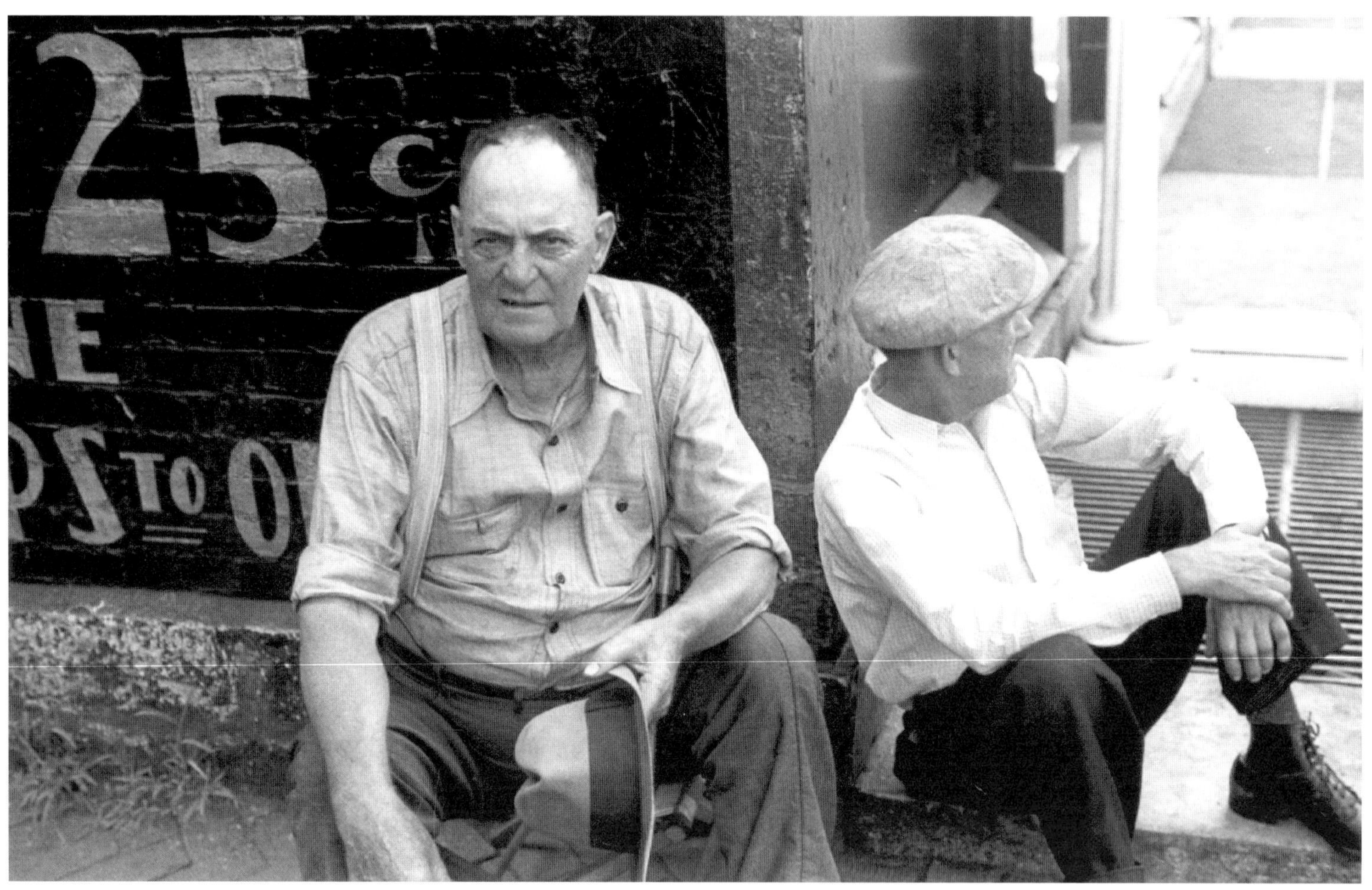

FIG 74 Residents of Columbus, Ohio

pression had ravaged individual lives. Shahn photographed such a vendor, a man seated on a newspaper and selling pencils on a Lancaster sidewalk, but while there was no question of his neediness, the portrait depicted him as a victim of ill fate rather than a casualty of hard times. His dignified, well-groomed appearance—a neat sport jacket, white shirt, and necktie—suggests that he has experienced a calamitous reverse in circumstances, which the crutch beside him serves to explain as the result of a physical misfortune. That Lancaster can do no better than to permit him sidewalk space to sell his humble goods is an indictment of its neglect of social welfare, but his tidy appearance and the specificity with which the photograph identifies his handicap militate against his being generalized as a representative of the Depression's ruinous effects (fig. 75).

Ragged children also featured regularly in thirties documentary as pitifully disadvantaged, innocent victims of the nation's economic calamity, and some of Shahn's earlier FSA work in the South had played masterful variations on that theme. One of the few children he photographed on Ohio's streets was a gap-toothed newsboy of eight or nine whose tattered shirt is the most woebegone garment Shahn depicted anywhere (fig. 76). Intense sunlight strikes his torso and face, making him squint against it and screwing his expression into a grimace that corresponds with his hard circumstances. The tonal contrast between his sun-drenched body and the pavement's cool shadow intensifies his pathos. His portrait is consonant with Depression documentary's iconography of victimized children, but another cultural trope of longer standing makes a singular interpretation of it problematic. Street-smart, entrepreneurial newsboys were enshrined in the American success mythology as the acorns from which mighty oaks grow to become tycoons. They populated the novels of Horatio Alger, were annually heralded on "National Newsboys Day," and hawked their papers in numerous Hollywood films. That conceit has had remarkable staying power, as a late-twentieth-century advertisement for *Fortune* magazine indicates: over a vintage photograph of a street urchin clutching his newspapers, it featured the headline "By diligence, a quick-witted young fellow can rise from rags to riches."[1] These cultural overtones do not cancel the portrait's social implications, but they do make it more equivocal than most depictions of children as victims of the Depression.

Although we cannot know for certain, it seems probable that less ambiguous indications of an upheaval as monumental as the Great Depression could have been discovered on downtown streets had Shahn been determined to emphasize its impact. In his earlier work in the South,

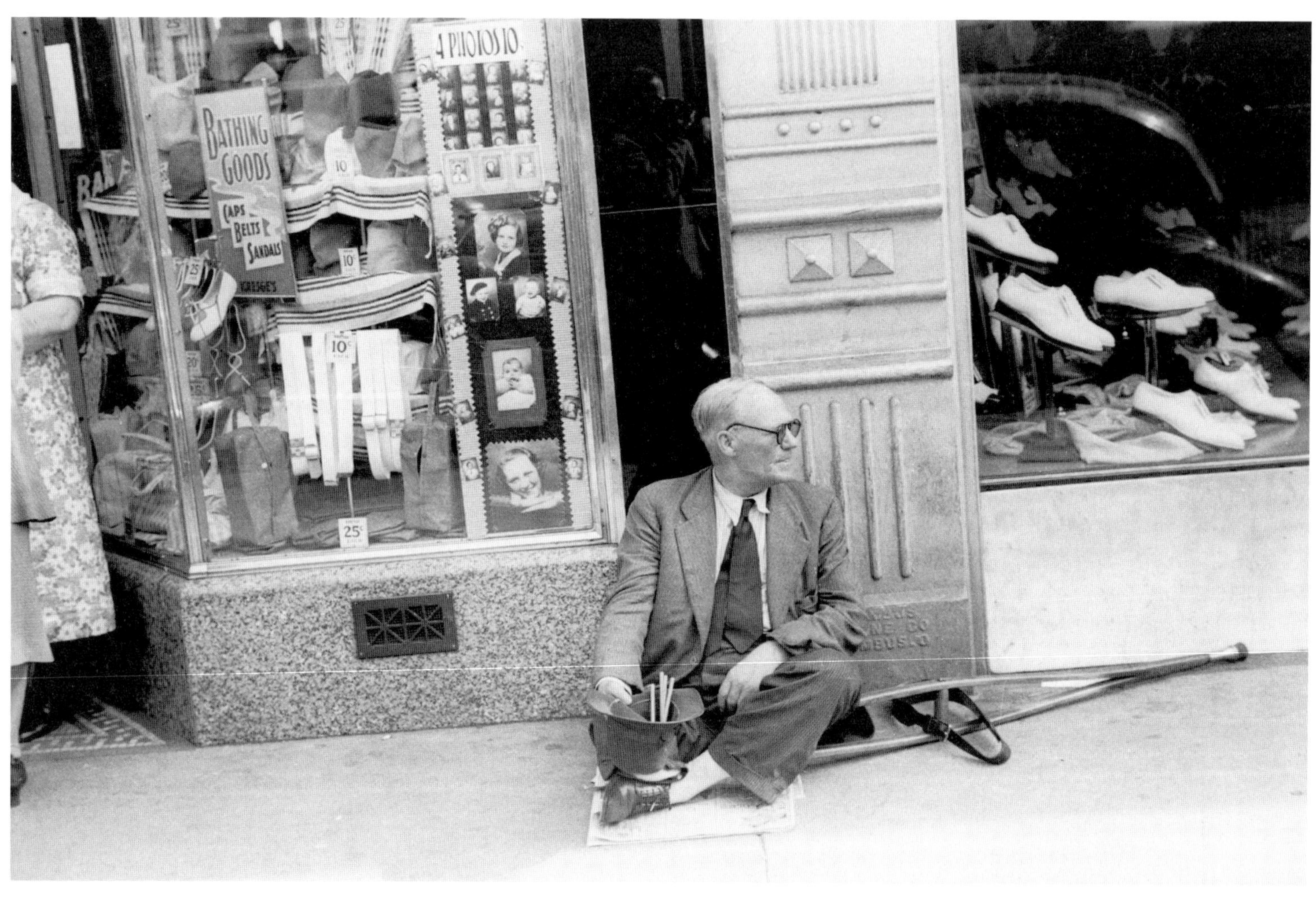

FIG 75 Main street scene, Lancaster, Ohio

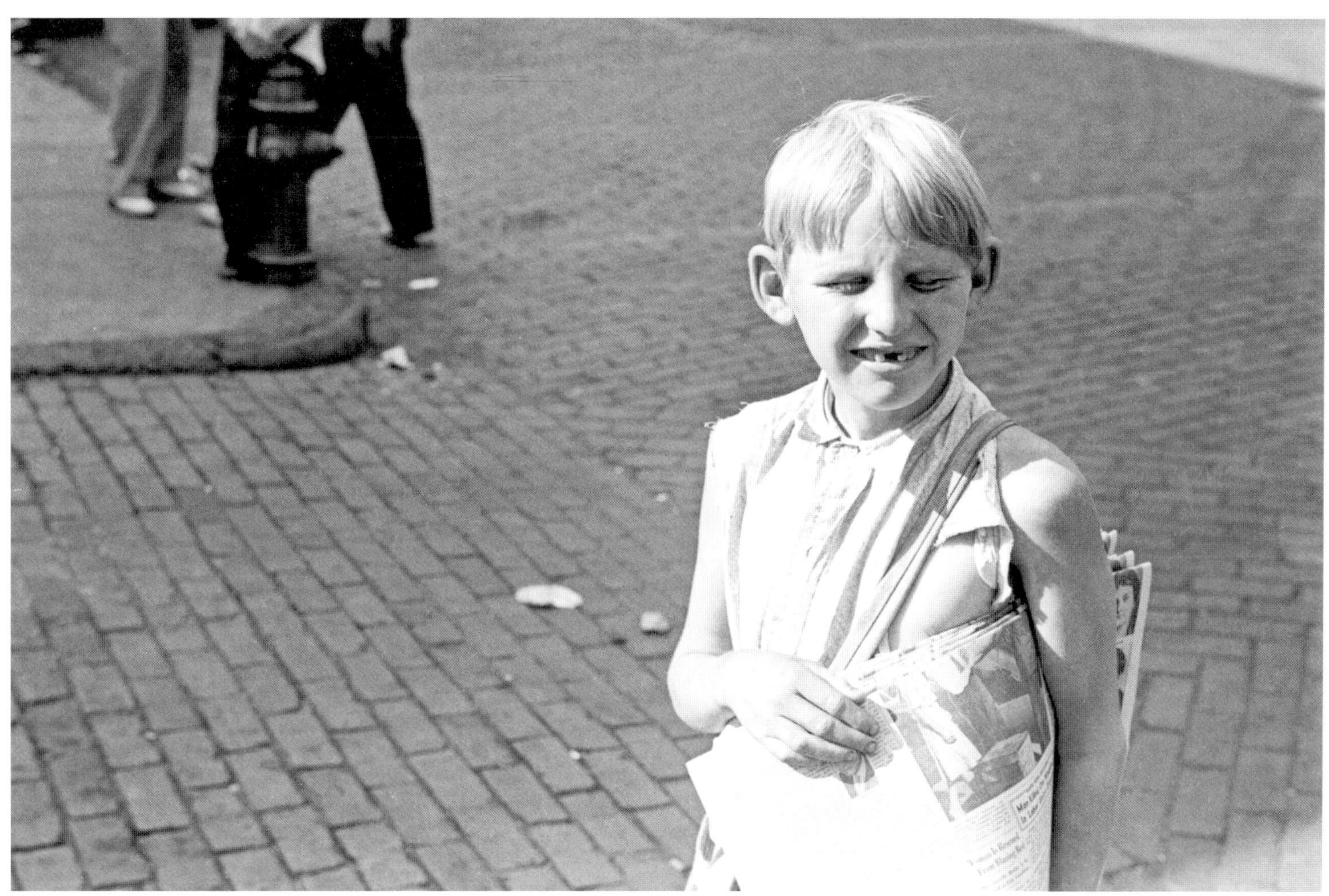

FIG 76 Newsboy, Newark, Ohio

he had found ample opportunities to do so. Moreover, in the summer of 1938, the nation was only beginning to recover from the "Roosevelt recession," which had begun the previous autumn when economic indicators plunged nearly to their lows of the early thirties. But guided by his new determination to photograph "the average American" and his conviction that he and his FSA colleagues had too single-mindedly stressed poverty, he instead concentrated on the expressions of normative culture that he observed as townspeople went about their daily round of activities.

But in fact the Depression's ravages did feature in Shahn's studies of the towns, just not in their business districts. Instead, impoverishment and need were evident in settings cordoned off from their everyday life, at a dispensary where Urbana officials distributed foodstuffs to relief recipients, and in a dismal Hooverville at the edge of Circleville. In both locales he made a sustained series of interrelated pictures, deviating from his usual procedure in downtowns of making discrete shots and indicating his determination to give poverty a prominent place in his survey.

In London he had photographed the entrance to the town's "relief office" from so close in that a sign specifying the hours between which "relief clients" were served constitutes the picture's only subject. While the office was open for six and a half hours daily, the majority of those hours were reserved for "other business"; citizens on relief were welcome during fewer than half of them, and not at all on Saturdays. Inasmuch as any other business was auxiliary to its mission, the office's arrangements laid bare an attitude about those who needed assistance: that as a public burden, they deserved no more than stiff-necked, grudging treatment from civic officials (fig. 77).

The relief office was not part of either of Shahn's sequences depicting life on the two sides of London's tracks, nor did he follow up with pictures of its clients, but the disdain for the needy that it represented is evident in more than a dozen photographs of Urbana relief clients waiting to receive surplus commodities. These handouts were an expedient, distributed when welfare budgets could not meet the need for assistance. Shahn emphasized the humiliating circumstances of their distribution and photographed only before people received their allotment; had he then shown them carrying away their foodstuffs, the series would have tilted more toward a photo-essay conveying the reassuring impression that at least the poor's basic needs were being met.

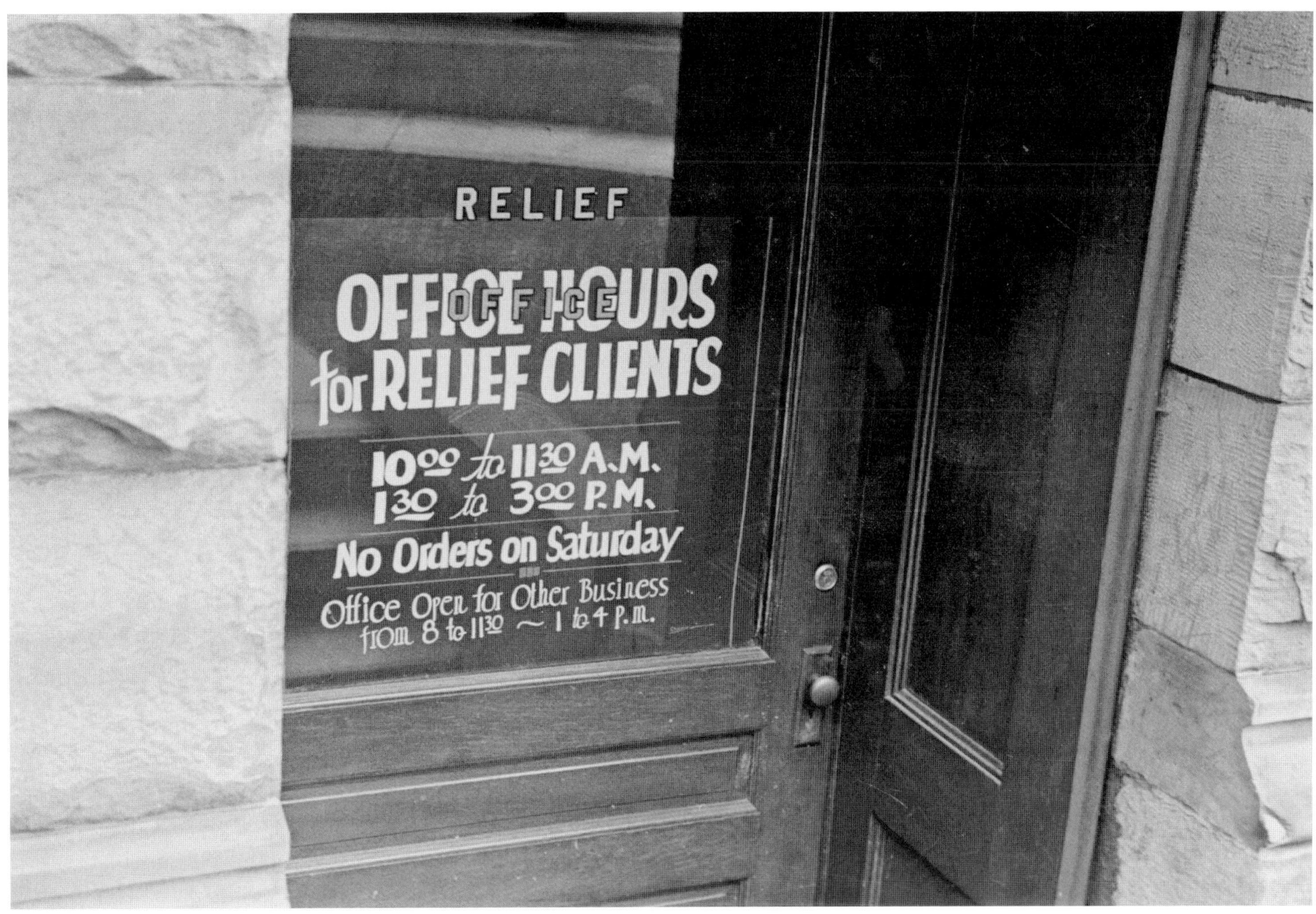

FIG 77 Relief office, London, Ohio

He began with two architectural views of Urbana's Town Hall, where the distribution occurred, of its ornately Victorian upper elevation and "City of Urbana" majestically incised above its arched entrance, before concentrating on the relief recipients patiently waiting for their goods on its sidewalk. The Town Hall was the only municipal building Shahn photographed that summer, and he did so to emphasize the highly visible setting in which these relief activities were taking place, an observation integral to his exposure of the callousness of relief officials. Urbana residents needing assistance were forced to wait for it in full public view, a shaming arrangement that exhibited their dependency to every passerby. Paradoxically, the photographs also suggested their stigmatization by portraying them as sequestered from the normal round of town life: none of the pictures includes even a glimpse of other downtown activity.

From the photographs it is not clear how the commodities were to be distributed, but since in many shots the crowd is turned to face the Town Hall, with those closest to it looking down, the likelihood is that the foodstuffs were to be doled out through a portal in the building's basement. The group includes a few children along with men and women of varying ages, including two black women, the only instance in Shahn's work that summer in which black and white citizens mingle. No seating is provided, and although some men sit on the Town Hall steps, women, several of them elderly, must wait on foot. Several people clutch a chit authorizing their allotment. Some have brought wagons to trundle away their goods, and most of the others carry shopping baskets. The crowd seems orderly enough, but officials have devised no plan to make this process less helter-skelter and more humanely dignified. The weather is fine on this particular day, but inclemency would add a further indignity to being required to wait outdoors (fig. 78).

Shahn alternated between mid-distance shots of the group and close-in portraits of individuals. Some of the latter convey the puzzled anguish that frequently characterizes individuals in Depression documentary. A grizzled father and son wearing similarly countrified hats and perching on their wagon present contrasting countenances, the boy's subdued, the father's stupefied and connoting the inexorable burden of familial responsibility (fig. 79). In a remarkable double portrait, the body language of two otherwise entirely unlike women—one elderly and wearing an old-fashioned bonnet, the other young with a fashionable bob—expresses similar ill ease and uncertainty, the older woman's fingers pensively to her lips, the younger one's mouth agape (fig. 80).

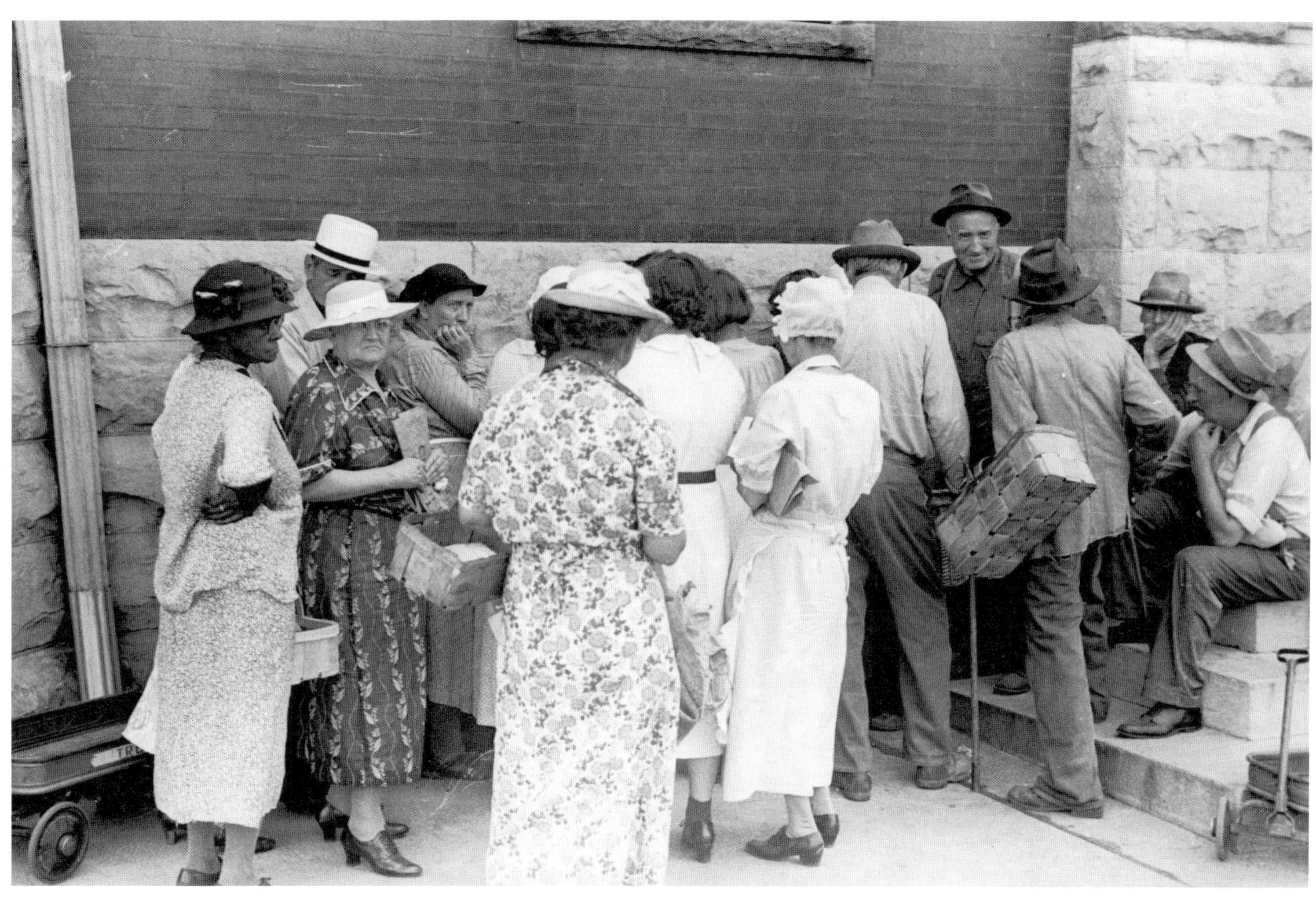

FIG 78 Outside relief station, Urbana, Ohio

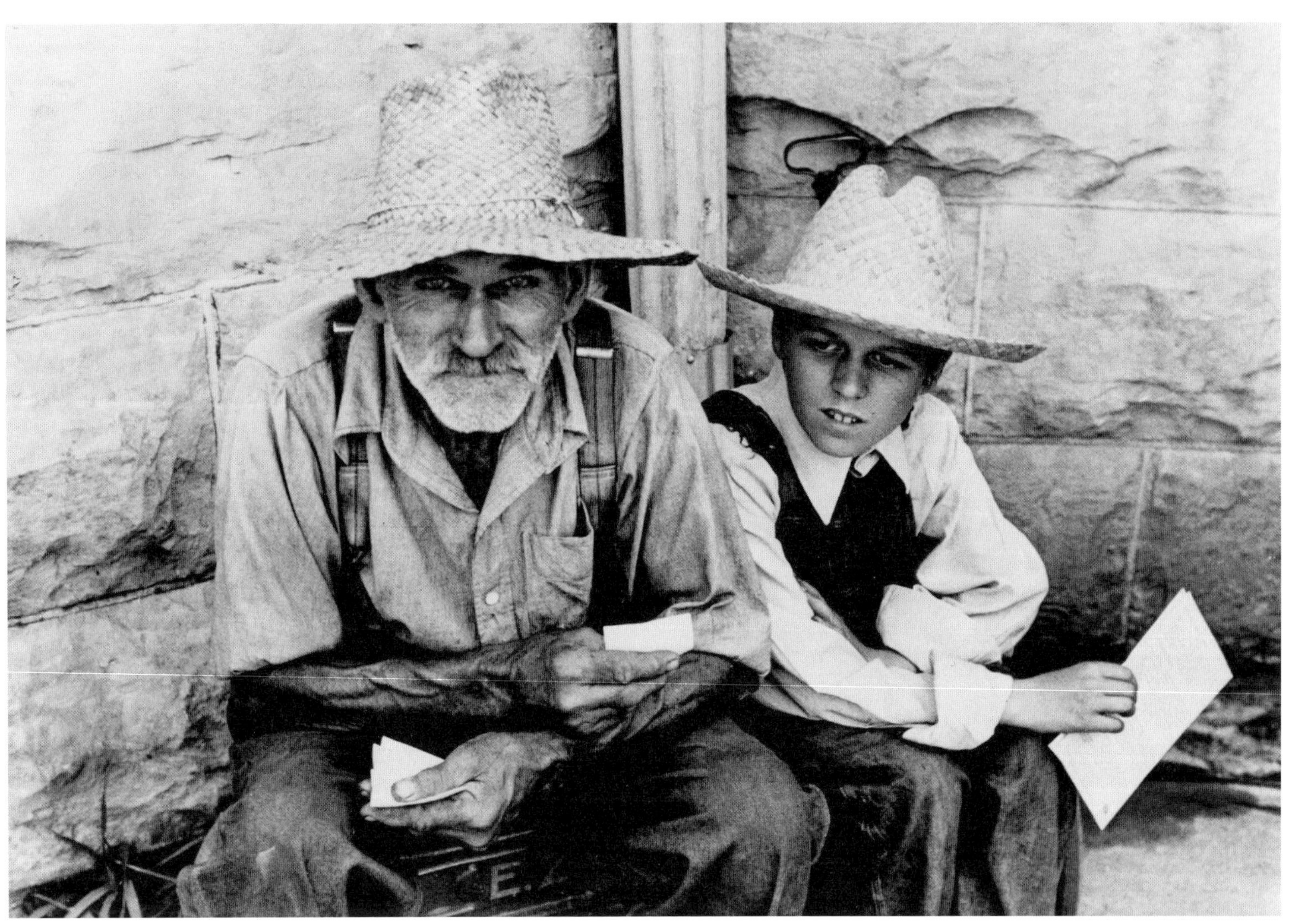

FIG 79 Waiting for relief commodities, Urbana, Ohio

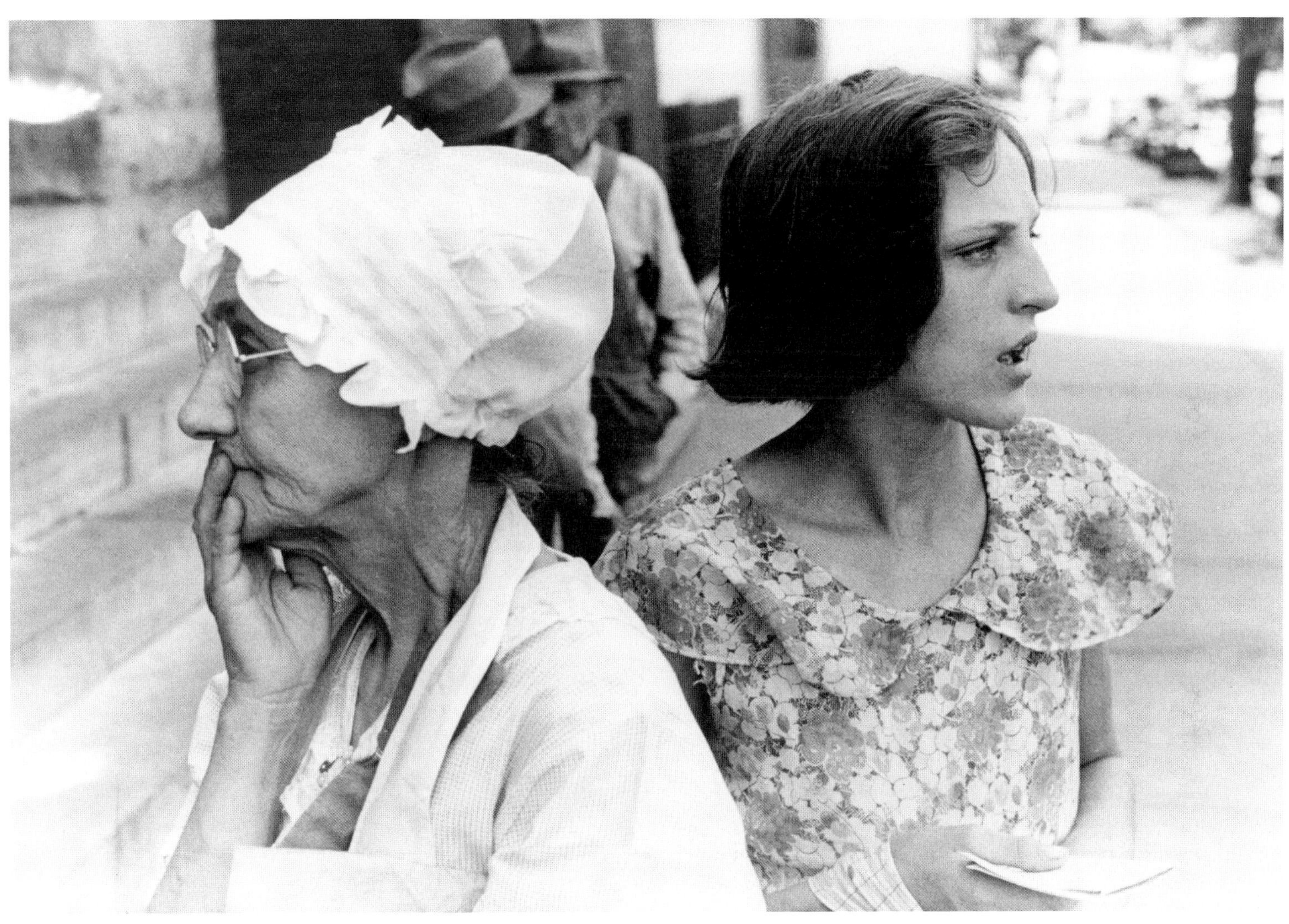

FIG 80 Waiting outside relief station, Urbana, Ohio

Yet what is most notable about the relief recipients is how indistinguishable most are in appearance and demeanor from other townspeople. Women are neatly dressed in print dresses as if for downtown shopping, most older ones also wearing ladylike straw hats. Like many of their counterparts on downtown streets, men are less carefully turned out and wear open-necked shirts, galluses, and sometimes well-worn hats, but none has ragged or inadequate clothing, and they engage in the same sort of sidewalk banter (fig. 81). A viewer of these group pictures without their titles might easily mistake them for depictions of some normative cultural activity such as the prelude to a community supper.

As a whole, Shahn's photographs of relief recipients invite two responses to their circumstances that are more emotionally than logically consistent. On the one hand, the portraits of individuals suggest that the vulnerability instigated by neediness can lead to despair and social morbidity, pathologies that do damage to the community fabric; on the other, the group pictures indicate that the needy are just like other townspeople, neighbors who have run into a bit of bad luck and need only a helping hand until they can weather it. Neither attitude warrants the humiliating, mean-spirited treatment they receive at the hands of public officials. In a photograph epitomizing his censure of it, Shahn employed a different compositional strategy than with other shots in the series by retreating several steps back to emphasize the group as a whole and aiming up so as to include a window in the Town Hall from which a stout woman is surveying the scene. This perspective reveals how uncomfortably jammed together the relief recipients had to be in order to receive their allotment and contrasts their moiling group with the solitary woman above them in the window, her elevated position, akimbo stance, and supercilious gaze symbolic of the patronizing official oversight of relief activities (fig. 82).

If Shahn's critique of official disdain for the needy struck a note uncommon in FSA photography, his pictures of Circleville's squalid Hooverville were squarely in documentary's mainstream, emphasizing the plight of families struggling to cope with appallingly inadequate living conditions. How its residents came to live in such a wretched place and what circumstances kept them there were propositions too abstract for the camera to explore; only language or statistics could satisfactorily address them, and in a "general caption" Shahn did proffer a minimal causal explanation. "During depression many farms of the district were foreclosed. People who lost homes naturally gravitated toward the town. A town of its char-

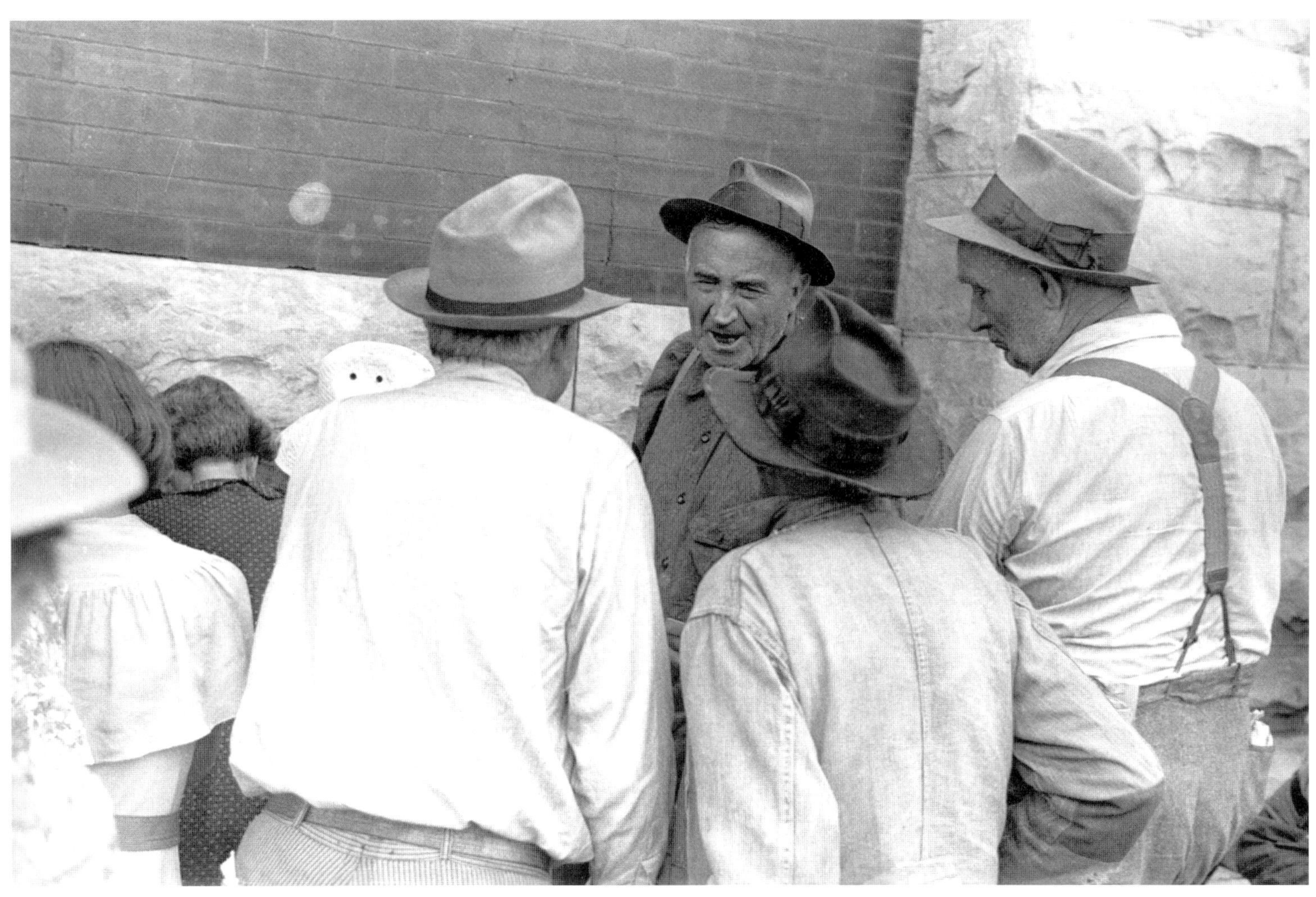

FIG 81 Waiting for relief commodities, Urbana, Ohio

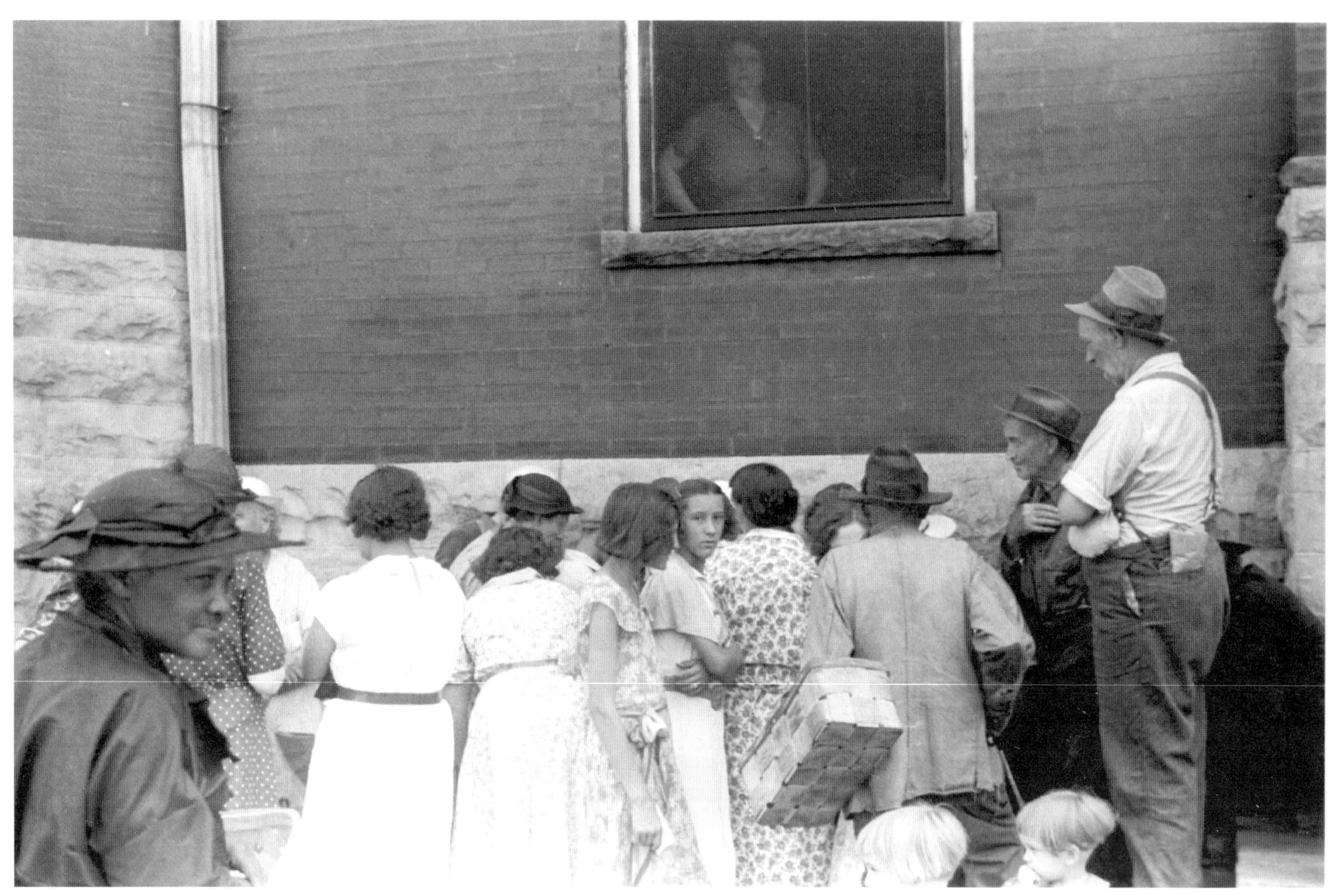

FIG 82 Rural relief near Urbana, Ohio

acter is unable to house new influx of population. Consequently there sprung up around it an extensive Hooverville." But with his camera he focused on the Hooverville's families, because it had an unparalleled capacity for delineating with graphic detail the human consequences of these larger societal disruptions, and also because viewers, inasmuch as they were members of families themselves, might more empathetically be convinced to respond to such egregiously disadvantaged ones.

Most of his Hooverville photographs concentrate on how pathetically inadequate its housing was for sustaining even a minimally decent existence for the families forced to live there. Their abodes were either jerry-built, boxy wooden structures of one or two rooms, or sagging older houses no less insalubrious and only slightly more commodious. In all of these shots he included at least one inhabitant of a hovel to give a human face to the sociological generalization the pictures cumulatively made about the inferiority of these living conditions. A few are of solitary men, but the rest all feature children, with or without their parents, and children are the subjects as well of the handful of pictures that do not depict housing. As William Stott has remarked, children are among "the natural heroes of photography" because they have not yet learned disguise; and in thirties documentary they could also exemplify poverty's corrosive effect on normative family life and the Depression's victimization of the weak and powerless.[2]

The contrast between a father and daughter posing in the entrance of their crude shack illustrates Stott's observation. The father, deeper in the doorway's recess and with his body turned slightly away from the camera, expresses both wariness and shame, while the girl faces it without embarrassment, her insouciant stance—her knee bent to rest her foot against the doorjamb—and direct gaze giving her an air of unaffected guilelessness. The child's transparency intensifies viewers' perception of the father's guarded distress over the circumstances in which his family is sunk. Their home is no better than a chicken coop, inadequate for anyone, and abysmally so for a family of at least four.[3] The good-luck horseshoe above its door is at once bleakly ironic and a touching testimony to the family's attempt to personalize their dismal living quarters (fig. 83).

Shahn employed a similar pairing in a shot of a blowsy older house from which a family is moving; whether by choice or compulsion is unclear. In its littered yard, a frowning mother carrying a toddler looks at the ground, avoiding the camera, while her son openly regards it from behind a screen door. The house's inferior condition testifies to the family's abjectness:

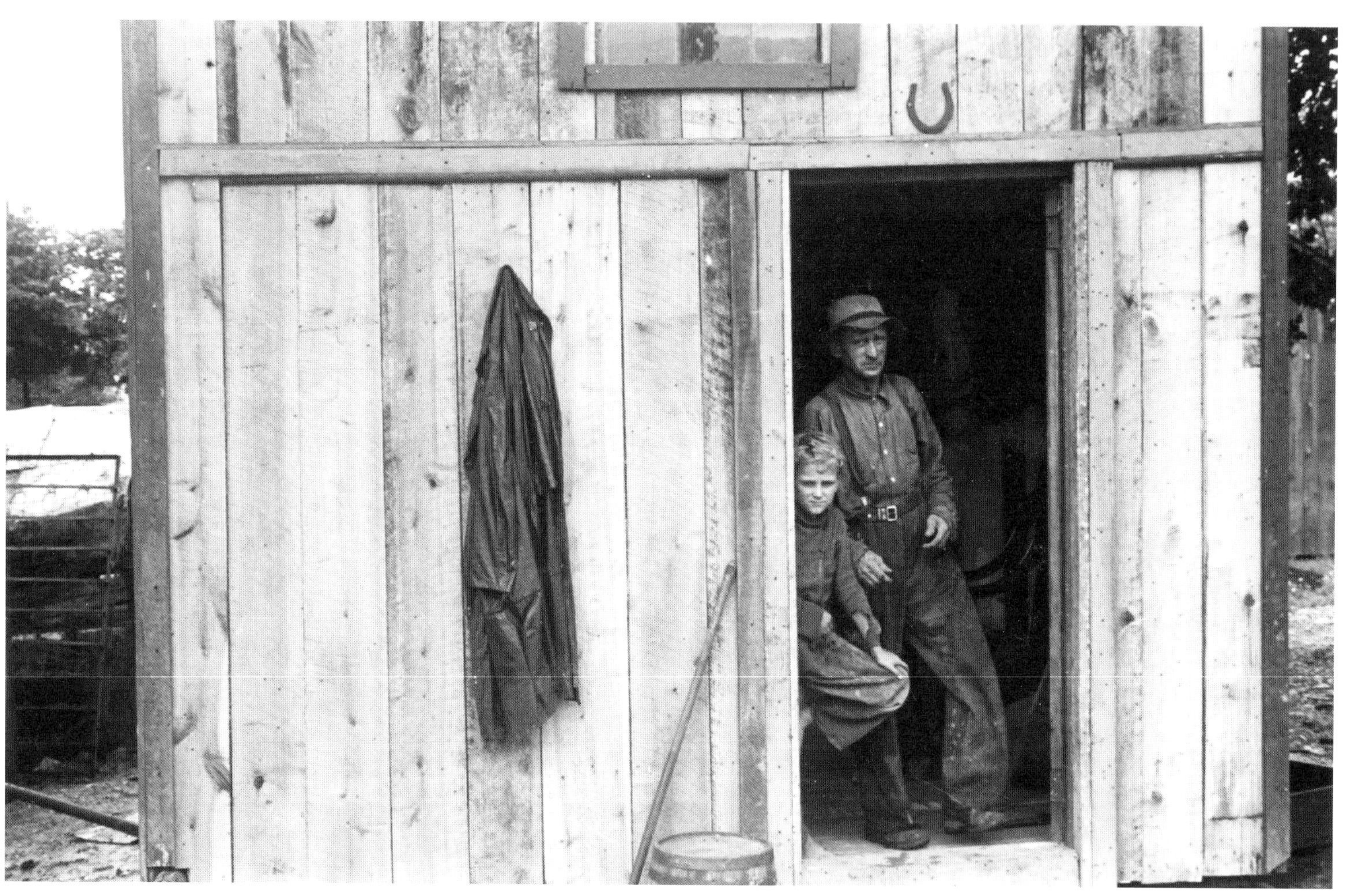

FIG 83 Dwellers in Circleville's "Hooverville," central Ohio

the siding sags, and the window and door frames are out of plumb and have never been painted; nor has a crude lath fence with several broken or missing boards. The title, "Dwellers in Circleville's 'Hooverville,'" gives no hint of why or where this family is moving, but if they have been evicted from even this inferior house, their prospects for one more adequate are negligible (fig. 84).

More circumstantial were the titles to three pictures of another Hooverville family, identifying the father as an ex-farmer employed by the Works Progress Administration (WPA), the New Deal's major work-relief effort. In July 1938 the agency employed 362 men in Pickaway County to maintain county roads and Circleville's streets; they were ordinarily limited to working thirty hours per week and earned an hourly wage equaling the average received by the area's most unskilled laborers. The WPA also employed 78 women in the public library or on domestic projects such as sewing and repairing schoolbook bindings. Only one family member was permitted to work for the agency. There were 1,000 families receiving relief in Pickaway County, some 15 percent of its population, and nearly half of them depended on the WPA.[4]

The WPA wages were insufficient to maintain anything approaching a decent standard of living for the family of at least seven, as the ramshackle condition of their home plainly indicates, the most pitiful of any Shahn photographed. It had been crudely constructed of what appear to be scavenged materials, with cardboard tacked on for insulation. A makeshift outdoor basin for washing up indicates that water must have been carried in from elsewhere. Attempts to repair the flimsy door had come to naught, and screening gapes from its frame. A fire insurance advertisement that served as insulation and perhaps decoration is cruelly ironic, inasmuch as such a flimsy shack has no insurable value, and in any case an underwriter would never offer a policy on a structure so perilously inflammable (fig. 85). A close-in shot of the family's second-youngest child, a girl of three or four in a sailor dress whose dismayed expression and body language belie her age, supplies a more intimate view of the house's loathsome living conditions: several flies are crawling on her arm (fig. 86).

Perhaps because these candid photographs made the family so pitiable, Shahn also shot a posed three-quarters portrait of the father enfolding his fretful youngest child in his arms. A woman holding an infant was a frequent subject in thirties documentary, echoing a long tradition in visual art of the Madonna and infant Jesus, but a father doing so was less common,

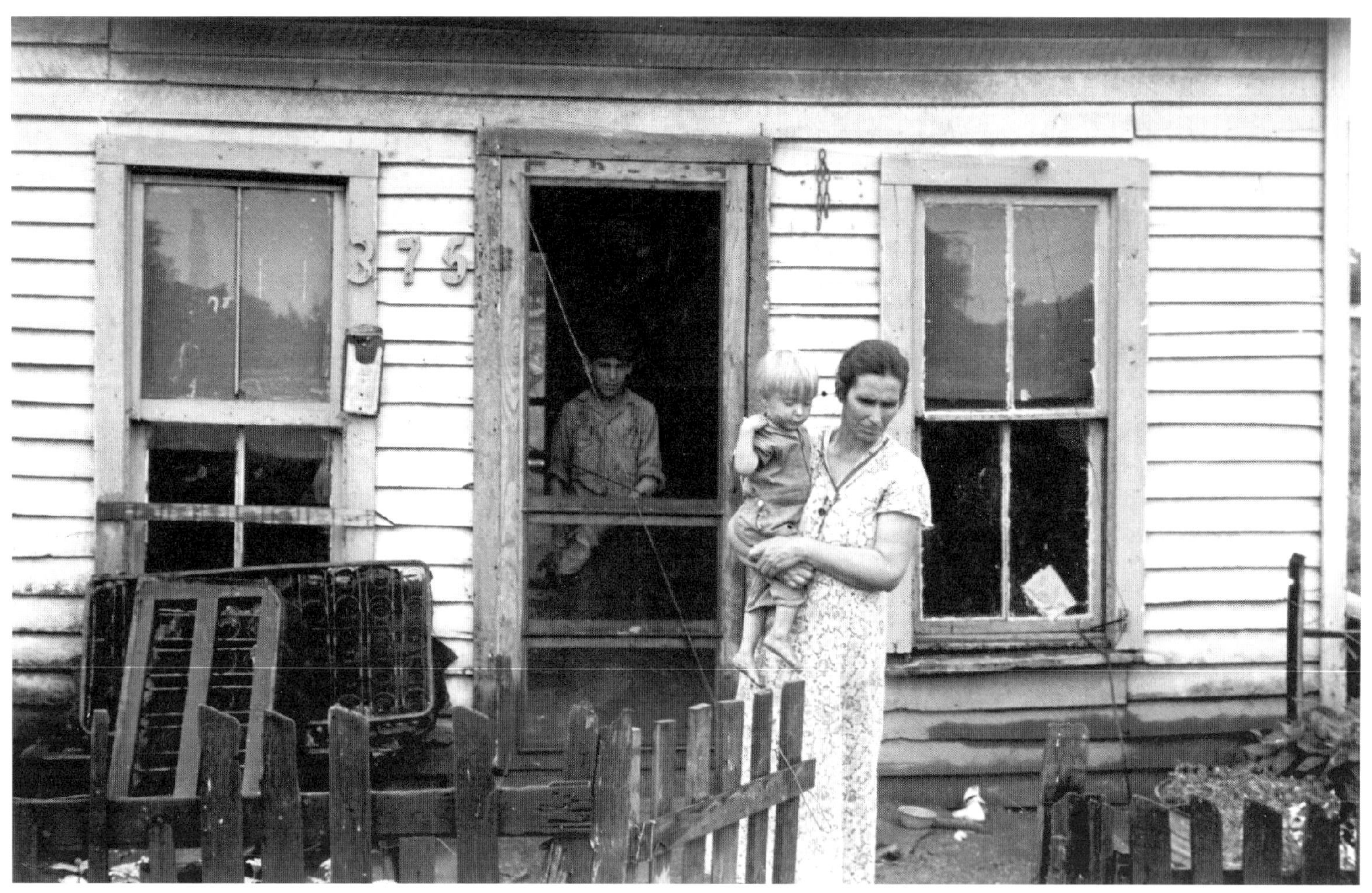

FIG 84 Dwellers in Circleville's "Hooverville," central Ohio

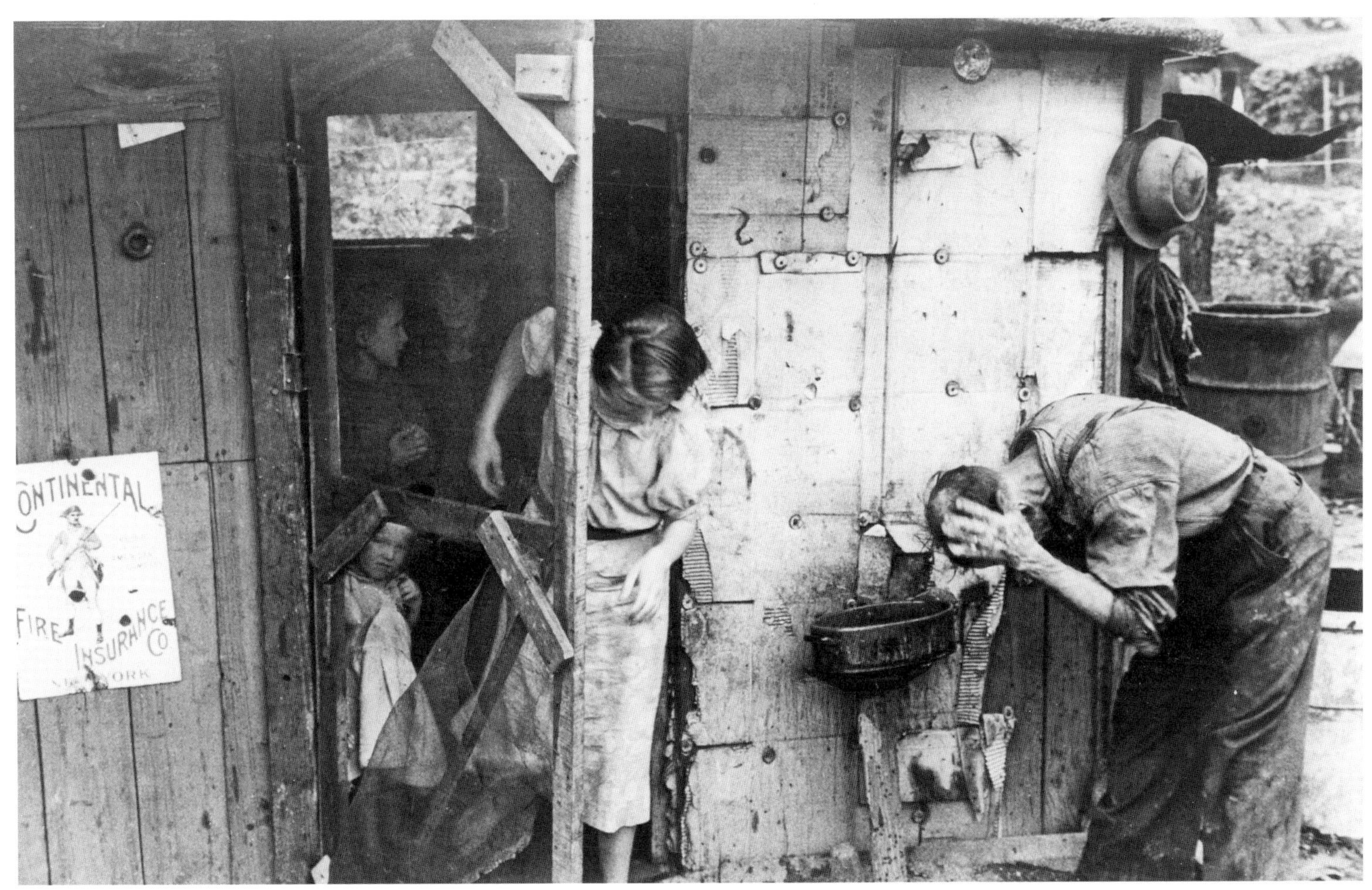

FIG 85 Ex-farmer now on W.P.A., central Ohio

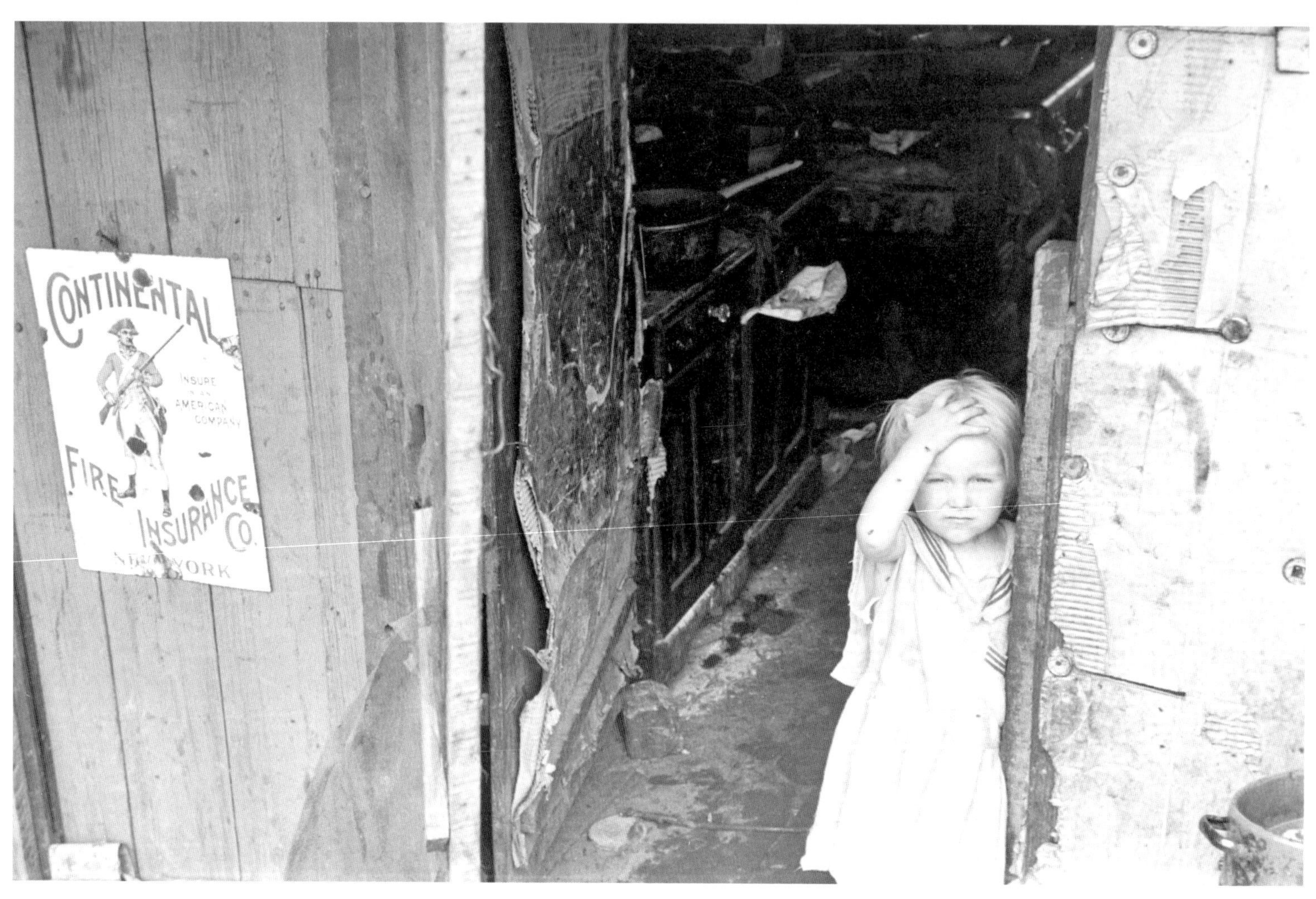

FIG 86 Child of ex-farmer now on W.P.A., central Ohio

no doubt because it was less frequent in life. The portrait's unconventionality alone makes it touching, but even more its poignancy depends on the remarkable duality that Shahn was able to capture in the father's bearing, between the anxiety that hoods his eyes and clenches his mouth, and the tenderness with which his hands cradle his child. Neither emotion cancels out the other, and the exposition of his human complexity brings forward the father and his family as something other than solely pathetic victims of cruel circumstances. While unmistakably exposing their home's inadequacy, the picture asks viewers to acknowledge that not only does desperate poverty characterize their lives, but so too does a circuit of intimate and supportive familial affection (fig. 87).

As a makeshift community segregated at the edge of town, Circleville's Hooverville would have had numerous other liabilities besides inferior housing—including poor sanitation, a lack of nearby stores for basic needs, no access to public utilities, and a relentlessly dreary ambiance—but of all such insufficiencies, Shahn focused only on one, the absence of any decent area where children could play. Not only was it the most amenable to visual representation, but even the most hardhearted viewer could not imagine that children bore any responsibility for their hardship.

All of Shahn's photographs of the Hooverville's children are composed to surround them with uninviting expanses of bare earth, only mud puddles and scattered stones varying its blankness. These spaces are not only uncongenial but unsafe as well, since it is apparent that they are also used by automobiles. As environmental portraits, these pictures at once delineate how bleak are the settings for children's activities and suggest the dismal circumference of their world.

The children's ages influence how they respond to the camera. A dark-eyed, swarthy boy is the most self-conscious, regarding it with a mixture of wary mistrust and challenge, so that he appears both vulnerable and to be striving not to show it. At thirteen or so, he has begun to adopt the disguises of adulthood, and photographing him from so close in allows Shahn to make his portrait a psychological study as well as an exposure of the barren environment that is shaping him (fig. 88). A ringleted girl of three or four is ingenuously inattentive to Shahn's camera, which he has aimed so as also to draw attention to her raw surroundings and her plaything, a crude pull toy scavenged from some ruined device. It and the abandoned tire on which she sits are rubbish, and they and this barren ground are abysmal makeshifts for the

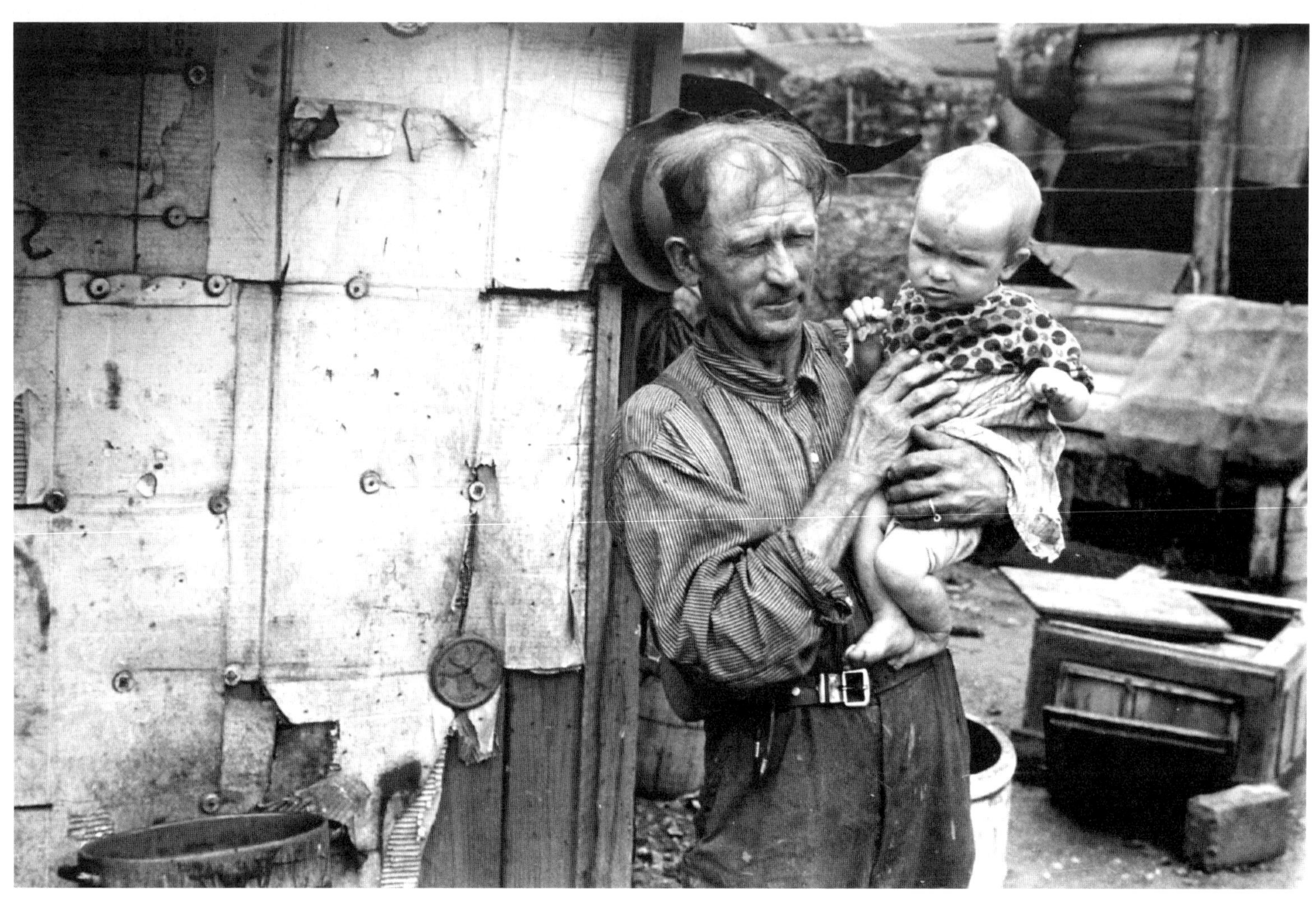

FIG 87 Ex-farmer and child, now on W.P.A., central Ohio

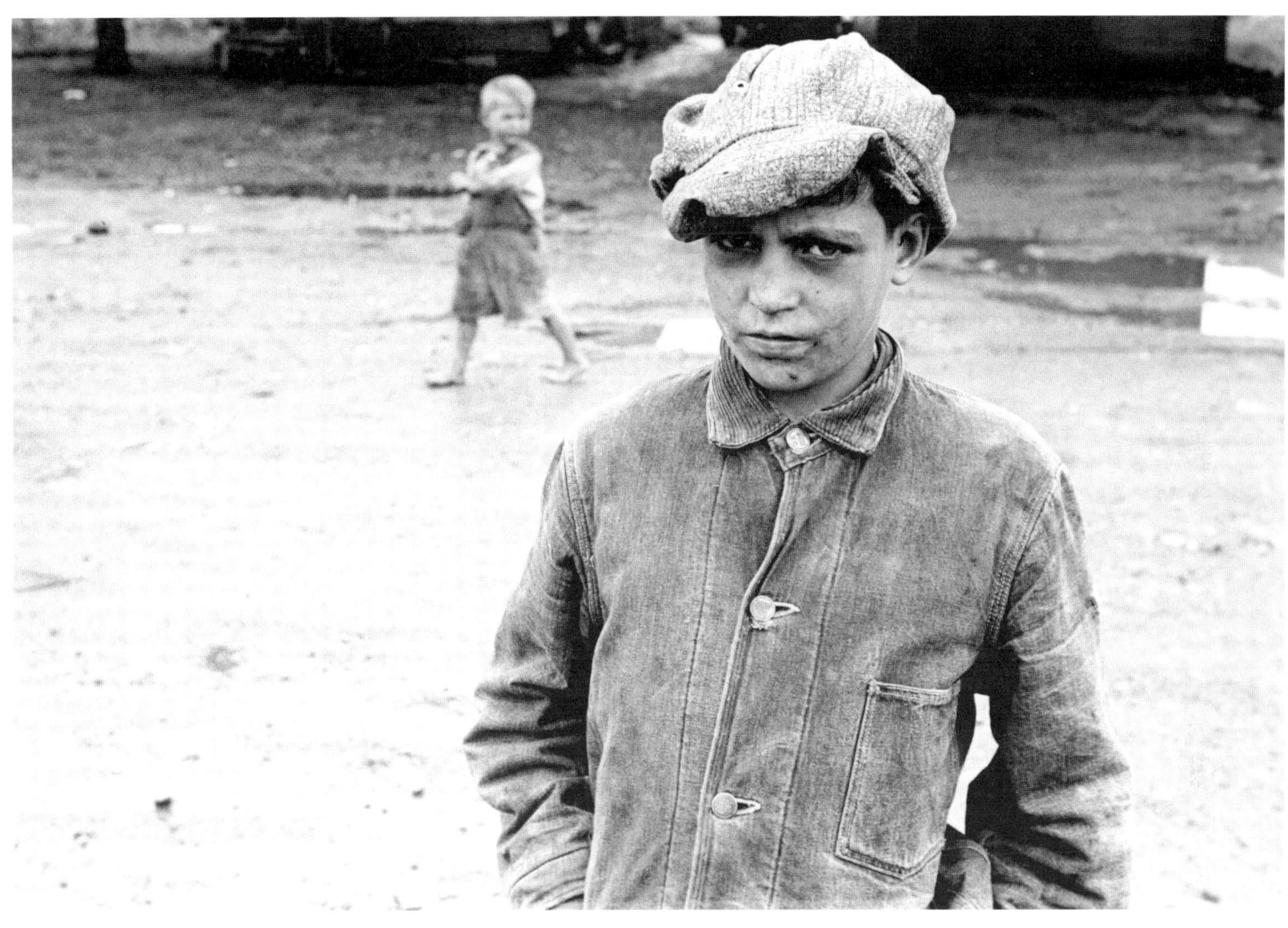

FIG 88 Dwellers in Circleville's "Hooverville," central Ohio

decent facilities for play that any child deserves (fig. 89). That portrait's implicit metaphor of human junk is explicitly delivered in a more expansive study of a tousle-haired boy of seven or eight striking a nonchalant pose with an elfin smile and his hands jauntily thrust into the pockets of his overalls. The photograph's asymmetrical composition gives equal emphasis to the engaging lad and the disorderly pile of refuse behind him, the juxtaposition revealing the dreariness of his surroundings, but even more intimating that he, like the trash, is regarded as a discard of little value or consequence (fig. 90).

That equation condoned the shantytown's existence and was the fruit of a general aversion to—and even contempt for—individuals disadvantaged by the Depression, who, like refuse, were judged unsightly and disposable, to be kept out of sight, or, if not, shamed. By making the metaphor's cruel abstraction tangible and then dramatizing its falsity with sympathetic portraits of the Hooverville's residents, Shahn meant to demolish it. What ideologies and values lay behind it were not ones the camera could readily portray, but Shahn could create a counternarrative by bringing impoverished citizens into public view with more sensitivity than relief officials, who intended to stigmatize their clients by requiring them to display their need to their neighbors. Just as in exposing this bureaucratic contempt he emphasized the relief recipients' indistinguishability from other citizens, when he photographed the Hooverville's pathological conditions he also invoked the normative by concentrating on families and especially their children, whose lives were being stunted despite their parents' tender ministrations. Deploying photography's unparalleled ability to illuminate the particular and making astute judgments about emphasis, Shahn strove to invite empathy with as well as pity for the Hooverville's dwellers, and against both responses, but especially empathy, the social abstraction that generalized them as disposable entities could not stand.

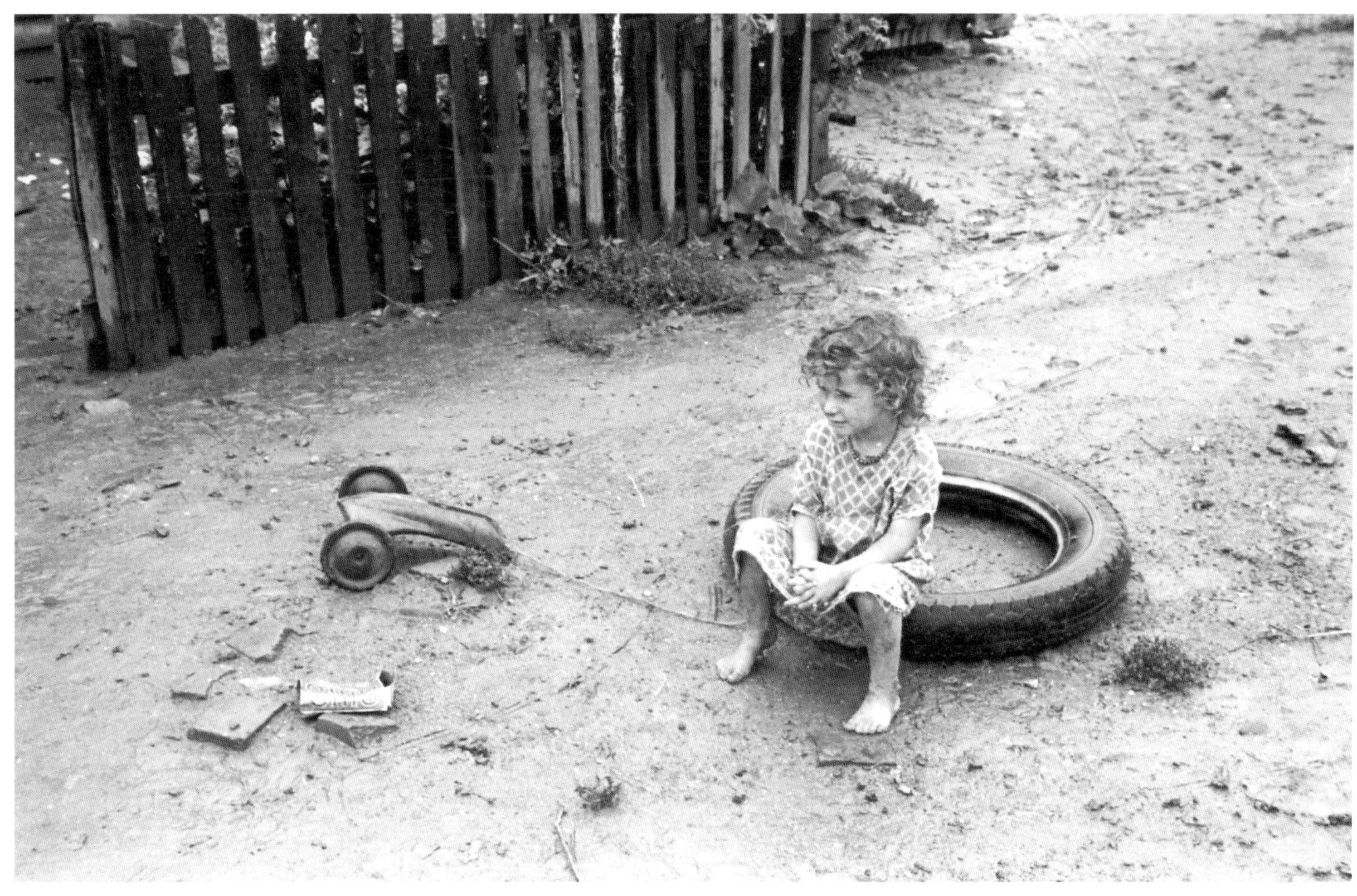

FIG 89 Dwellers in Circleville's "Hooverville," central Ohio

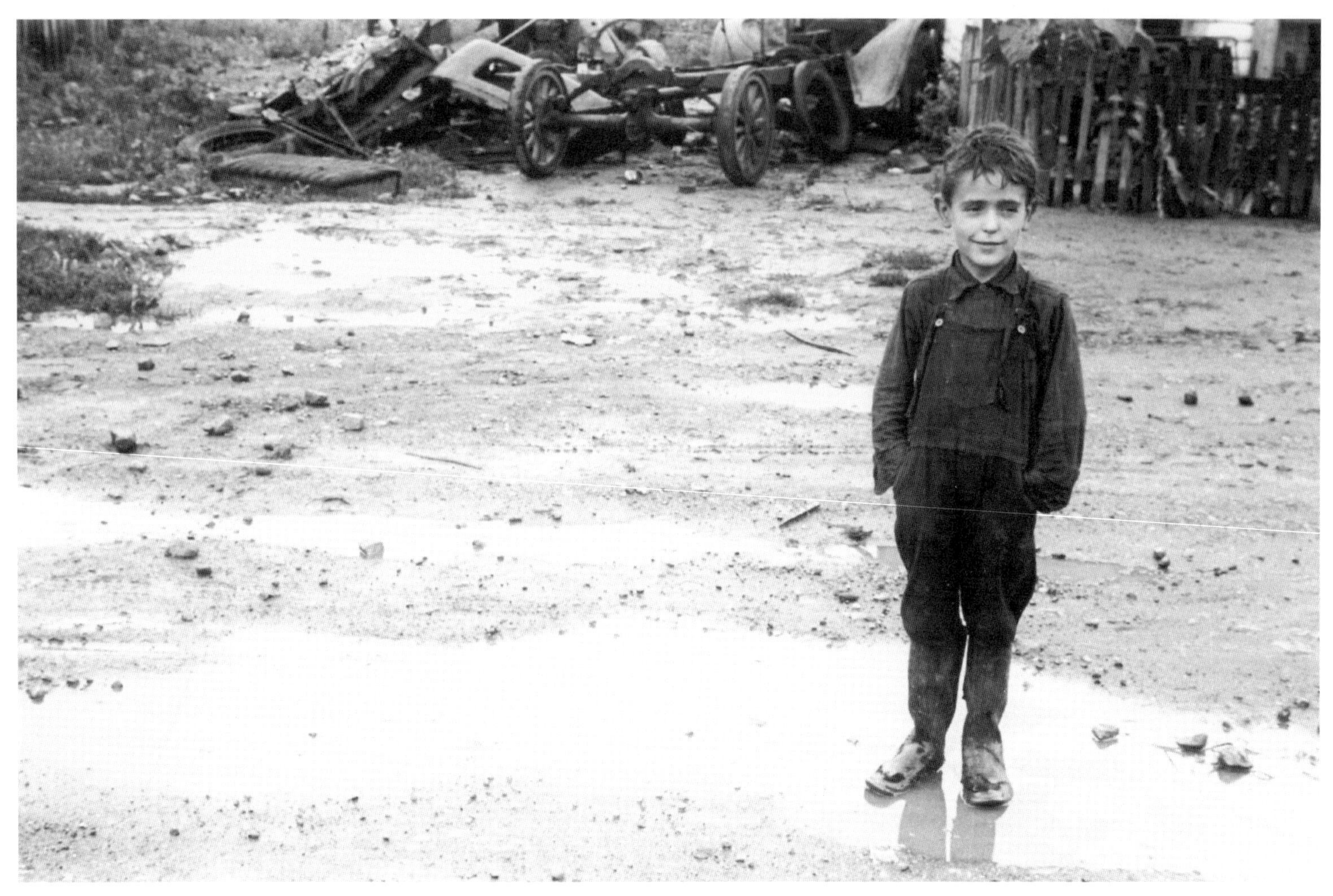

FIG 90 Dwellers in Circleville's "Hooverville," central Ohio

INDIGNATION RATHER THAN commiseration fueled Shahn's photographs of African Americans, who, like the poor, were marginalized in Ohio's towns, but indelibly so, because their experiences as citizens were shaped by such pervasive, entrenched, and apparently immutable codes of racial discrimination as to defy melioration short of a national determination to redefine the scope of American democracy. Because the will to undertake that revaluation was not so much as faintly on the horizon in the late 1930s—Congress could not even pass anti-lynching legislation, nor would President Roosevelt support it—the white majority's virtually uncontested embrace of racism presented such a blatant contradiction to Stryker's belief in small-town egalitarianism that his script expediently refrained from indicating that these communities could contain any African Americans at all. But central Ohio towns did have black residents, more than 5,000 in the eight rural counties where Shahn photographed, about 2 percent of their population. Evidence of his indignation at the script's tendentious color blindness is that nearly 8 percent of his photographs depict black subjects, considerably more than a proportional representation would require, and that his tone in several of these studies is more corrosive than in his other work from that summer.

Not all, or even most, directly reference the habitual racial discrimination of the thirties, although *any* photograph of African Americans inevitably evoked it, because even the most oblivious viewer could not fail to identify its subjects as members of a pariah caste consigned by inviolable custom if not law to a subordinate social and usually economic station beneath all whites. "A cleaning and pressing shop in Urbana, Ohio" is titled without reference to the young African American in its doorway; nor does the photograph reveal any obvious signs of racial discrimination. Without him it would be another of Shahn's studies of artistic signage, three lettering styles specifying the Pantitorium's faux-Latin name and services, with the bonus of a rich set of reflections in the window. One of these is of Shahn himself, seen in profile and using his angle finder as he apparently aims down the sidewalk, although a post obscures some of his reflection. The young man, looking in the same direction, has likely been drawn to the doorway to see what Shahn is photographing. The shot was almost certainly a lucky accident, and the young man's unexpected presence provided an opportunity to add to the photograph a resonance it would not have had were he white. Not only does it document the presence of African Americans in Urbana and thus contradict their invisibility in Stryker's script, but so encompassing and universally understood was the regime of subordination based on racial phenotype that the young man's body is inevitably, for black and white viewers alike, an unmistakable signifier of it (fig. 91).

A Marysville photograph is also nominally of a local business and has a similarly denotative title, "Real estate and loan office." Vernacular signage is again the picture's most assertive element, but Shahn composed asymmetrically and from a great enough distance so as also to include a black man seated on the windowsill of an adjacent barbershop. In this case his inclusion is not fortuitous: had Shahn wanted only the titular subject, he could easily have moved a few feet closer to eliminate the man. His body emits the same cultural implications as the young man's in the Pantitorium's door, but the photograph also hints at how racial codes circumscribe African Americans' economic opportunities, relegating them to menial work. While there is no way of knowing for sure, this man is almost certainly the shoeshine "boy" employed by this barbershop and is passing time while business is slack. Even if his trim appearance and proximity to the barber's pole did not suggest it, that he lounges on the shop's windowsill does, inasmuch as racial convention would prohibit any black man not an employee from perching himself so in front of a white business (fig. 92).[1]

Shahn made just a handful of close-in, individual portraits in Ohio. His study of a brawny, broad-shouldered African American of middle years is among the most compelling. The man's concentrated gaze, clenched pipe, and akimbo stance give him an air of self-possession that dominates the photograph, despite its exceptionally busy background of a menswear store's window displaying hats and haberdashery. Although it is likely that Shahn used his angle finder, the portrait's lighting is so adeptly managed—sunlight angling from the side so as to

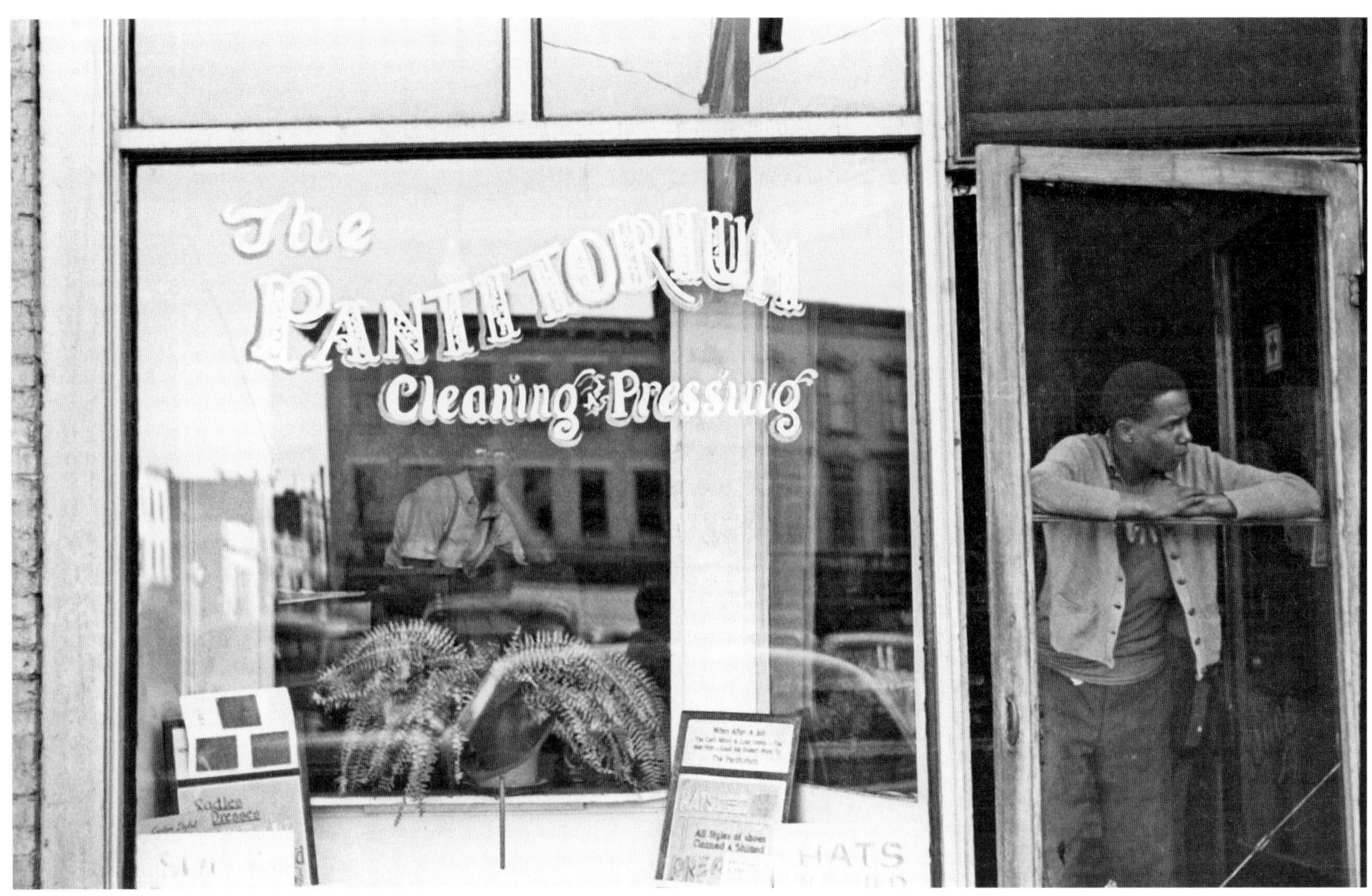

FIG 91 A cleaning and pressing shop in Urbana, Ohio

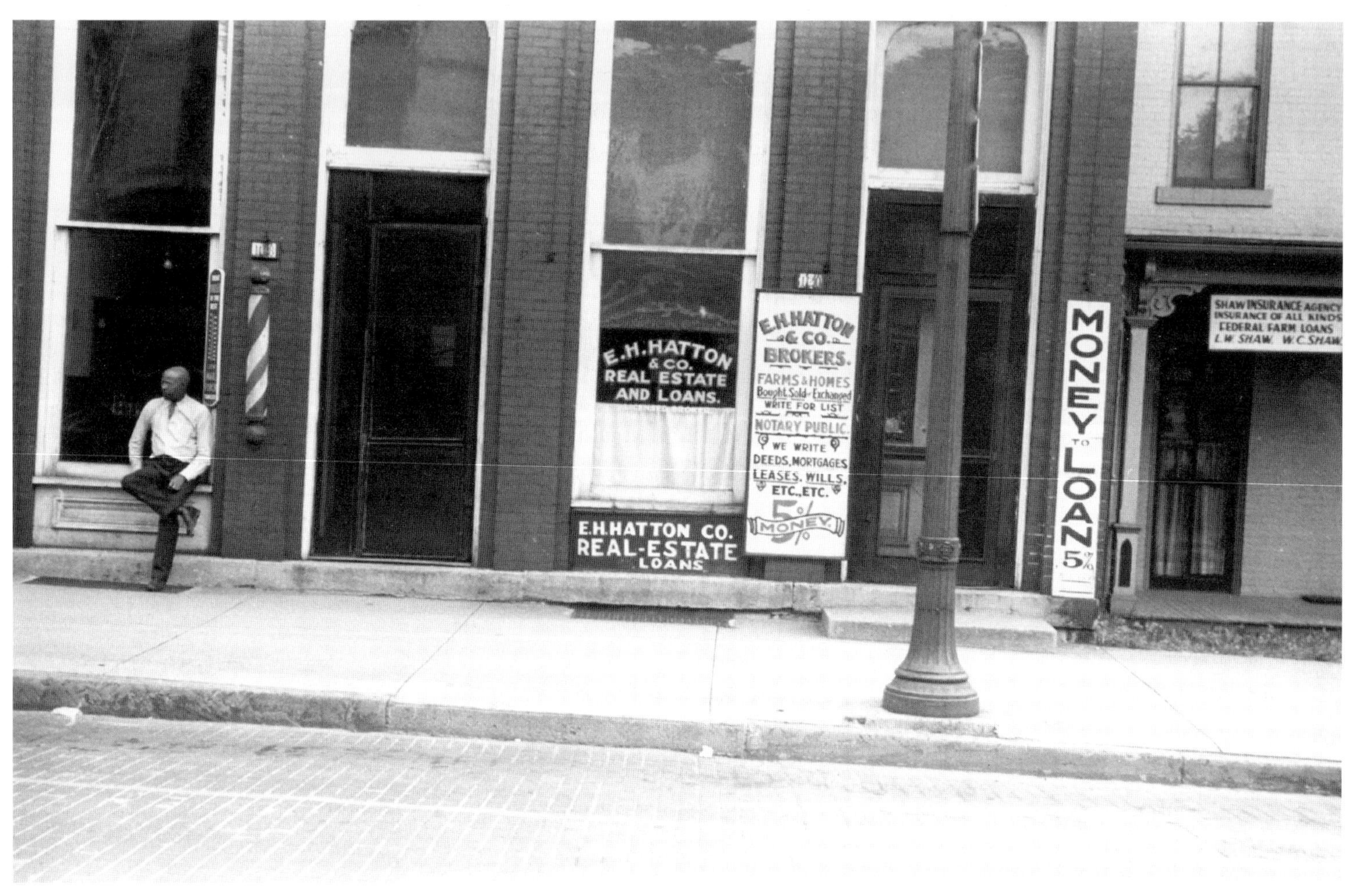

FIG 92 Real estate and loan office, Marysville, Ohio

fall on just the man's hat and right shoulder and sleeve—and the subject is so composed that it is impossible to know for certain. Shahn titled it "Resident of Plain City, Ohio," which was consonant with his practice of not using the word "Negro" or "colored" (the era's polite terms) or "black," all of which were common in titles and captions by his FSA colleagues. Instead, in addition to "residents," Shahn denominated African Americans as "citizens," or he used a generic title such as "street scene," or, as with the Marysville and Urbana photographs, one that pointedly elided their human subjects. Titles and photographs thus went in different although not contradictory directions. If the photographs could not avoid invoking socially constructed notions of difference, their verbal gloss implied that they were (or ought to be) immaterial, a consistency in nomenclature for black and white subjects proclaiming his conviction that race was an artificial and undemocratic category.

Just beyond the Plain City man's shoulder at the frame's edge is an advertising thermometer prominently displaying the word "FREE." This juxtaposition serves as both a historical allusion and a counterpoint to his stalwartness. By recalling emancipation seventy-five years earlier, it heralds his standing as a citizen, but it is also a sardonic reminder that most of the privileges guaranteed by his citizenship had since been so systematically undermined by endemic racism that the concept had become an empty legalism (fig. 93).

The many customary forms of subordination that racism had given rise to were often tacit and thus difficult for the camera to reveal, in that they designated such intimate behaviors as physical and verbal deference in blacks' interactions with whites and more generally their "knowing their place." In his shot of the shoeshine attendant, Shahn managed to find a way to imply one of these, racially defined differential access to public spaces, and to suggest a structural feature of segregation that permitted blacks only low-status work, but these observations were oblique, and he looked for sites that would make the atmosphere of bigotry more explicit.

As with the chain-store signage that indicated modernity's inroads, he employed graphic elements to vivify this abstract perception. In two photographs of signs he moved closer than usual, eliminating much of their settings to magnify their racial content. On a street hoarding, a minstrel show poster unabashedly flaunts a set of derogatory stereotypes that were unchanged since slavery and in fact often referenced it. The advertisement features repetitive representations of white performers in blackface, their lips and popping eyes exaggerated,

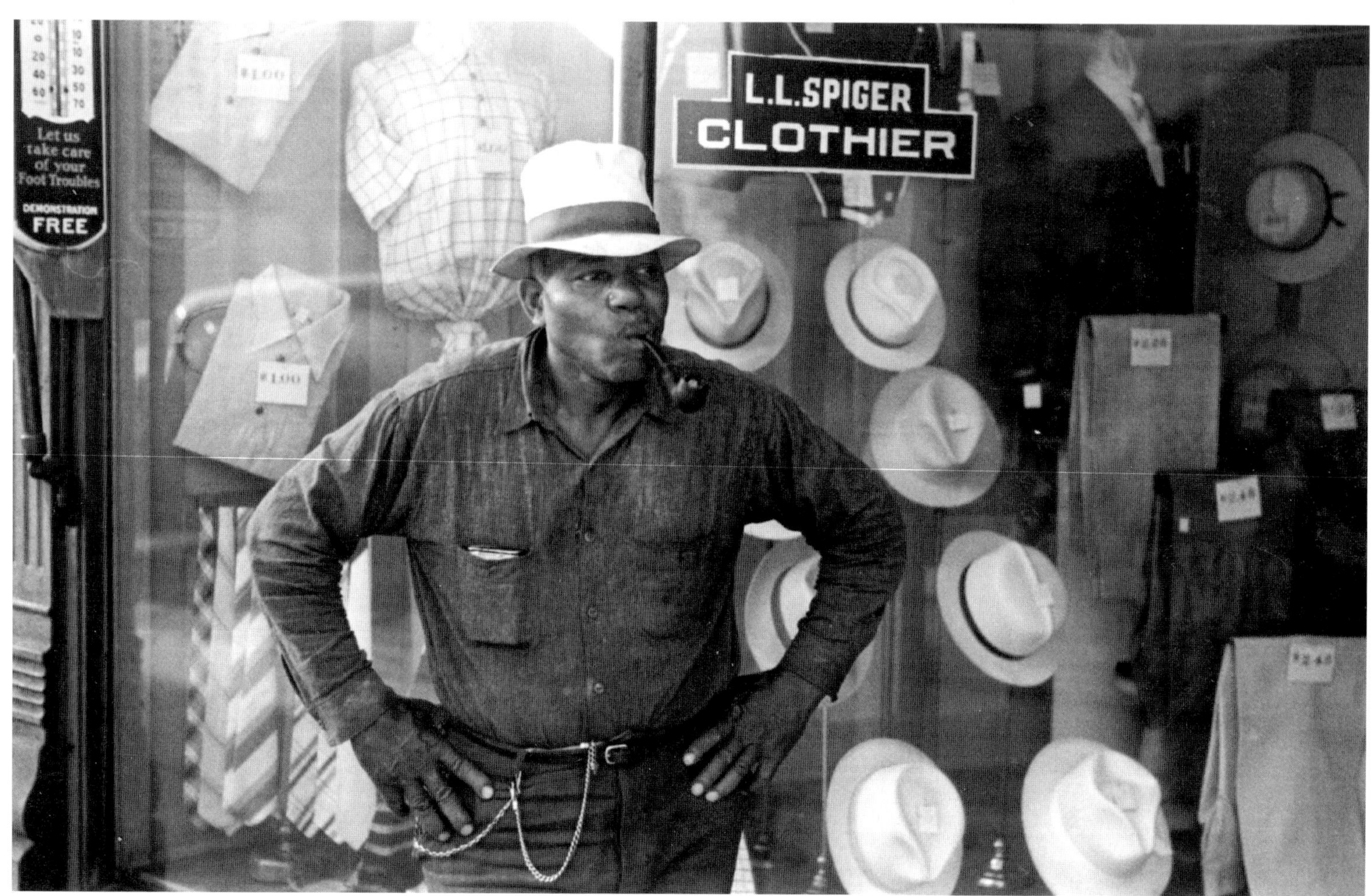

FIG 93 Resident of Plain City, Ohio

their formal dress absurdly anomalous, and their capabilities confined to music, dance, and self-demeaning verbal humor that depended on the audience's preconceptions about blacks' gullibility, ignorance, and loose morality. Whether this minstrel show was a sideshow of the Downie Bros. Circus, also advertised, is unclear, but the proximate representation of a circus elephant suggested that both it and the performers were exotic, nonindigenous representatives of a primitive "darkest Africa" (fig. 94). Minstrel shows were a nearly defunct form of entertainment by the late thirties, but not because of any general revulsion toward the demeaning stereotypes they purveyed: the movies and radio that had supplanted them regularly drew on the same stereotypes, as the enormous contemporary popularity of the *Amos 'n' Andy* radio program indicated.

A sign in a restaurant window—"We cater to white trade only"—provides the most categorical evidence of how utterly racism permeated the towns' daily life. Jim Crow was not legally prescribed as in the South, but its customary practice in Ohio was similarly intended to be an omnipresent reminder to African American residents of their inferior status. Especially it strove to prohibit occasions on which social mixing of the races might occur. Shahn composed to center the sign in the picture's upper half, so that a dining table is visible through the window as an emblem of what the exclusion of African Americans from the restaurant was determined to prevent (fig. 95).

Two linked photographs that Shahn made at a bus station intimate how universally social interactions were racially segregated. The first centers on two African American men in front of the station, and aside from their shared skin color, it emphasizes their dissimilarity. One is young and slender, the other middle-aged and stocky. The younger man's double-pocketed work shirt and cloth cap indicate that he is a manual laborer, as does his lunchbox, while the older one's white shirt and billed cap mark him as a service employee. The younger man stares quizzically at something down the street (possibly trying to see what Shahn seems to be photographing); the older man looks ruminatively straight ahead. The photograph is an uncommonly expressive double portrait, distinctly individualizing each man as they participate in the sort of sidewalk gathering that Shahn photographed elsewhere. He evenly divided the composition between the men and a view of the bus station's window and waiting room. Possibly he wanted to include the signage and interior for their visual interest, but

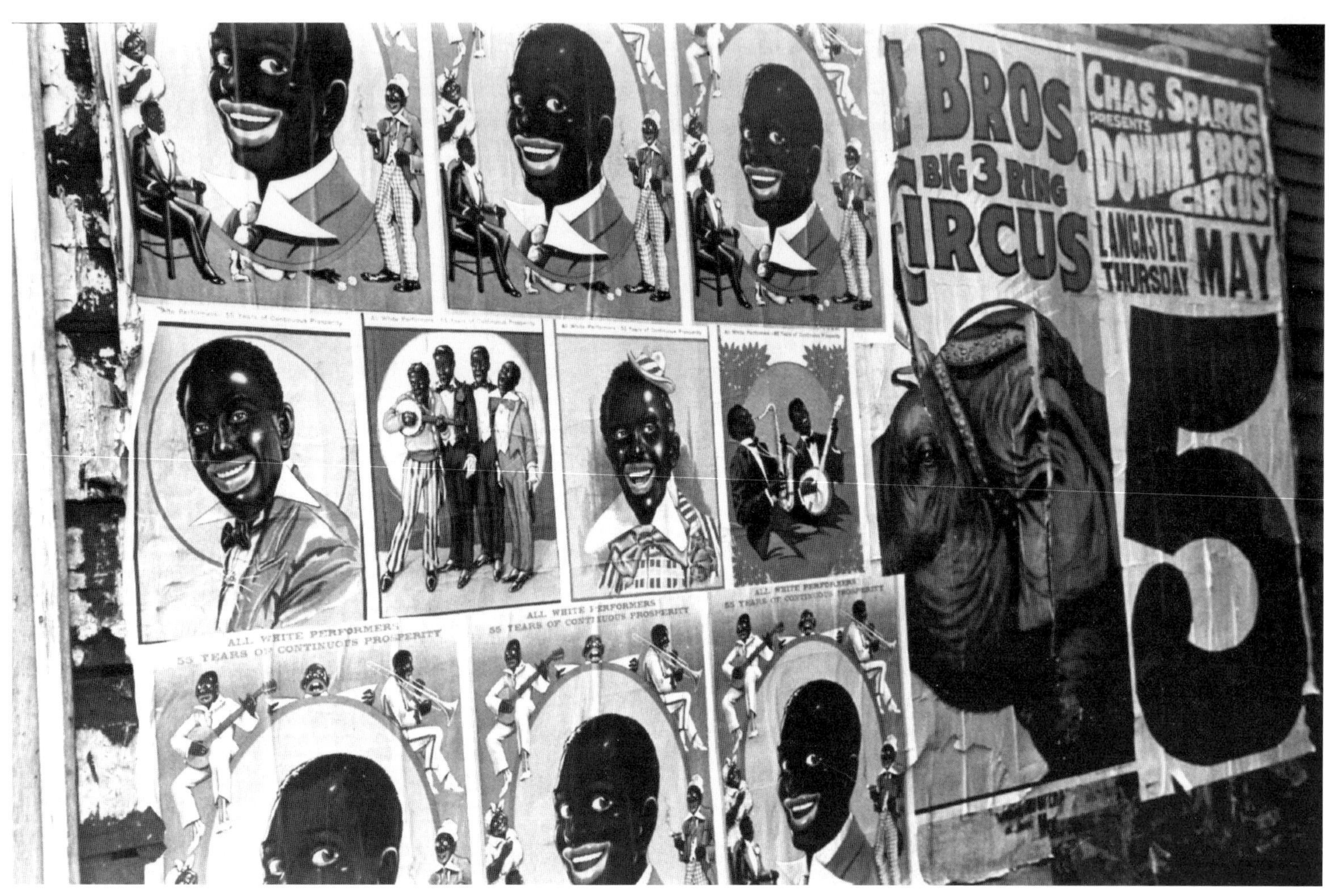

FIG 94 Circus poster, Circleville, Ohio

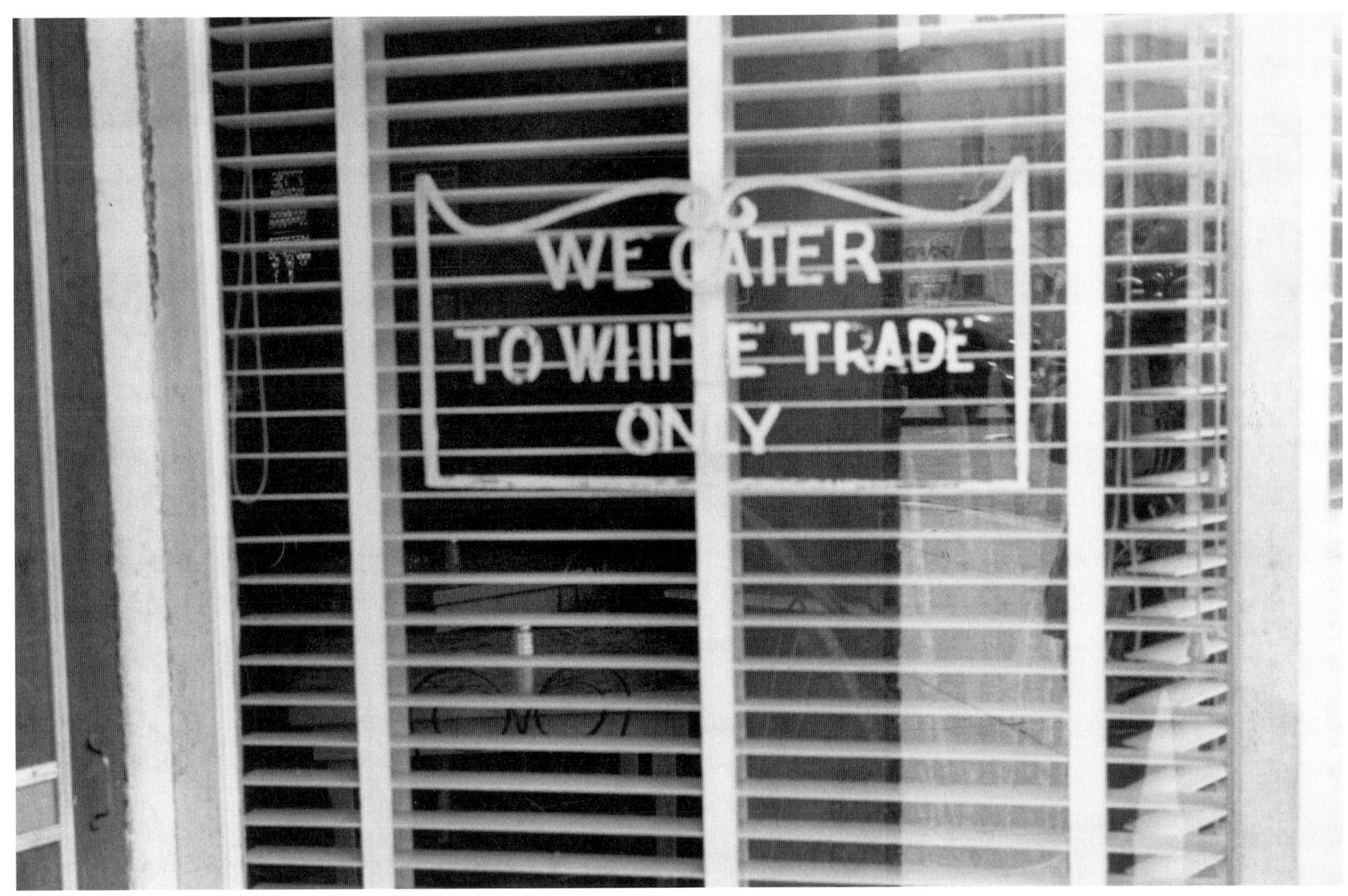

FIG 95 Sign on restaurant, Lancaster, Ohio

that framing also suggests that the men wait on the sidewalk because their race would make them unwelcome inside (fig. 96).

A side view of the bus station portrays a second conversational group, this one composed of whites whose sidewalk kibitzing, as in other of Shahn's photographs, melts normative social distinctions: its participants include a man in overalls, another in suit and tie, and a third sporting a natty straw skimmer. Shahn was careful in composing to include the two black men in front of the station. These adjacent gatherings make it clear that the small town's sidewalk democracy does not transcend racial difference. Each view of the bus station can stand alone, but paired they make visible the tacit racial codes that regulate the small town's daily life (fig. 97).[2]

Another pair of photographs, of a tavern's black piano player, are the most caustic Shahn made that summer, and also unique inasmuch as they are interior views shot with a flash. The use of artificial lighting was contrary to his professed principle, and that he overrode it on this single occasion suggests that he believed the malignancy of the racism expressed in the tavern was emblematic and could not be as unequivocally revealed using his usual methods. The bar presented an opportunity to observe a racial interaction that would be difficult or perhaps impossible to document on town streets. His indignation about racial injustice fueled these photographs, and it is also evident in two other of their features. He added them to the FSA file even though their harsh, awkward lighting made them the least esthetically controlled of his small-town pictures, and he also uniquely gave them a title reeking with sarcasm: "Wonder Bar, hot spot of Circleville, Ohio."[3]

The first depicts a black man, seen from behind, playing an upright piano; the intensity of the artificial light saturates his white shirt and the piano's keys to give him heightened emphasis in the otherwise murky barroom. Shahn framed him slightly off-center, even though the flash creates an unpleasant glare on the varnished surface of an adjacent screen, so as to include in the composition only enough of the bar's counter to show a single patron and thus supply the context for the piano player without diminishing his centrality. His job is to entertain patrons, and while he is at the piano they are indifferent to his presence, as the turned back of the one at the bar indicates (fig. 98).

In the second picture he has finished his set and is timorously exiting the barroom. His hunched posture and deferentially downcast expression do not discourage the white patrons

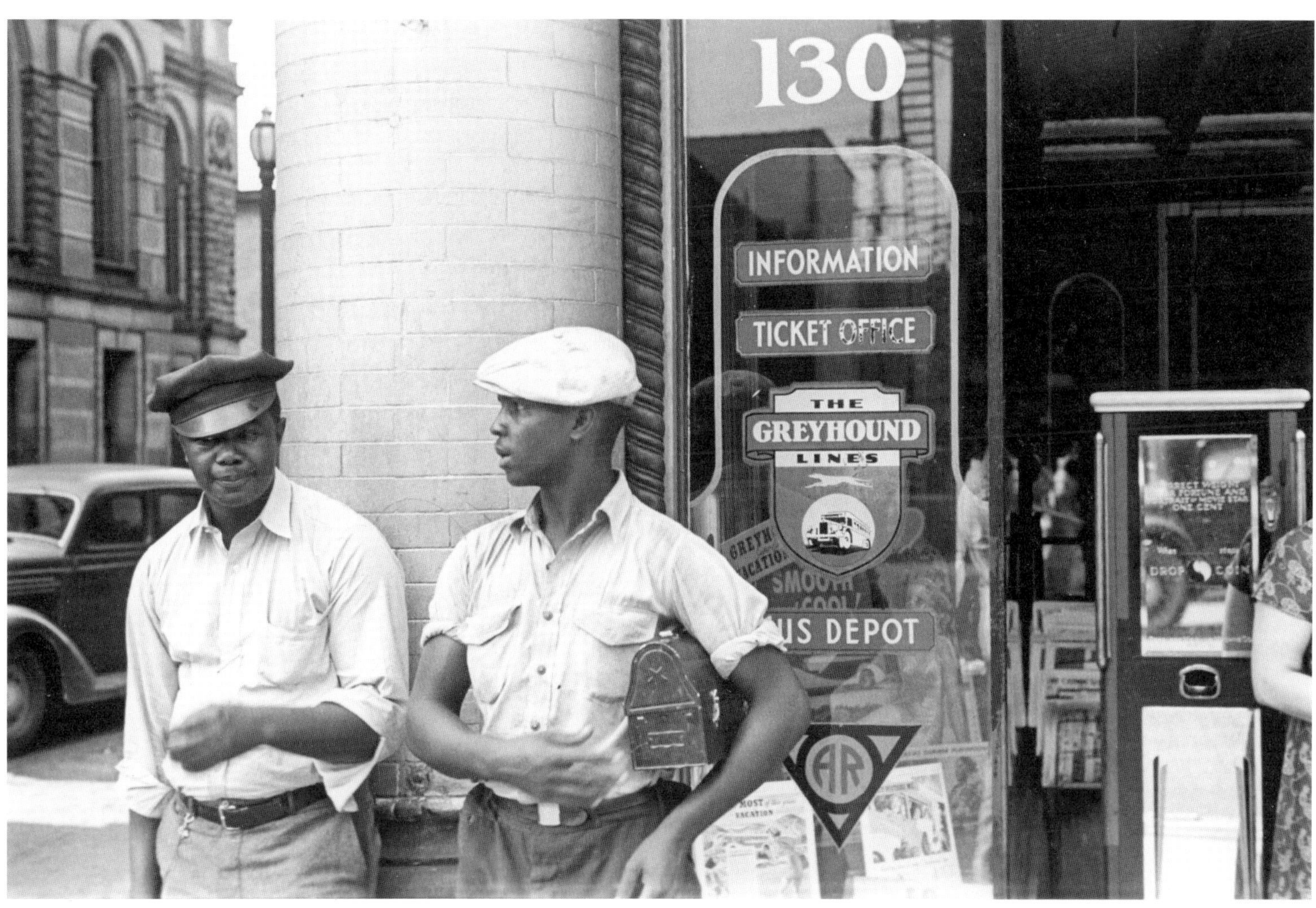

FIG 96 Bus station, Marion, Ohio

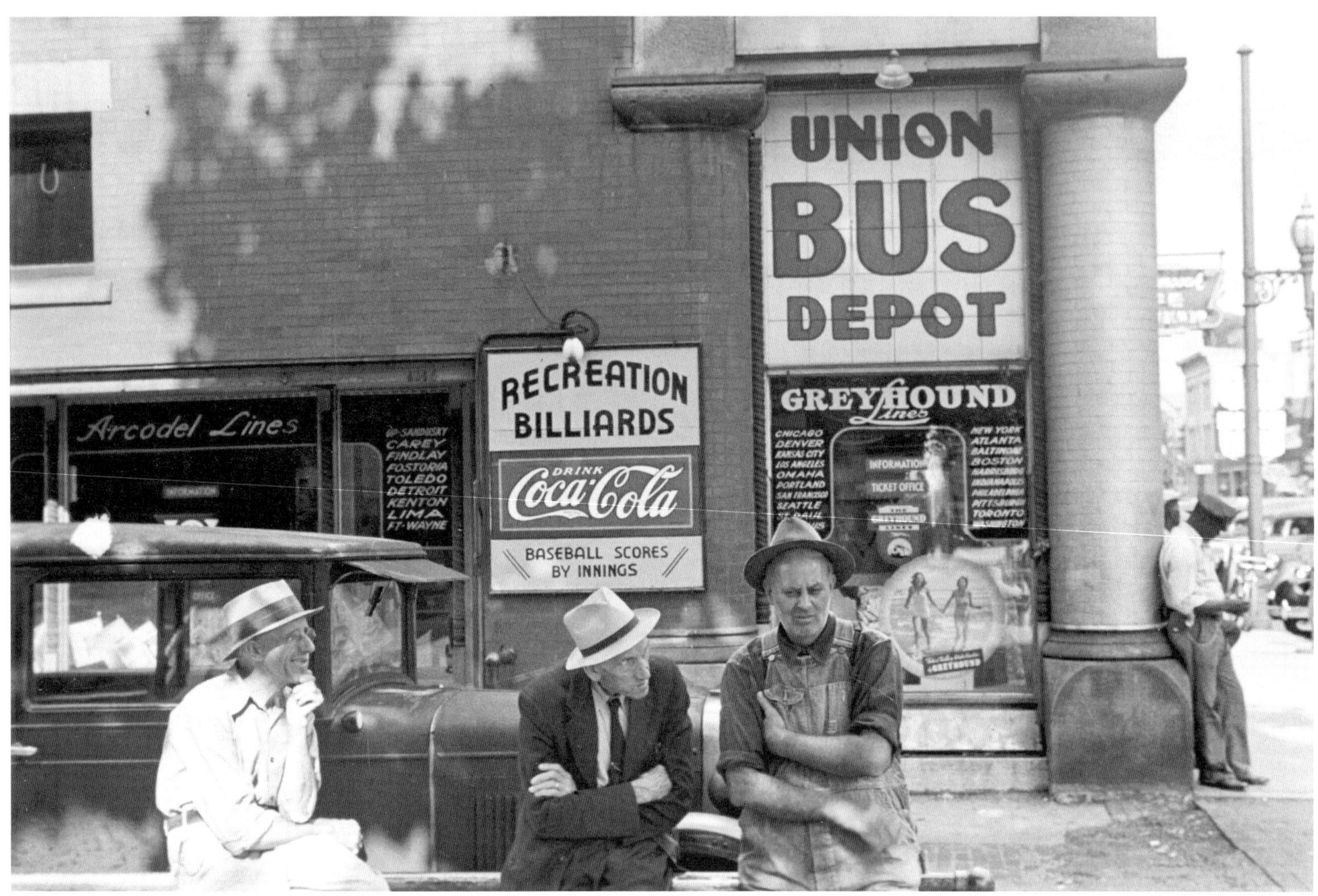

FIG 97 Bus station, Marion, Ohio

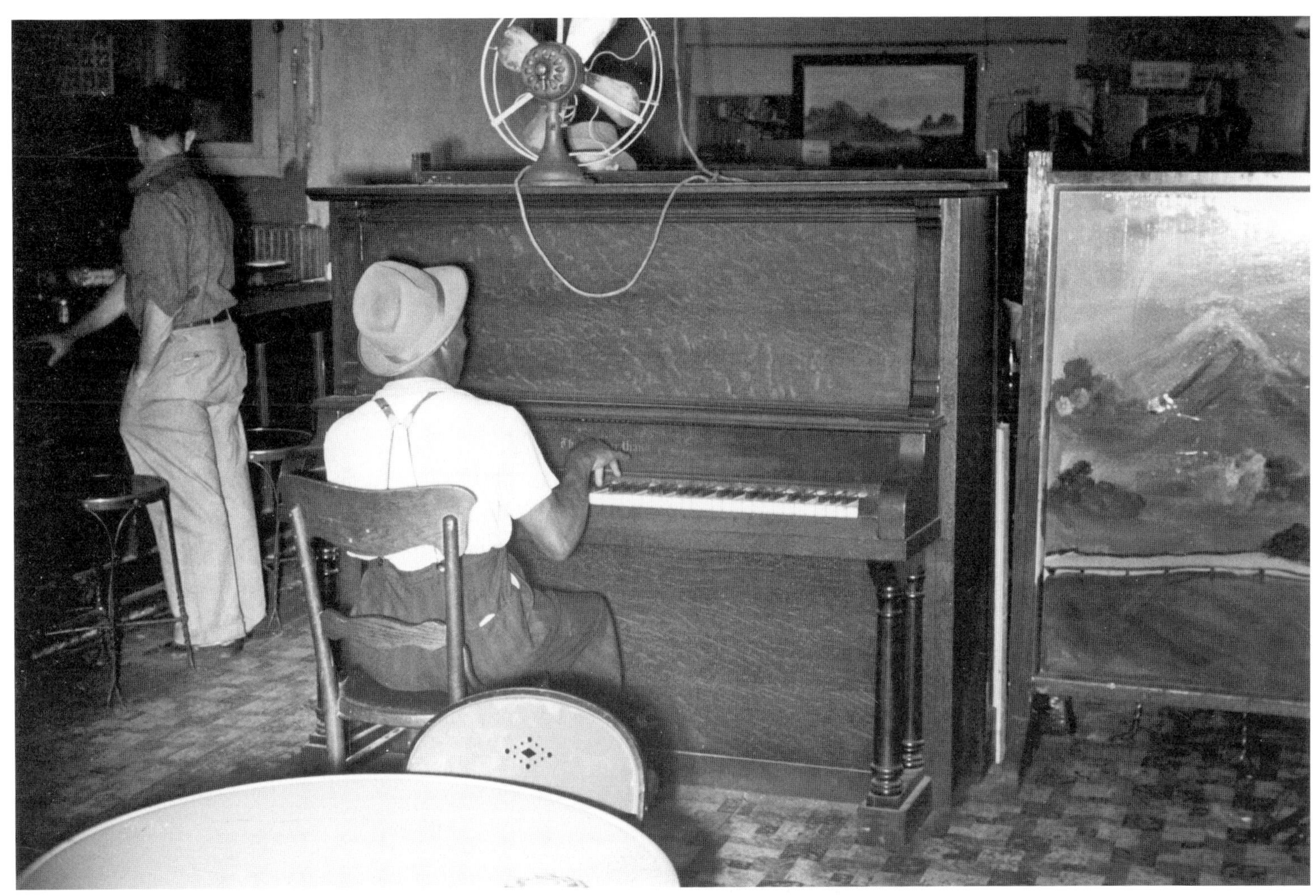

FIG 98 Wonder Bar, hot spot in Circleville, Ohio

from a glowering surveillance of his passage. While seated at the piano and providing entertainment, he is essentially invisible to them, but away from it they regard his presence as not only unwelcome but a transgression. All present acknowledge it, the piano player by his abjectness and the patrons by their surliness. The culture's poisonous racism is not solely structural but deforms even the most commonplace personal behaviors, encouraging whites to become arrogant bullies and blacks to be obsequious ciphers (fig. 99).

Shahn, however, did not assume that the appearance of servility this piano player was obliged to adopt accurately represented black consciousness any more than did the caricatures flaunted by the minstrel poster, although both indicated how thoroughly racism pervaded these small towns. Thus he also took care to make expressive portraits of African American individuals that owed nothing to such notions, such as the images of the pair in front of the bus station or the sturdy Plain City man. If Ohio's black citizens were unquestionably victims of a gross injustice, in his survey that fact alone did not define them. The strongest of these portraits is of an African American photographer, in which Shahn presents his subject with a remarkable gravitas and which is also rich in self-reflexivity.

The photographer specialized in tintypes, playing-card-sized portraits on a thin metal plate that could be rapidly developed on the spot and then delivered to the sitter. Their convenience and inexpensiveness made them the most popular photographic process during the nineteenth century, and until the development of the Polaroid camera in 1948, they were the nearest that photographic technology came to producing an instant picture. Following the wide diffusion of simple box cameras loaded with flexible film, the popularity of tintypes waned around the turn of the twentieth century, but into the thirties, itinerant photographers continued to make them, mostly serving a clientele for whom portrait studios or personal cameras were too dear.

Although there is no knowing with certainty, in making this portrait Shahn must have had his angle finder switched off. His nearness to the sitter, the tintypist's direct, frank gaze into the lens, and the careful composition all indicate that it is posed. For many of his photographs depicting individuals, Shahn used his angle finder to imbue his pictures with a spontaneous air—a fragment of emblematic daily life caught on the fly—but a more deliberate, formal address was required with this fellow craftsman, especially to honor in kind his métier of artful portraiture. Such a posed, intimate representation also documents that the two photographers had been engaged in a social interaction, and in that sense it flouts the basic premise underly-

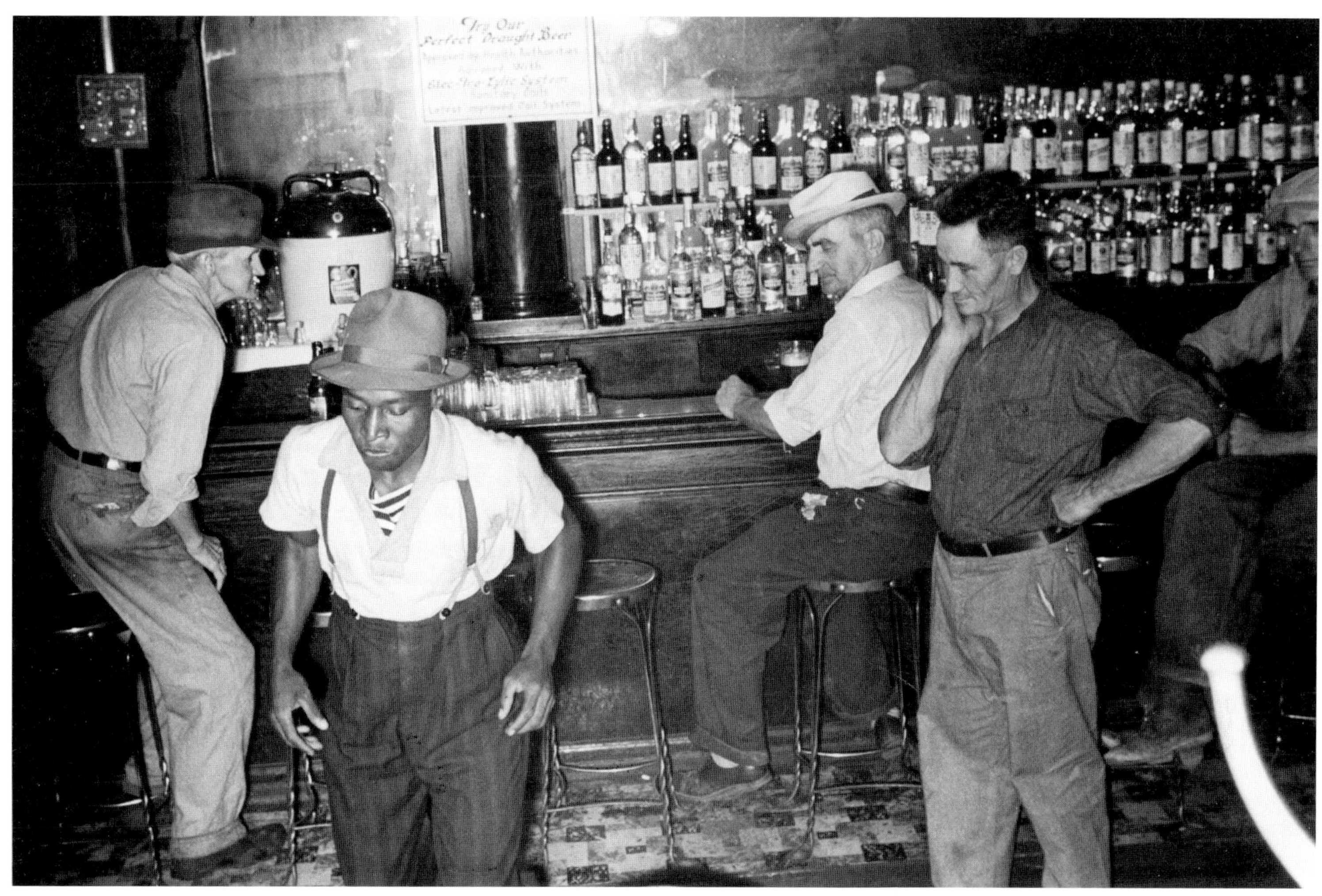

FIG 99 Wonder Bar, hot spot of Circleville, Ohio

ing codes of racial separation. Behind his camera the tintypist is an artist at work—his sleeves rolled up, his apron draped to protect his clothing during the developing process, his hand steadying his tripod, his work exhibited on the camera's long side. Shooting obliquely, Shahn composed to make a restaurant window occupy the frame's nearest third, so as to avoid the diffuseness that a more expansive view including more of the receding storefronts and sidewalk would have produced, and he made the focus shallow to establish an envelope of defining space around the tintypist.

The portrait not only emphasizes the tintypist's unimpeachable dignity, it also hails him as Shahn's artistic colleague, in spite of the differences in their equipment, working methods, and intentions. The tintypist employed a cumbersome camera and an archaic process to make commissioned portraits for private consumption, whereas Shahn used his portable, up-to-date 35 mm Leica to shoot documentary studies, many candid, for a mammoth federal archive. But they shared more fundamental similarities. As itinerant workers discovering their subjects along unfamiliar sidewalks, both relied on the camera's inherent capacity to isolate the subject of a photograph from the inchoate flux of ordinary experience, and on their visual imagination to bring out that subject's essential qualities; both, moreover, concentrated their attention on "the average American," on that segment of society that Shahn believed was insufficiently represented in documentary's corpus (fig. 100).

In light of the portrait's valorization of the tintypist as a fellow citizen in the republic of photography, the fact that he is black is immaterial. To disregard the prevailing ideology of race and advertise such an equality, though, was to adopt a profoundly heterodox stance, as Shahn well knew. His pictures had documented the pervasiveness of racial discrimination and its effects on the daily experience of black Ohioans, from limiting their access to public space or where they might eat lunch to the deference they were expected to show in the presence of their white neighbors. Shahn's respectful portrait of his fellow professional—the strongest he made of anyone that summer—contradicted the white majority's stigmatization of African Americans based on the assumption that their black skin proclaimed them to be inherently unequal, and it also reflected his conviction that an artist's obligation was to hold a mirror up to society at such an angle as to require people to confront what they otherwise tried to avoid seeing—in this case a black man whose composed dignity left no doubt of his claim to social equality.

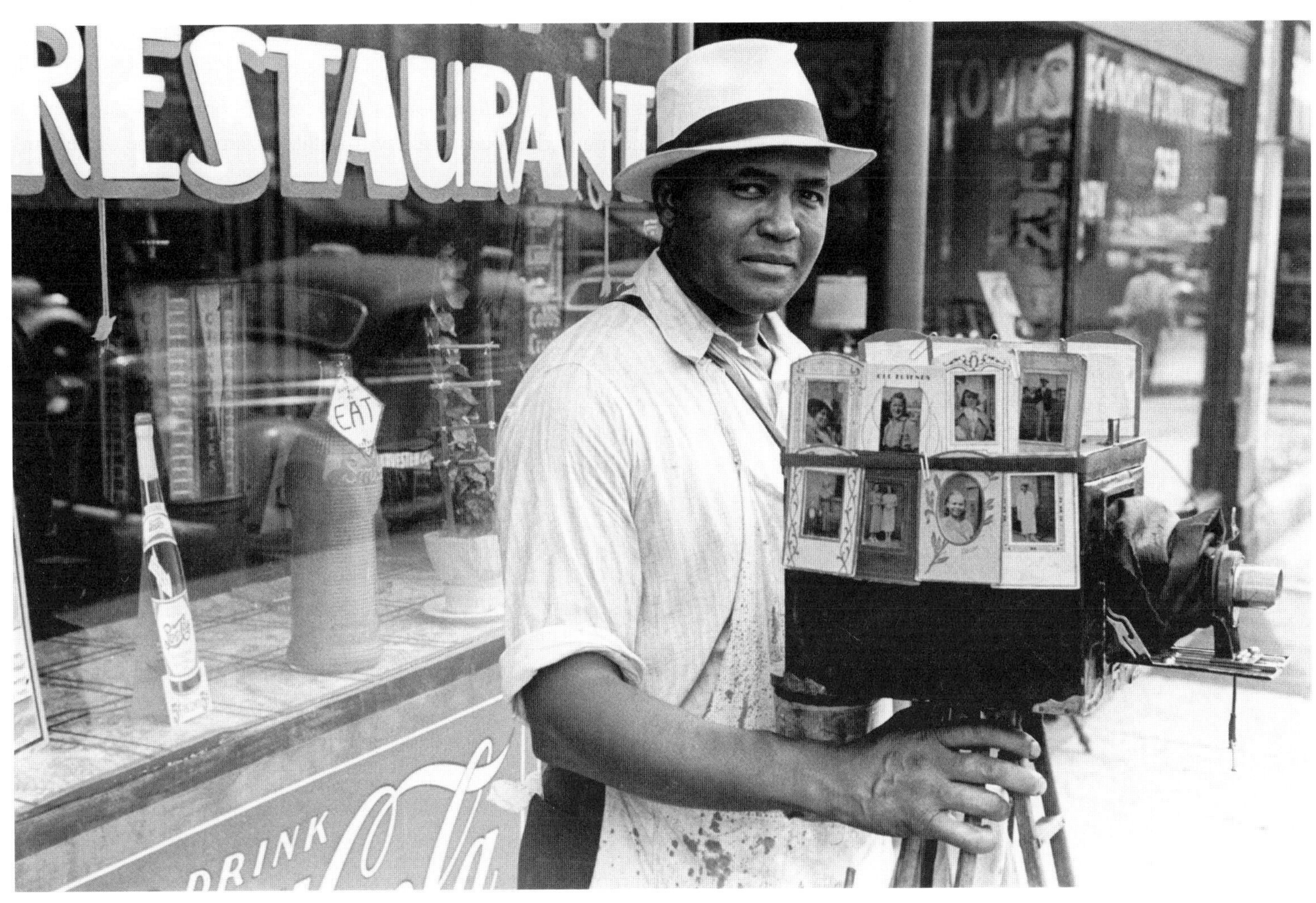

FIG 100 Itinerant photographer in Columbus, Ohio

Shahn's portrait of the tintypist, no less than his more obvious depictions of racial injustice, reflected his indignation at the script's erasure of black citizens and his determination
to make them visible, even though that invalidated Stryker's assumption that the small town
was a bastion of the democratic ethos. While the script's premise was one that Shahn had
also seconded in a number of his studies, the skepticism that is an essential feature of the
artist's sensibility also made him receptive to what contradicted it, as the small town's racial
discrimination and scorn for the depression's victims most egregiously did. Eliding these
victims of social prejudice—Stryker's response to what discomfited his views—was thus for
Shahn an impossibility.

Shahn's Negative Capability

SHAHN'S DIVERGENCES from Stryker's script seem to suggest a venerable narrative in which an uncompromising artist thwarts a patron's—in this case a government bureaucrat's—determination to manage, contain, and shackle the artist's afflatus in order to make it serve the interests of state power or flatter the patron's ego. In fact, such an indictment of Stryker as an overbearing martinet who tyrannized the photographers has been made in some appraisals of the FSA's Historical Section, which have singled out his shooting scripts as evidence of his high-handedness.[1] But this critique greatly exaggerates the scripts' prescriptive authority and depends on a naïve view of how photographs make meaning. More specifically, its simplistic binary is inadequate for understanding Shahn's small-town survey, its congruities as well as incongruities with Stryker's views.

The scripts were not grids circumscribing authorized picture topics. Stryker drew them up, he said, to stimulate the photographers' "curiosity and ingenuity," and there is no evidence that a script ever restrained their individual creativity.[2] As several of the photographers later testified, he consistently urged them to follow wherever their own eyes led them, irrespective of what a script proposed. He "wouldn't tell you what to photograph at all, ever," one unequivocally declared.[3] In any case, a script merely enumerated subject possibilities without any hint, much less specification, of how they ought to be addressed, and to suppose that a list of topics is tantamount to a set of actual photographs requires disregarding how decisive a photographer's formal choices are to the interpretation that any picture puts forward.

Nevertheless, behind any such list are guiding assumptions, the most basic of which is that the cultural realm being itemized is especially worth photographing. Stryker's conviction that

small towns were such a realm rested on the supporting assumptions that these communities were fundamentally healthy and intrinsically democratic, and that they had resolutely
maintained their traditional ways in the face of modernity's transforming energies and the
exigencies of the Depression. These characteristics, he believed, made a photographic survey
of small towns the ideal vehicle with which to meet the incipient demand he sensed for representations of the enduring strengths of American democracy as reproof to antidemocratic
ideologies on the march abroad.[4]

It would be a mistake to conclude that Stryker's oversight coerced Shahn into making
the fraction of his small-town pictures that corresponded to the director's ambition. Shahn's
turn toward wanting to concentrate on "the average American" indicates his sympathy with
the broad political aim that lay behind the script, one that resonated with the photographer's
ardent anti-fascism. While all of the FSA photographers with the exception of Evans thought
of themselves as liberals or "progressives," as did Stryker, Shahn had the most obvious leftist
commitments. His twenty-three gouaches from the early thirties centering on the Sacco and
Vanzetti case had become icons for the left, and he had been an editor of the radical publication
Art Front until he resigned in 1935 to protest the magazine's acquiescence to the Communist
Party's demand that it condemn Diego Rivera for his anti-Stalinism.[5] After joining the FSA
later that year, he became a stout believer in the federal agency's often controversial programs
to relieve rural distress and was zealous to create propaganda to support them. His readiness
in Ohio to participate in the new direction the Historical Section's propaganda efforts were
beginning to take also stemmed from his political commitments. For him, as for many others
on the left in the late thirties, the apparently inexorable triumphs of fascism abroad made the
defense of democratic values an ever more pressing priority. In mid-1938, Shahn was on the
cusp of this wave in the FSA. After the Nazis' annexation of the Sudetenland and *Kristall-
nacht* later that year and the fascists' victory in the Spanish civil war the following spring, the
other photographers would begin to make more pictures in a similar vein, and following the
outbreak of the European war in September 1939, they would copiously do so.

Were the entirety of Shahn's survey to consist of his photographs of small-town democracy,
it would have only a narrow significance for anticipating the Historical Section's new direction,
and perhaps as an example of the degree to which international developments toward the end

of the thirties encouraged an uncritical celebration of American cultural practices. But the achievement of his project greatly exceeds the instrumental goal for it implicit in Stryker's script, because while Shahn did not entirely disregard the script's sanguine view of the small town, neither did he scruple at dissenting from its assumptions. If main streets provided him with numerous instances of democratic egalitarianism among white male citizens, he also gave considerable attention to the systemic racial discrimination that flagrantly violated democracy's most hallowed tenets. His pictures of downtowns revealed few if any signs of the Depression and implied that the towns had transcended its tribulations, but the destitute residents he photographed at other locations indicated the insufficiency of that impression. Some of his pictures made the physical environment of the towns beguiling, and a few suggested their vibrancy, but many others conveyed an impression of utilitarian banality and declining vitality. He equivocated most about Stryker's assumption that the small town was a bedrock of tradition. On the one hand, he downplayed such key expressions of modernity as the movies, mass media, and consumer culture, underreporting the degree to which these twentieth-century developments had penetrated Ohio's towns; on the other, he emphasized the ubiquity of the automobile and the transformations, environmental and psychological, that pivotal development was bringing about.

Shahn's receptivity to ambiguity—his portrayal of small-town culture as made up of a complex admixture of divergent tendencies—is his survey's most distinguishing hallmark. It was not heedless inconsistency: his photographs group around several related if contrasting motifs in sufficient numbers to indicate his intention to underscore the cultural conflicts they exposed. Assessing the outlook of creative workers in the Depression's waning years, Richard Pells observes that an attitude of skeptical ambivalence such as Shahn exhibited was rare. "In the late 1930s," he writes, "intellectuals as well as ordinary people were attracted to either-or propositions, yes-or-no answers"; they "could not live with ambiguity, paradox, and contradiction." That craving for certitude converged with the increasingly urgent resolve to defend democratic values, Pells says, to encourage "an indiscriminate celebration" of culture that "emphasized the rediscovery of tradition and folklore, national identity, and the common man" and swept aside whatever might darken an affirmative view of the American way of life.[6] Shahn's avoidance of that tendency and his project's nuanced multivalences not only rank his small-town studies among the FSA's outstanding achievements, but by disclosing rather than papering over some of the key cultural tensions of the thirties, these qualities also testify, in Lawrence Levine's formulation, to his photographs' "essential soundness as guides for the historian."[7]

Shahn's politics lay behind some of the ambiguities of his survey. If the growing menace of international fascism encouraged his positive depictions of Main Street egalitarianism, so did his fierce and longer-standing commitment to social justice make it impossible for him to overlook the racism and scorn for the impoverished that blighted small-town democracy. Unlike Stryker, at least in his small-town script, Shahn was unable to compartmentalize his politics even to serve a propaganda effort with which he sympathized.

The script's staunchly upbeat tone also served to spur his determination to test its assumptions. If it goes too far to say that it imagined a photographic version of a Potemkin village, its celebratory air, and omission of whatever might be an embarrassment to it, could only be a goad to an observer as independent and skeptical as Shahn. In London, at the outset of the summer's work, his critique of the script's tendentiousness became immediately apparent when he pointedly titled a sequence "the other side of the tracks," which with his depictions of democratic manners along "the main street" proposed a more nuanced view of London's social organization than the script allowed for. His dissent from the script was evident not only when he concentrated on topics it avoided, but also in how he composed some views that corresponded with it. In these photographs his formal decisions frequently, although not always, embedded an interpretation at variance with the script's assumptions, as in some downtown panoramas that intimated civic fatigue. Somewhat ironically, the script succeeded in stimulating his "curiosity and ingenuity," and in doing so contributed to his survey's rebuttal of its certitudes.

But most decisive, once Shahn was behind his camera, the artist more often than not trumped the propagandist. His omnivorous, implacable eye made him constitutionally unable to dissimulate the cultural tensions he discovered in the towns, which in his photographs were both pleasing and prosaic, democratic and bigoted, traditional and modern, sturdy and languishing. These clashing perspectives reflected the conflict between his aspiration to contribute to the defense of democratic culture by depicting its everyday practice in a quintessentially

American setting, and the irrepressibility of his artist's vocation, which demanded fidelity to the principle of unflinchingly depicting life as he found it. In theory these objectives need not have been in opposition, but once he was on the ground in Ohio, the discontinuities he discovered made a unified point of view impossible.

As an artist foremost, Shahn abundantly possessed what John Keats in 1817 called "negative capability," a disposition in which the artist is "capable of being in uncertainty, mysteries, doubts without any irritable reaching after fact and reason," and which the poet believed essential in the creation of superior works of the imagination.[8] Shahn's resolution not to be blinkered by the certainties of Stryker's script in spite of his own sympathy with its broad aims, his refusal to either idealize or debunk the towns, his incisive portrayal of them as replete with cultural tensions and contradictions, and his tolerance for ambiguity in both individual pictures and his project as a whole, all indicate how amply he possessed the negative capability that Keats saw as essential to the gifted artist's mental makeup. If these indeterminacies rendered some of his pictures ill-suited to the propaganda purposes Stryker hoped they would serve, they made Shahn's survey as a whole of enduring value to the historical archive of 1930s culture that the director was even more ambitious for the FSA photographs to become.

Notes

INTRODUCTION

1. The Farm Security Administration (FSA) began as the Resettlement Administration (RA), an independent agency created by executive order in 1935 as part of the Second New Deal. Many of its programs provided assistance to small and tenant farmers overlooked and even disabled by the Roosevelt administration's agricultural policies, initially outlined in the Agricultural Adjustment Act of 1933. In 1937, after Congress gave the RA legislative legitimacy with the Bankhead-Jones Farm Tenancy Act, it was renamed the FSA and housed in the Department of Agriculture. Under both names it was a vast, sprawling bureaucratic agency, in which the Historical Section (photographs) and Special Skills Division (fine arts) were small publicity units. In 1942, the Historical Section was detached from the FSA and assigned to the Office of War Information, operating under its aegis for another year before being shut down. In the photographic literature, it has become commonplace to conflate the Historical Section with "the FSA," a convenient usage even if it disregards the Section's administrative history and gives the impression that photography was the agency's major undertaking. That convention is followed here.

"THE AMERICAN INSTITUTION SMALL TOWN"

1. Shahn to Stryker, ca. March 27, 1938; Stryker to Shahn, April 5, 1938; Stryker to Shahn, May 21, 1938; FSA Textual Files, reel 2, Library of Congress.
2. Shahn interview with Richard Doud, April 14, 1964, 2, Archives of American Art, Smithsonian Institution, http://artarchives.si.edu/oralhist/shahn64.htm; Bernarda Shahn telephone interview with Robert W. Wagner, March 15, 1988, quoted in *Ben Shahn in Ohio: The Summer of 1938,* ed. Wagner (Upper Arlington, Ohio: The City of Upper Arlington, Cultural Arts Commission, 1988), unpaginated.
3. All of Shahn's Ohio small-town pictures can be viewed on the Library of Congress's "American Memory" website, http://memory.loc.gov/ammem/fsowhome.html, with keyword searches using

the towns' names. Also viewable are at least some of his "killed" (unprinted) shots, which are untitled but are accessible with the "Display images with neighboring call numbers" function.

4. Two versions of the small-town script exist in the Roy Stryker Papers, neither dated, although it is clear from internal evidence that the lengthier one (8 pages, plus 2 pages of additions), titled "The Small Town," came first; its composition in late 1937 is indicated by Stryker's November letter to Russell Lee asking him to look over a draft of it. The second, considerably briefer document (3 pages) contains a new preamble, "sample items" from the earlier script, and a few new items; it is titled "The Farm Security Administration Photographer Covers the American *Small Town.*" What purpose that redaction was to serve is unclear, although it may have been prepared for Marion Post Wolcott, who was hired in July 1938, because it is followed in the Stryker Papers by a memorandum about photographing in Florida, one of her earliest assignments. The Roy Stryker Papers are housed at the University of Louisville, and have been microfilmed by Chadwyck-Healey, Inc. Stryker's letter to Lee, dated November 30, 1937, is also in the Stryker Papers. Since the later script mostly condenses the earlier one and their tone is identical, they are treated here as a single document.

5. Some historians of the FSA have erroneously identified a shooting script titled "American Background," which Stryker drew up in 1936 after a conversation with Robert S. Lynd, as the small-town script, even though it refers to photographing "towns of various sizes" of up to 100,000 population. This was Stryker's earliest script and more accurately should be understood as anticipating the small-town script he composed a year or so later. Lynd was the co-author of *Middletown: A Study in American Culture* (1929) and a professor of sociology at Columbia University; Stryker had become acquainted with him during his graduate studies at Columbia. Lynd's book, a community

study of the small city of Muncie, Indiana, had been well received critically and even became a modest best-seller.

6. Shahn interview with Doud, 4.

7. Stryker's conviction that the small town fostered democracy was not uncommon, as the title of a book by Arthur E. Morgan, the former head of the TVA and sitting president of Antioch College, indicated: *The Small Community: Foundation of Democratic Life—What It Is and How to Achieve It* (New York: Harper, 1942).

8. D. W. Meinig, "Symbolic Landscapes: Some Idealizations of American Communities," in *The Interpretation of Ordinary Landscapes: Geographical Essays,* ed. Meinig (New York: Oxford University Press, 1979), 167–168.

9. Roland Marchand, *Advertising the American Dream: Making Way for Modernity* (Berkeley: University of California Press, 1985), 260. The source for Capra's first exposition of small-town virtues, the Oscar-winning *Mr. Deeds Goes to Town* (1936), was just such a *Saturday Evening Post* short story, "Opera Hat" by Clarence Buddington Kelland.

10. Shahn interview with Doud, 4.

11. Ibid., 1, 3.

12. Ibid., 5. Shahn also remembered that Stryker was taken aback by this critique and only later came to share Shahn's view; but in this case his memory seems unreliable, since the new direction he proposed had already been implemented by Stryker in his small-town script.

13. Ibid., 2.

14. An informative brief discussion of the relationship between a photographer's subjectivity and interpretation is Richard Whelan, "Preface," in *Double Take: A Comparative Look at Photographs* (New York: Clarkson N. Potter, 1981), 15–38.

15. Edward Weston, "Photographing California," *Camera Craft* 46 (March 1939): 105.

16. Shahn interview with Doud, 1, 4.

17. Lawrence W. Levine, "The Historian and the Icon: Photography and the History of the American People in the 1930s and 1940s," in *Documenting America, 1935–1943,* ed.

Carl Fleischhauer and Beverly W. Brannan (Berkeley: University of California Press, 1988), 22.

PHOTOGRAPHING OHIO

1. "Small town" is an amorphous taxonomic category with no commonly accepted definition. Places with a population of under 1,000 are often denominated "hamlets" or "villages," those between 1,000 and 10,000 "small towns," and those between 10,000 and 35,000 "larger towns." By treating Ohio's towns as interchangeable, Shahn avoided the need to address these distinctions.

2. Robert S. Lynd and Helen Merrell Lynd, *Middletown* (New York: Harcourt Brace, 1929).

3. Shahn's exclusions from among the Lynds' "main-trunk activities" are education and home life, and since he photographed so few public buildings, the sense of political arrangements is minimal.

4. Shahn interview with Doud, 3.

5. In addition to this Circleville photograph, Shahn's reflection is also visible in shots of a farmer looking into the window of a Washington Court House savings and loan, a crippled man selling pencils on a Lancaster street, an Urbana cleaning and pressing concern, and an unprinted (killed), untitled picture of a barbershop exterior, probably made in London. In *Myself among the Churchgoers,* a 1939 self-portrait, he depicted himself aiming his angle finder at the painting's viewers.

6. James Agee and Walker Evans, *Let Us Now Praise Famous Men* (1941; reprint, Boston: Houghton Mifflin, 1988), 450–454; Erskine Caldwell and Margaret Bourke-White, *You Have Seen Their Faces* (1937; reprint, New York: Arno, 1975), 187.

7. Lionel Trilling, "Greatness with One Fault in It," *Kenyon Review* 4 (1942): 99–102.

8. Susan Sontag, *On Photography* (New York: Farrar, Straus and Giroux, 1977), especially 3–24.

9. Shahn interview with Doud, 4.

10. Only eight photographs have a vertical format, just 2.5 percent of his small-town coverage.

THE TWO SIDES OF THE TRACKS

1. Shahn told Doud that he worked in Ohio for about six weeks. The Shahns' child was born on June 17, and assuming two or so weeks for Bernarda to be recovered enough to chauffeur her husband, it seems probable that he began photographing in earnest early in July; a number of London pictures depict an annual street carnival that in 1938 took place July 4–9.

2. Figure 3 is the only photograph of London's main street that depicts both black and white residents, and one of the few Shahn made anywhere that does, likely because such propinquity was uncommon. Besides documenting the traditional Saturday shopping day, the photograph reveals the guarded surveillance of the two African American shoppers by at least one of the white women, and in that way it anticipates a more corrosive shot that Shahn would make of white male patrons of a Circleville bar glowering at a black employee as he exits it (fig. 99). While overt antagonism is more apparent in the Circleville bar, this London photograph hints that a similar attitude toward black townspeople was common among white residents.

3. John A. Jakle, *The American Small Town: Twentieth-Century Place Images* (Hamden, Conn.: Archon, 1982), 129. Besides the removal of trees, Jakle also notes other changes in the appearance of small towns that characterized this era: many merchants modernized their storefronts; streets were widened to accommodate automobile traffic; spaces formerly dedicated to pedestrians were converted to berths for cars; and angle parking became the norm.

4. *Madison Press* (London, Ohio), June 30, 1938. The State Theater does appear in figure 8 and probably figure 70, but in the first so distantly, peripherally, and out of focus as to be nearly invisible, and in the second so fragmentarily as to baffle firm identification.

5. [Federal Writers' Project], *The Ohio Guide* (New York: Oxford University Press, 1940), 527.

6. In 1937, photographs of African Americans in *Life* magazine amounted to only .001 percent of the total that centered on everyday life, and that was the highest percentage the magazine achieved before its demise in 1972; coverage of ordinary white Americans appeared 120 times more often. Mary Alice Sentman, "Black and White: Disparity in Coverage by *Life* Magazine," *Journalism Quarterly* 60 (Autumn 1983): 506.

SEEING MAIN STREET

1. *The Ohio Guide,* unpaginated portfolio between 528 and 529.

2. This building is referred to in the architectural literature as the Home Building Association; by the time Shahn photographed it, that savings and loan institution had failed and the building was occupied by the Newark Union Trust Company. In later years it became a jewelry store, a clothing store, and an ice cream parlor. Lauren S. Weingarden, *Louis H. Sullivan: The Banks* (Cambridge, Mass.: MIT Press, 1987), 98–109.

3. "Opening of New Quarters Home Building Ass'n," *Newark American Tribune,* August 25, 1915, 3; "Editorial: Neglected Treasure Located in Newark," *Newark Advocate,* March 7, 1979, 2; both cited in Weingarden, *Louis H. Sullivan,* 108–109. *The Ohio Guide's* section on Newark does not include Sullivan's bank among the town's "points of interest," which suggests that it had become anonymous by the time Shahn photographed it.

4. *Urbana and Champaign County* (Urbana, Ohio: Federal Writers' Project, 1942).

5. *The Ohio Guide,* 589.

6. Alternatively, this effect could have been achieved in the darkroom by an FSA technician, since Shahn did not print his pictures. He did, though, routinely include directions for making file prints after he had edited the "first prints" (preliminary proofs from his negatives) sent to him by the Washington office after developing.

7. Lewis Atherton, *Main Street on the Middle Border* (Bloomington: Indiana University Press, 1954), 345.

8. A sign also indicates that the Circle movie theater is just outside the frame's right edge. It had recently acquired a modernized front, and had Shahn recomposed to include it, the two shabby buildings would have been excluded and the photograph would have become more a study of modernity's alteration of the townscape.

9. An imposing hotel such as the American Hotel was much coveted by Ohio's towns, as a photograph Shahn made in Lancaster illustrates, showing a billboard mapping an ambitious civic campaign to raise funds to build a seventy-room hotel. According to the *Lancaster Eagle Gazette* (July 24, 1938), citizens had pledged more than $250,000 to the campaign.

10. For an informative composite diagram of commercial architectural styles from about 1820 to 1915—and a glossary of terms to describe them—see Richard V. Francaviglia, *Main Street Revisited: Time, Space, and Image Building in Small-Town America* (Iowa City: University of Iowa Press, 1996), 6–7.

11. Circleville's Roundtown Conservancy website displays contemporary photographs of these structures: http://www.roundtownconservancy.org/circleville._historic._district.html. The upper portion of a white Federal-style building identified there as "Gibsons" closely resembles the one in figure 26, except with only six windows across its upper floors rather than nine. Most likely it is the same building, and the portion that formerly housed Miller Shoes had been demolished.

SIDEWALKS

1. This shooting sequence is conjectural, but it is possibly confirmed by another picture that Shahn did not have printed for the FSA file, a close-up with only the young man and one other behind the window, likely made before those outside arrived on the scene. By itself it is a strong photograph, but including it in the sequence would have

suggested that the men inside and outside the tavern are of independent interest, detracting from the emphasis on their contrasting identities that is conveyed by the three pictures included in the file.

PUBLIC AND RELIGIOUS INSTITUTIONS

1. *The Ohio Guide*, 92.

MODERNITY AND TRADITION

1. Jakle, *The American Small Town*, 132.
2. The *Circleville Union-Herald* published several accounts of these parking controversies during the summer Shahn worked in Ohio; see especially the issues of July 13, July 27, and August 3, 1938.
3. Shahn interview with Forrest Selvig, September 27, 1968, Archives of American Art, 6.
4. In Muncie, Indiana, during the worst years of the Depression, 1929–1933, gasoline sales fell just 4 percent, far less than other commodities; the next-lowest reductions were 38 percent in variety store purchases and 49 percent in food expenditures. Robert S. Lynd and Helen Merrell Lynd, *Middletown in Transition* (New York: Harcourt Brace, 1937), 10–11.
5. Ibid., 46.
6. *Madison Press*, June 9, 1938.
7. The Kroger chain spread across nineteen Midwestern states and boasted that it advertised regularly in 1,053 newspapers; besides its London outlet, it maintained stores in Newark and Lancaster and likely elsewhere. *Madison Press*, June 2, 1938. A&P was by far the largest national grocery chain: it had outlets in Lancaster, Newark, Plain City, and Somerset, and almost certainly in other towns.
8. Atherton, *Main Street on the Middle Border*, 240–241.
9. Ben Shahn, *Love and Joy about Letters* (New York: Grossman, 1963), 15, 17. I am grateful to Martha Langford for calling my attention to Shahn's comment on signage.
10. E. L. Doctorow, *Ragtime* (1975; reprint, New York: Plume, 1996), 98. The novel adduces many examples of duplicated events, and near its end provides an ironic counterpoint to them, when a racist fire chief is compelled to rebuild single-handedly, like a premodern mechanic, an African American character's Ford automobile that the fire chief had been responsible for ravaging. But in the novel's final scene, another character is inspired to create the "Little Rascals/Our Gang" film comedy series, fables of democracy that turned out to be such quintessential duplicated events that their popularity continued for the entire duration of the twentieth century.
11. See, for instance, Rothstein's of a St. Louis newsstand (1939), Vachon's in Omaha (1938) and Norfolk, Virginia (1941), and Lee's in Cook, Minnesota (1937), Taylor, Texas, and Windsor Locks, Connecticut (both 1939).
12. Tacked above the newsboy's head is an advertisement for the *Daily Racing Form*, its juxtaposition with the admonition not to "forget your CITIZEN" and the headline about the neglect of relief creating a montage of clashing cultural beliefs and actions—civic responsibility, political pusillanimity, and the gambler's hopes for a lucky fortune.
13. Tino Ballio, *Grand Design: Hollywood as a Modern Business Enterprise, 1930–39* (Berkeley: University of California Press, 1993), 2. For a contemporary examination of the significance of the movies in thirties culture, see Margaret Farrand Thorp, *America at the Movies* (New Haven: Yale University Press, 1939).
14. Shahn's title for this picture is equivocal about where it was made, "probably in the vicinity of Lancaster, Ohio"; it may have been Newark, where *One Wild Night* played in July. Despite its racy title, this film was a comedy about four small-town men who contrived their own kidnapping so as to have a vacation together without their wives. The contrast between the film's title and the stolid group under the marquee ventures a gently ironic witticism.
15. The *Circleville Union-Herald* reported on the new facades of the Circle and Grand theaters, June 8 and July 27, 1938, and the *Newark Advocate* and *American Tribune* reported on the refurbishing of that town's Lyric Theater, August 6, 1938.

16. *The Ohio Guide,* 566, 527, 465.

17. Lynd and Lynd, *Middletown in Transition,* 378–379, 379 n. 7.

18. Robert H. Wiebe, *The Search for Order, 1877–1920* (New York: Hill and Wang, 1967), especially xiii.

19. Warren I. Susman, "The Culture of the Thirties," in his *Culture as History: The Transformation of American Society in the Twentieth Century* (New York: Pantheon, 1984), 153–158. His quotation from Lynd is from *Knowledge for What? The Place of the Social Sciences in American Culture* (Princeton, N.J.: Princeton University Press, 1939), 9.

THE VISIBLE AND INVISIBLE POOR

1. This advertisement appeared in the *New Yorker,* February 14, 1983, 99.

2. William Stott, *Documentary Expression and Thirties America* (New York: Oxford University Press, 1973), 275.

3. In another shot, two boys stand in the shack's entrance, presumably other members of the family inhabiting it.

4. *Circleville Union-Herald,* July 27 and August 10, 1938. In computing the number of Pickaway County residents requiring relief, the newspaper postulated the average family as four persons, which may have been too low.

"WE CATER TO WHITE TRADE ONLY"

1. An alternative interpretation might be that this was a black barbershop and the man an idle barber or waiting customer, but it seems unlikely inasmuch as Union County, of which Marysville was the county seat, had the fewest number of African Americans (261) of any of the eight counties.

2. In Worthington he made a similar pair of shots, each of a group of men gathered on a meat market's steps, one group composed of three white men, the other of five African Americans. While these pictures indicate the customary racial segregation of such gatherings, they were probably made on two visits and do not juxtapose the groups as the bus station picture does.

3. Three pictures share this title, one of the Wonder Bar's interior and two more of its exterior. One interior view is titled "Wonder Bar, hot spot in Circleville, Ohio," and the different preposition was likely a mistake in the caption's transcription.

CONCLUSION

1. Among others, James Curtis makes this argument in *Mind's Eye, Mind's Truth: FSA Photography Reconsidered* (Philadelphia: Temple University Press, 1989), 3–20.

2. Stryker uses the quoted phrase in the preface to his redaction of the small-town script. Roy Stryker Papers.

3. Jack Delano interview with Richard Doud, June 12, 1965, Archives of American Art.

4. If Stryker's impetus for encouraging a photographic study of small towns was broadly political, it also went hand in hand with an administrative goal: as the Historical Section's director, he labored to sustain its federal support and if possible to increase it, and if his intuition was correct that such "positive" photographs were going to be in demand, having a supply of them in the file would position his unit at the forefront of a developing trend and enhance its standing in Washington.

5. A useful summary of Shahn's political interests and activities in the first half of the thirties is Deborah Martin Kao, "Ben Shahn and the Public Use of Art," in *Ben Shahn's New York: The Photography of Modern Times,* by Kao, Laura Katzman, and Jenna Webster (Cambridge, Mass.: Fogg Art Museum and the Harvard and Yale University Presses, 2000), 39–73. Kao intimates that Shahn joined the Communist Party, although her evidence (an entry in Lincoln Kirstein's diary) is not very persuasive. There is little question, though, that he sympathized with many of the party's causes.

6. Richard H. Pells, *Radical Visions and American Dreams: Culture and Social Thought in the Depression Years* (New York: Harper and Row, 1973), 327–328.

7. Levine, "The Historian and the Icon," 22.

8. Lord Houghton, *Life and Letters of John Keats* (London: George Routledge and Sons, 1906), 67.

Index

John Raeburn is a professor of American studies and English
at the University of Iowa. He is the author of, most recently,
A Staggering Revolution: A Cultural History of Thirties Photography.

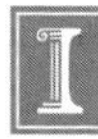

The University of Illinois Press
is a founding member of the
Association of American University Presses.

Designed by Kelly Gray
Composed in 10.5/15 Adobe Caslon
with Avenir display
by Jim Proefrock
at the University of Illinois Press
Manufactured by Bang Printing

University of Illinois Press
1325 South Oak Street
Champaign, IL 61820-6903
www.press.uillinois.edu